Farms, Gardens & Countryside Trails

of Western North Carolina

Author
Jan J. Love

Contributing Writers
Elizabeth Hunter,
Mary Lynn White & LM Sawyer

Designer
Scott Smith
1250 Design

Project Coordinator
Jan J. Love

Published by HandMade in America, Inc.
111 Central Avenue, Asheville, North Carolina 28801• (828) 252-0121
For book orders, call 1-800-331-4154
http://www.wnccrafts.org

Acknowledgments

This guidebook was developed under the auspices of HandMade in America, an organization dedicated to the nurturance of craft culture and community in Western North Carolina. Research, creative development and printing of this guidebook were funded with grants from North Carolina Travel and Tourism, North Carolina Department of Cultural Resources, the North Carolina Folk Life Division, the Appalachian Regional Commission, the North Carolina Community Development Initiative and The Conservation Fund. Special thanks for the participation of the North Carolina Division of Community Assistance, the North Carolina Cooperative Extension Service, and various Chambers of Commerce and tourism offices in Western North Carolina.

Library of Congress Catalog Card Number 2001-1333-74. ISBN 0-9651905-3-6

Table of Contents

FYI
Helpful Stuff to know 10

Quilt Top Ramble 18

HERITAGE SITE 50
Grandfather Mountain

Jewels & Gems Meander 52

HERITAGE SITE 80
Orchard at Altapass

Arbors & Orchards 82

HERITAGE SITE 118
Big Botanicals

The Ribbon Garden 120

Whistlestop Tour 124

HERITAGE SITE 160
Oconaluftee Indian Village

Foothill Forays 162

HERITAGE SITE 196
Waldensian Heritage Wines

Water Ways Trail 198

HERITAGE SITE
The Garden of John C. Campbell Folk School 218

Index 220

Map **Inside Back Cover**

You are now in possession of a handy guide to hundreds of gardens, farms, botanical inns and bed & breakfasts, garden art shops, nifty nurseries, restaurants with exquisite renditions of local fare, orchards, vineyards, ranches, mills, corn mazes, historic sites and trails full of wildflowers and wild adventure. Even so, this book is much more than that. It's a written recollection of one-on-one encounters with the remarkably varied and vastly passionate people who have sunk their roots deep into the dirt of the Blue Ridge region. ❁ Life imitates art as two sisters transform a 19th century farm into a haven of hospitality with gardens of gourmet vegetables and organic flowers to complement an upscale restaurant and espresso bar. Around the bend, a couple entertains and educates with their alpaca husbandry. A few ridges north in the Bethel community, elk graze in a green glade between slopes of Fraser firs pruned with pride by several generations of the Cornett family. A widow honors the memory of her husband by converting their little farm in Ennice into a miniature animal petting farm – an instantly successful field trip for city kids. Meanwhile, in the far west corner of Ashe County, a fifth generation son of the Miller family keeps the blood of the century-old farmstead flowing through walking trails and wild tales of toiling in corn and wheat fields, raising cattle and making molasses. ✿ Up from the Sandy Mush valley, a wife and husband tend to multitudes of rare and exotic plants at their mountaintop Shangri-La. Over Doggett Mountain on the down slope, a woman has created a door into a magical garden realm forever open to kindred spirits in search of herbs of grace and blooms of bliss. Through a meander of goldenseal and goat farms, two Madison County men hone a tobacco field into ageless bonsai and lotus gardens. Past bow-legged scarecrows and flowering labyrinth pathways, a youthful but experienced organic farmer reaps harvests of garlic, tuberoses and eggplants on the banks of the South Toe River. Heirloom apples, ground corn, homestead goat cheese and handmade soap are family legacies that live on, time out of mind, in the valleys and on the ridges around Mt. Mitchell. ❁ In Asheville suburbia, two good-hearted souls teach permaculture and walk-the-talk with bare feet at their organic herb, flower and forest gardens. An upscale-downtown restaurant owner and apple expert blends flavors, flowers and culinary finesse with a Barnardsville garden guru and holistic bed & breakfast operator to create "garden to gourmet" workshops. A floral décor artist with Memphis roots, a Parisian background and a rooster named Daisy, revives an Asheville alley with an eclectic Appalachia to the Orient garden adjacent to his studio of garden art, exotic orchids and flowers such as lady's slippers and lily of the valley. A Hendersonville native renovates a gas station into a garden shop full of carnivorous swamp plants, herbs, vegetables, twig furniture and funky nature art. Nearby, on an avenue of apples, Highway 64 East, a family of five

stands firm in the face of encroaching development, to continue the fifty-year legacy of their orchard and produce market that yields a cornucopia of fruits and vegetables annually. ❁ In Waynesville, a woman spends a winter, and her savings, to renovate a room of her garden center into a mountain museum honoring her Blue Ridge heritage. Where the wind dances up Jonathan's Creek, a family with dreams and determination dedicates the bigger part of its 270-acre farm to nature preservation while creating a luxury lodge and llama-trekking destination. A bishop, a wildflower enthusiast and the Tuscola Garden Club put their hearts and heads together to create a nature center as a memorial to the bishop's wife, a place for her flowers and a trail of 500 different species of native plants for the club members to maintain. A man of gives the same honor to Kituhwa, Mother Town of the Cherokee, as he designs a corn maze adjoining the original Council House Mound on the brim of Bryson City. ❁ The Dalmas family and other Waldensian descendants pay daily tribute to their heritage along the trail of fermented grapes and continuous faith in Valdese. In a valley fed by Fiddler's Run, a tributary of the Catawba River,

Don Chapman, nurturing optimist/horticulturist, gives vision to disabled students on how to create functional propagation pots for mums, pansies, cabbage and kale. A '46 Ford pick-up forever hauls a bed of petunias with the same tenacity as its owner, the Morganton man under whose care thousands of daylilies live large in meadows of millstone. In Sandy Plains some 45 years ago, a determined girl pledged to fulfill her grandfather's wistful dream of owning a legendary plantation by the Green River. She makes good on her promise by buying it years later and converts it into an exquisitely restored home with historic tours, water and boxwood gardens, emus and garden weddings. The Carillon family of Old Fort daily and diligently release waters from their inn and fruit orchard reservoir to create the public Andrew's Geyser by day and the private Mill Creek waterfall for their guests by night. ✿ A young couple leaves the high life of "Hotlanta" and escapes to the Highlands to provide safari tour escapism for others in the Nantahala rainforest. An Otto dairy farmer brings back memories of the nifty 50's with his coup de grâce creamery tempting travelers on Highway 441 with fresh ice cream, butter, milk,

cheese and eggs. Within shouting distance, a man stands guardian at the gates of his native nursery enclosed on all sides by nature, while doling out silky dogwood and dog hobble, sunup to sundown, day in and day out, with his dog Dee to keep him company. A community center of garden art and crafts, weaving, a beeswax business and a walking trail emerges out of a tightly-knit effort of conscientious, Mayberry-minded citizens in Stecoah Valley. In Franklin, the retirement plan of a Water Lily Hall of Famer turned into the largest aquatic nursery in the nation and a site reminiscent of the magic of Monet. ❁ This book is the key to unlock the door into the lives of the good people who live and breathe, create and connect with the good earth of Western North Carolina. Free your mind and follow your heart and this handy guidebook on a surprisingly entertaining and educational journey returning to our innovative agricultural roots.

FYI
Helpful Stuff To Know

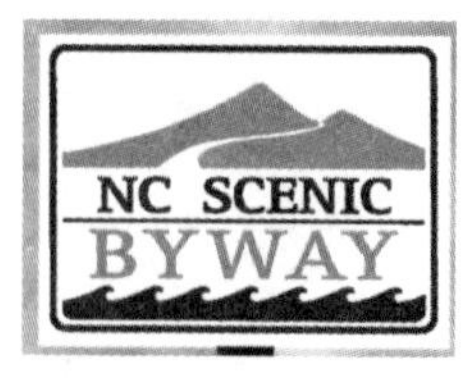

CELEBRATING THE ROAD LESS TRAVELED.

Throughout North Carolina 44 scenic byways are designated and maintained by the Department of Transportation. The byways offer something more than a simple route from one point to another. They lead you past shifting landscapes of natural beauty and wonder. Panoramic vistas give way to intimate drives under the evergreen canopies and quickly open up again to the sight of distant mountains. Whitewater rivers and quiet streams sidle up for a stretch then wander off. Patchwork fields and hillsides stretch to the horizon, sown with colors of the season.

HOW TO USE THIS GUIDEBOOK

We've detailed six driving loops of varying lengths, with almost 500 stops listed. There is no set time for discovering the farms, gardens and attractions on a single trail. Depending on the time you have to invest, you can bite off all or part of any loop.

For each trail a map shows the location and category of the stops. Listings are numbered sequentially based on a starting point and routing that seemed most natural to the editors. However, feel free to pick up the loop at any point and go in any direction you please. You may even wish to combine parts of two adjoining loops. A map of North Carolina, which is available by calling the N.C. Division of Travel and Tourism at (919)733-7600 in-state or 800-847-4862 out-of-state, is a nice item to have handy for jumping from one trail to the next and complements the maps provided.

In addition to the specific trails, which in most cases are often actual loops, there are "spurs" indicated that strike out from the loop to capture a destination, such as a special interest garden or farm. We encourage you to include these excursions as part of your overall tour.

FYI
Helpful Stuff To Know

PLANNING YOUR TRIP

To enrich your experience, we suggest that you:

Come ready to enjoy yourself

According to your interest, sample some of the books listed on pages 16 and 17 under "Recommended Reading".

Go with the flow

The mountains have a rhythm and a pace of their own. The more slowly you go, the richer the experience. Here's a rule to go by: Determine how long it normally takes you to do something. Then double it.

Learn about the maker

The real treasure is often the story behind the garden. Ask questions. Gardening is close to the heart; people like to talk about it. On the other hand, it's good to remember that a gardener's time is precious. Please respect posted hours for all sites listed in this book.

Strike out on your own

If you see an interesting road that's off the map, take it. Getting lost (and found again) is half the fun.

Wherever practical, our trails overlay the N.C. Scenic Byways routes.

A RED, WHITE AND BLUE RIDGE PARKWAY

The North Carolina section of the Blue Ridge Parkway, the connecting ribbon of our Farms, Gardens and Countryside Trails system has been recognized as an "All American Road" by the Federal Highway Administration. To find out more visit www.blueridgeparkway.org on the web.

TAKING THE KIDS (OR GRANDKIDS) ALONG WITH YOU?

While most of the sites in this book are open to families, a number of them are especially kid friendly. We've made it easy for you to find these sites by noting them with our special Kid Friendly icon.

For more information about HandMade in America, check out www.wnccrafts.org

FYI

Helpful Stuff To Know

STUFF THE KNAPSACK (OR TRUNK)

How about: binoculars; *Peterson Field Guides* to birds, trees, and wildflowers; extra sweater; shoes to wade in; copy of *War and Peace* (unabridged) for pressing dried flowers, four leaf clovers and other treasures; compass; a tin of Altoids (or other mints); flashlight; pocket-knife for slicing apples or spreading peanut butter for sandwiches on the run; a blanket for naps on hillsides or for stargazing on mountain tops; reading glasses; sunscreen; floppy hat, and walking-stick.

And, be sure to bring your checkbook since many farms, garden sites and some stores are not set up for credit cards.

Record your good times

Whether you choose a notebook, sketch pad, camera or watercolors, recording your journey will allow you to revisit your experiences.

Call ahead about special needs

If you or someone in your party has physical restrictions and needs special assistance, we strongly suggest you call ahead. Some of the sites may vary in handicap accessibility.

Pick up the phone

Some of the sites featured are open for business on a limited basis. If their schedules and yours don't mesh, give them a call. Often you can arrange special meeting times.

LISTING CRITERIA

Individual committees and host groups within the 21-county region submitted sites for consideration. Site criteria:

- *Sites that celebrate the horticultural/agricultural diversity of the region.*
- *Sites that are garden, farm or countryside related with an interpretive/educational slant.*
- *Easy to access with adequate parking and usually adequate restroom facilities. Some sites due to the nature of business may be more rustic and remote.*

FYI

Helpful Stuff To Know

- *Farms and garden sites that offer dependable times for guests to visit.*
- *Restaurants with a reputation for fine food and featuring dishes indigenous to the region.*
- *Inns and B&B's with a historical underpinning and/or gardens and grounds deserving recognition.*

We double-checked each site against these criteria and visited them personally to capture a working knowledge of the unique qualities of each site. We toured over 900 sites, many of which are anxious to be listed in an upcoming second edition. Telephone numbers, addresses, websites and other information contained within is accurate, to the best of our knowledge, as of the date of publication. We are certain that there are other farms, gardens, produce stands, restaurants, and inns in the region that qualify for a listing in this directory. For those we missed in this initial volume, we apologize and urge you to ask for a listing in subsequent editions.

TO FIND EVEN MORE FARMS, GARDENS AND FARMER'S MARKETS

We encourage you to inquire further at each county extension office and at other information centers about demonstration sites and other garden sites that are open on a "by appointment only" basis and, for that reason, not included in this book.

Another good starting place for finding more sites to visit is the directory of local chambers of commerce and host group organizations on the following pages.

And, if you enjoy this guidebook, make sure you get a copy of HandMade in America's *Craft Heritage Trails of WNC* as well.

Happy Trails!

FYI

Helpful Stuff To Know

There's a great tradition of music in these mountains. Here is just a sampling of places where you can catch our talented local artists live on stage:

Asheville

Asheville Music Zone
(828) 255-8811
Barley's Tap Room
(828) 255-0504
Bean Streets
(828) 255-8180
The Bier Garden
(828) 285-0002
Broadway's
(828) 285-0400
Kat's Music and Food
(828) 225-0371
Grey Eagle
(828) 232-5800
Hannah Flannagan's
(828) 252-1922
Jack of the Wood
(828) 252-5445
KarmaSonics
(828) 259-9949
Malaprops
(828) 254-6734
Stella Blue
(828) 236-2424
Stoney Knob Cafe & Patio
(828) 645-3309
Tressa's
(828) 254-7072
Tuna Tini's
(828) 285-9110

HELPFUL PHONE NUMBERS

North Carolina Travel & Tourism...(919) 733-4171

Blue Ridge Mountain Host
(Polk, Rutherford, McDowell, Yancey, Buncombe, Transylvania, Henderson and Madison Counties)
........................(800) 807-3391

High Country Host
(Mitchell, Alleghany, Ashe, Avery, and Watauga Counties)
........................(828) 264-1299
........................(800) 438-7500

Smoky Mountain Host
(Jackson, Graham, Clay, Swain, Cherokee, Macon, and Haywood Counties)..........(828) 369-9606

Great Smoky Mtn. Nat. Park...........(423) 436-1200
Pisgah National Forest...................(828) 877-3265
Blue Ridge Parkway........................(828) 298-0398

Chambers of Commerce & Visitors Centers

Andrews .... (828) 321-3584
Asheville/Buncombe County.......... (800) 257-5583
(828) 258-6111
Banner Elk/Avery County...............(800) 972-2183
(828) 898-5905
Black Mountain/Swannanoa...........(800) 669-2301
(828) 669-2300
Blowing Rock...........................(800) 295-7851
(828) 295-7851
Boone.................................. (800) 852-9506
(828) 262-3516
Brevard/Transylvania County..........(800) 648-4523
(828) 883-3700
Bryson City/Swain County ....(800) 867-9246
(828) 488-3681

FYI

Helpful Stuff To Know

Burnsville/Yancey County..........(800) 948-4632
(828) 682-7413
Cashiers/Jackson County............(828) 743-5191
Cherokee Reservation Info.........(800) 438-1601
(828) 497-9195
Franklin/Macon County.............(800) 336-7829
(828) 524-3161
Hayesville/Clay County...............(828) 389-3704
Hendersonville/Henderson County
....(800) 828-4244
(828) 693-9708
Hickory Nut Gorge..................... (828) 625-2725
Highlands....................................(828) 526-2112
Maggie Valley.............................. (800) 624-4431
Marion/McDowell County .... (888) 233-6111
Mars Hill/Madison County........(828) 680-9031
Morganton/Burke County .... (828) 437-3021
Murphy/Cherokee County ....(828) 837-2242
Robbinsville/Graham County ...(800) 470-3790
(828) 479-3790
Rutherfordton/Rutherford County
....(800) 849-5998
Sparta/Alleghany County ....(800) 372-5473
(336) 372-5473
Spruce Pine/Mitchell County ...(800) 227-3912
(828) 765-9483
Sylva/Jackson County.................(800) 962-1911
(828) 586-2155
Tryon/Polk County....................(800) 440-7848
(828) 859-2300
Waynesville/Haywood County...(800) 334-9036
West Jefferson/Ashe County ..... (336) 246-9550
(888) 343-2743

Emergency Numbers

N.C. Highway Patrol..................(800) 445-1772
Cellular phones............................*47 (Toll free)

Black Mountain
Monte Vista
(828) 669-2119
Town Pump
(828) 669-9151
Blowing Rock
Twigs
(828) 295-5050
Boone
Caribbean Cafe
(828) 265-2233
Brevard
Falls Landing
(828) 884-2835
Celo
Celo Inn
(828) 675-5132
Flat Rock
Highland Lake Inn
(828) 693-6812
Franklin
Sweet Carolina Nights
(828) 349-1961
Hot Springs
Bridge Street Cafe
(828) 622-0002
Saluda
The Purple Onion
(828) 749-1179
Sylva
Soul Infusion Tea House
(828) 586-1717
Spring Street Cafe
(828) 586-1600
Morganton
Comma
(828) 433-SHOW
or (828) 433-7409
Rutherfordton
The Vineyard
(828) 288-0240
Valdese
Old Rock School
(828) 879-2129

RECOMMENDED READING

Allan M. Armitage, *Armitage's Garden Perennials,* Timber Press, 2000

Allan M. Armitage, *Herbaceous Perennial Plants,* Second Edition, Stipes Publishing, 1989.

Steve Bender and Felder Rushing, *Passalong Plants,* UNC Press, 1993.

Stanely L. Bently, *Native Orchids of the Southern Appalachian Mountains*, UNC Press, 2000.

Dick Bir, *Growing and Propagating Showy Native Woody Plants,* UNC Press, 1992

Toby Bost, *North Carolina Gardener's Guide,* Cool Springs Press, 1997.

Creighton Lee Calhoun, Jr., *Old Southern Apples*, MacDonald & Woodward Publishing Co., 1995.

Brian Capon, *Botany for Gardeners,* Timber Press, 1990.

Timothy Coffey, *The History and Folklore of North American Wildflowers*, Facts on File, Inc., 1993.

Rick Darke, *The Color Encyclopedia of Ornamental Grasses,* Timber Press, 1999.

Michael A. Dirr, *Dirr's Hardy Trees and Shrubs,* Timber Press, 1997.

Michael A. Dirr, *Manual of Woody Landscape Plants,* Fifth Edition, Stipes Publishing, 1975.

Ken Druse, *The Natural Garden*, Clarkson N. Potter, Inc., 1989.

Foote and Jones, *Native Shrubs and Woody Vines of the Southeast*, Timber Press, 1989.

Fred Galle, *Azaleas,* Timber Press, 1987.

CONTEMPORARY FOLK MUSIC

The mountains of Western North Carolina have become home to a number of contemporary folk singers/songwriters who travel all over the world as ambassadors of the area. Here is a list of the current titles from some area musicians:

"Here We Are" by **An Asheville Area Acoustic Songwriters' Sampler**

"Letters in the Dirt", "Radio" and "Last of the Old Time" by **Chuck Brodsky**

"Casting Shadows" by **Leigh Hilger**

"A Hundred Lies" by **Malcolm Holcombe**

"Life So Far" by **Billy Jonas**

"A Thousand Girls" and "This Time Last Year" by **Christine Kane**

"Promise" by **Annie Lalley**

"Good Again" by **Josh Lamkin**

FYI

Helpful Stuff To Know

Brent and Becky Heath, *Daffodils for American Gardens,* Elliott & Clark, 1995

Jones and Foote, *Gardening with Native Wildflowers,* Timber Press, 1990.

Justice and Bell, *Wildflowers of North Carolina,* UNC Press, 1968.

Sandra F. Ladendorf, *Successful Southern Gardening, A Practical Guide for Year-Round Beauty,* UNC Press, 1989.

Elizabeth Lawrence, *A Southern Garden,* UNC Press, 2001.

Peter Loewer, *The Evening Garden,* Timber Press, 1993.

Peter Loewer, *The Wild Gardener,* Stackpole Press, 1991.

Peter Loewer and Larry Mellichamp, *The Winter Garden: Planning and Planting for the Southeast,* Stackpole Books, 1997.

Lynda McDaniel, *Highroad Guide to the North Carolina Mountains,* Longstreet Publishing, 1998.

Jan W. Midgley, *Southeastern Wildflowers*, Crane Hill Publishers, 1999.

Robert Polomski, *Month By Month Gardening in the Carolinas*, Cool Spring Press, 2000.

Radford, Ahles and Bell, *Manual of the Vascular Flora of the Carolinas*, UNC Press, 1968.

Lois G. Rosenfeld, *The Garden Tourist,*

Southeast edition, The Garden Tourist Press, 2001.

Ruth D. Wrensch, *The Essence of Herbs,* University Press of Mississippi, 1992.

"Hard Earned Smile" and "Flying" by **David LaMotte**
"Life is Good" and "Let Go" by **Jimmy Landry**
"Archaeology" and "The Holy Fool" by **Chris Rosser**
"Late Night Radio" and "New Blood" by **Beth Wood**

Also, John Ludovico of KarmaSonics recommends these local artists:

Jazz:
"Hold Back the Rain" and "Bittersweet" by **Evans & Coppola**
"Anthem" and "Chelsea Bridge" by **Frank Southecorvo Jazz Band**

Bluegrass:
"Real Live Music" by **Greasy Beans**
"Grab a Root and Growl" by **Sons of Ralph**
"Old Dreams and New Dreams" by **Steep Canyon Rangers**

Old Time Bluegrass:
"Neighbor Girl" by **Cary Fridley**

Instrumental:
"Kadotume" and "Dancing with Shadows" by **Bonfield & Ebel**

Quilt Top Ramble

"Choose and Cut" applies to more than Christmas trees on this ramble through a quilted High Country landscape. Within an ever-present border of mountains, a patchwork of pastures and patterned evergreens is seamed by ancient rivers and meandering creeks. Broad valleys are hemmed by angular uplands. Thread your way from Linville Falls' thundering cascades to the Avery County seat of Newland. Pass through picturesque Linville, its cottages clothed in chestnut bark, to the thriving college town of Banner Elk. Trace a creek's snake-like turns to Elk Park for tea and scones in a fairyland corner of an old gas station turned antique store. Or, follow the road more traveled—shadowed by Grandfather Mountain's dominating profile—to Valle Crucis. Gear down at Mast Store, a must-see mercantile where farm folk bartered chickens for dry goods. Feeling peckish? Grab a Moon Pie and an RC, and explore the grounds of two historic B&B's. At one, a venerable oak overspreads a rustic springhouse; at the other, silver laced Wyandottes and Buff Orpingtons provide eggs and early wake-up calls. Animal lovers can gaze into the gorgeous baby browns of an alpaca at Fireweed Ranch—or detour to Watauga's outback to marvel at herds of grazing elk. Frontiersman Daniel Boone was the first tourist to visit these mountains. Remember his stories as you head into the town that bears his name. Navigate hairpin turns through rhododendron on a back road to Blowing Rock, featuring gardens both ragged and

A perfect patchwork of people and places.

High Above the Trail

refined. A gardener's care is always apparent on the grounds of gracious Glendale Springs Inn. Within sight: Holy Trinity Church, whose natural wood interior, Last Supper fresco and encircling gardens restore and refresh. Up the Parkway in Laurel Springs, a "retired" pharmacist has concocted a crazy quilt combo—B&B, bocci ball court, mountain music dancehall and winemaking supply shop—at his ancestral homeplace. Follow a stitchery of split rail fences to the Parkway's splendid vistas, then walk a garden labyrinth at the Inn of the Red Thread. In the hilltop town of Sparta, prepare to ride through pastures of plenty. There's order wherever you look. An applique of white fences and horse paddocks. Young firs tufting hillside swatches. Tired of driving? Canoe the New River. Pedal a bike. Take a hike. Ride astride a proud palomino. Or, kick up your heels to the rhythm of a bluegrass band. Ashe County's fertile crescents, embellished by Christmas tree plantations and the old New River, offer Shatley Springs, where you can fill a few jugs with their famous water. Then trundle up the road to River House Inn for a Currier-and-Ives view. Nearby, Mt. Jefferson presides over twin towns that share its name. Zigzag up one last mountain, and descend, to the tiny hamlet of Todd. "The Virginia Creeper" once brought the world to Todd's doorstep on its rails. The train's long gone, but the river remains. And, Todd General Store awaits your coming with a slice of pizza and a tapestry of tales—ample provisions for the drive home.

Quilt Top Ramble

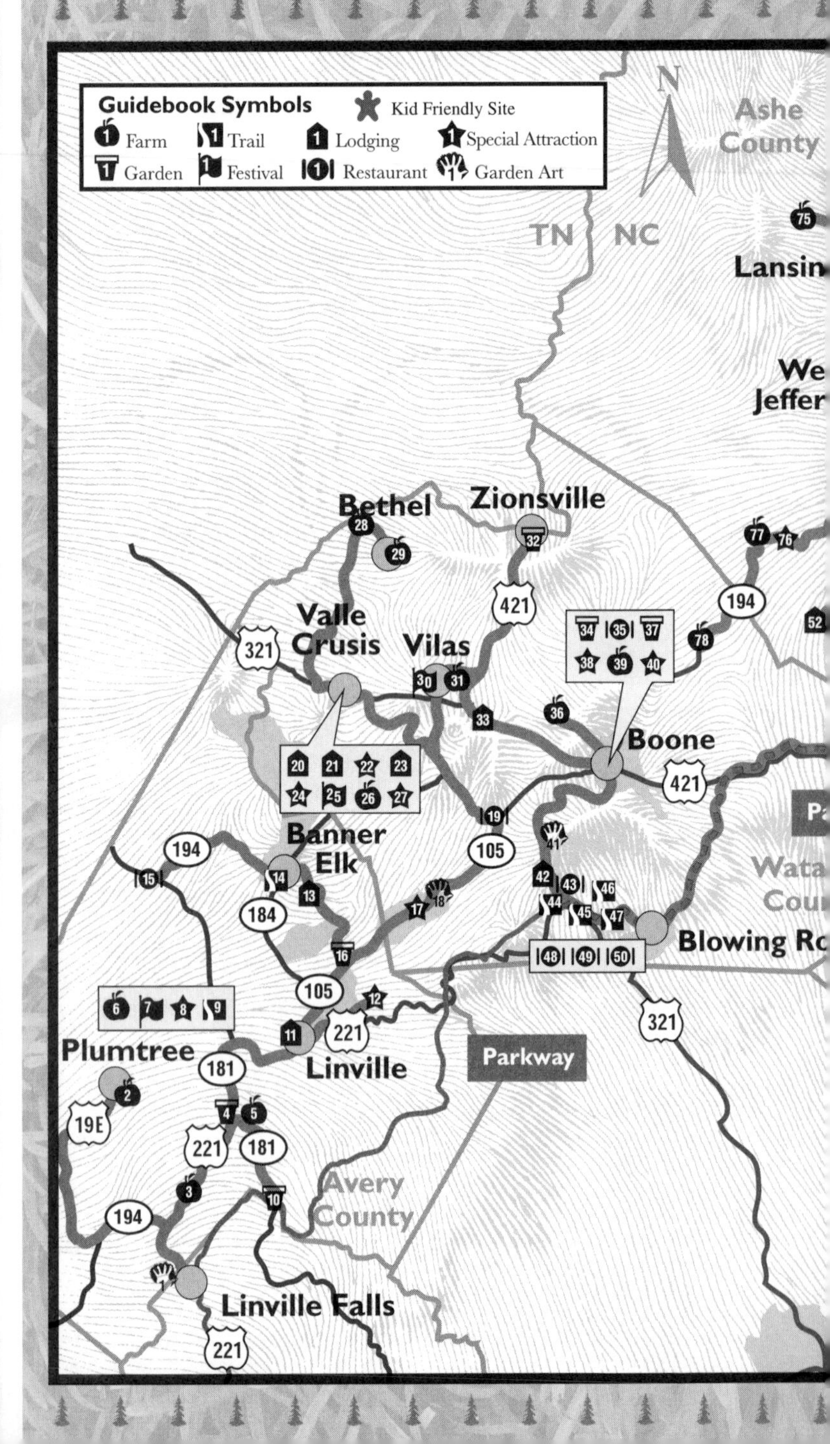

VA
Piney Creek
Ennice
Grassy Creek
16
69
194
Shatley Springs
68
67
221
Sparta
63
18
64
65
62
21
Alleghany County
Laural Springs
71
70
Jefferson
72
88
57
58
56
61
59
60
73
Parkway
55
54
53
Glendale Springs
74
163
Fleetwood
421

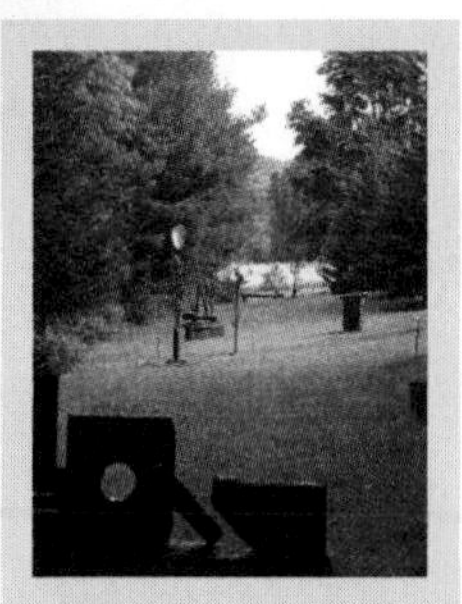

The first stop on the Quilt Top Ramble is the Anvil Arts Studio and Sculpture Gardens. Most times you can catch Bill in his studio and hang around to watch him work. Or, spend some quiet time in his picturesque sculpture garden. It's the perfect place to relax before beginning your day of adventure.

SCULPTURE
Garden
&
Gallery

LINVILLE FALLS

Anvil Arts Studio and Sculpture Gardens 9600 LINVILLE FALLS HWY 221 – It may be a garden on only one acre, but Bill Brown makes it count. Between six and 20 steel garden structures grace the grounds outside the studio. If it's high drama that appeals to you, you'll be drawn into these stories contrived through steel, copper, bronze and other materials. Mon–Fri 8:30am–5pm & Sat by appointment. (828) 765-6226. www.billbrownsculptor.com

Exit the BRP at Mile Post 316.3 at Linville Falls Community exit. Turn R onto Hwy 221 and travel 1 mi. Look for green steel building on L.

Side trip...

Sugar Plum Farms 1263 ISAACS BRANCH RD – Fraser firs are native only to the narrow band of highlands along the top of the Blue Ridge. A great stop year-round for the history of the Fraser is this working choose and cut farm. Views are spectacular. The air should be bottled. During the holiday season you can enjoy hay rides, trout fishing and hobnobbing with Santa. Open year-round for educational tours. Call for appointment. Open daily Thanksgiving–Dec 24 10am–5pm. (828) 765-0019. www.sugarplumfarm.com

From Linville Falls take L onto Hwy 194 S. Travel 4 mi and take R onto 19E (N) 5 mi to Plumtree. Take R onto Big Plumtree Creek Rd. Stay R at fork. Continue .5 mi until L onto Isaacs Branch Rd. 1.5 mi on L.

...Meanwhile, back on the trail

CROSSNORE

Quincy's Produce Market 5009 LINVILLE FALLS HWY – A line of colorful flags beckons travelers and locals alike to this roadside, open-air market. Quincy herself runs the 35-year-old, family owned and operated produce and plant

Yes, we have cold watermelons

The Road Goes On Forever

Side trips, tidbits, adventures, and treasure hunts

market. Offerings include bedding and vegetable plants, local and seasonal produce, jams, jellies, honey and molasses. In October, visitors can enjoy the annual Fall Festival. Open daily 8:30am–8:30pm. (828)733-0974.
In Crossnore on Hwy 221, 4 mi past Sculpture Garden on R.

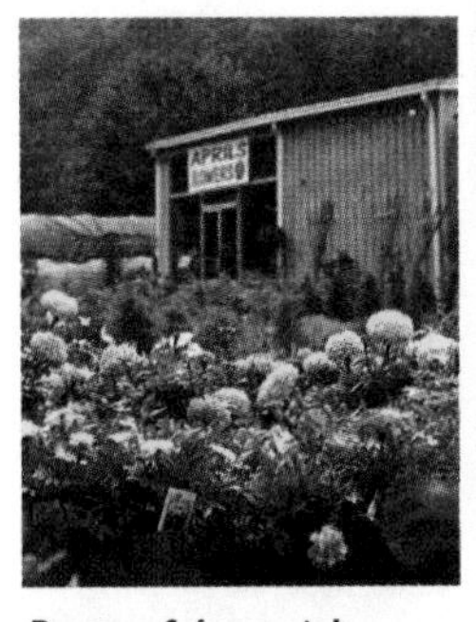

Be careful, a quick stop at April's Flowers can turn into an afternoon of advice, inspiration and a car load of perennials.

4 April's Flowers 4699 LINVILLE FALLS HWY – Rows of indigenous plants and flowers greet you before April can reach you at this impressive garden center. It is difficult to find a young woman more enthusiastic about gardening. Customers may overhear her bragging about her niece's first greenhouse or offering helpful advice and information. Mon–Sat 8am–5pm. (828)733-0774.
Just past Quincy's .4 mi on R.

NEWLAND

5 Three Oaks, Ltd. 201 BOWMAN RD – What was once the 1890 home of Civil War Major George R. Watkins now serves as the office and Christmas craft shop for this well-known choose and cut Christmas tree operation. After wandering through the forest of Fraser fir, white pine, Norway and blue spruce, and Dwarf Albertas, you'll want to explore the four rooms of holiday crafts on the second floor of the house for handmade ornaments, quilts and other seasonal treasures. Open daily from Nov 20–Dec 20 8am–5pm. (828)733-2662.
3 mi N of Linville Falls on Hwy 221 on R.

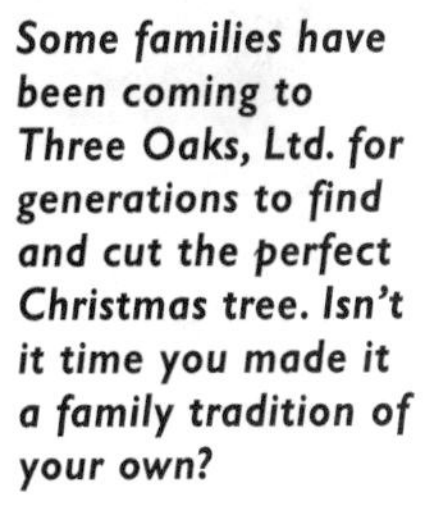

Some families have been coming to Three Oaks, Ltd. for generations to find and cut the perfect Christmas tree. Isn't it time you made it a family tradition of your own?

6 Sugar Mountain Nursery 675 PINEOLA ST– Step into a green world of Lecuthoe, Leyland, Mountain Laurel, Hemlock, Hydrangea, log moss and Galax–some of the 106 varieties of plants, shade trees and ornamentals found on this high-energy site. Locally crafted bark berry baskets, log fern stands, Sassafras candelabra and mossy hanging bird perches will delight and intrigue. Christmas trees, too. Mon–Fri 8:30am–5pm & Sat 9am–1pm. (828)733-2844. www.sugarmtnnursery.com
Coming into Newland on Hwy 194 on R next to BP Station.

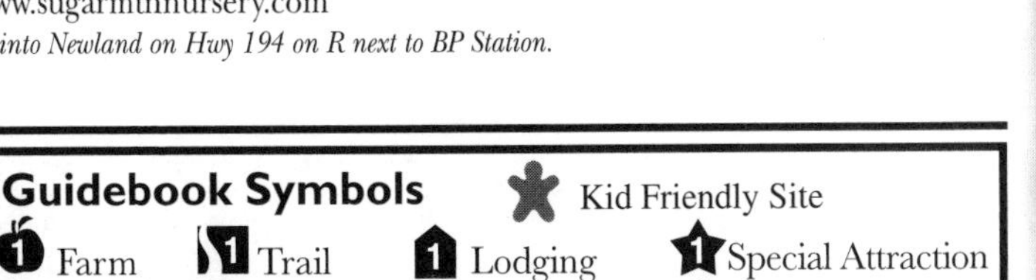

The Newland Riverwalk is host to many festivals throughout the year. If you happen to be there during one of these festivals you might just find the best Bar-B-Que sandwich you've ever eaten.

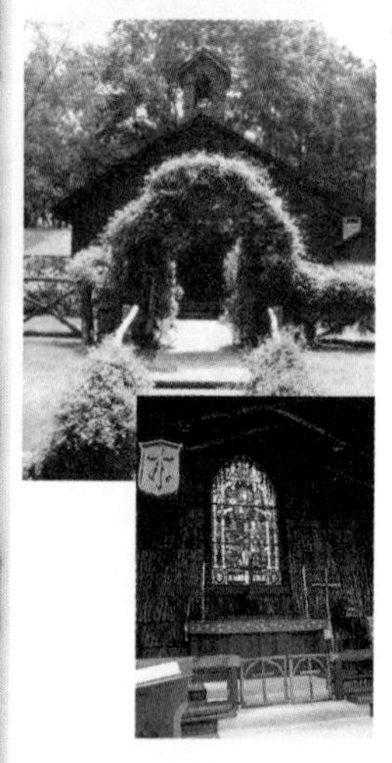

At one with nature: All Souls Epsicopal Church. Look for it in Linville.

7 **Avery County Agricultural and Horticultural Fair** – If you time your trip for September, you can catch this five-day annual event featuring a bountiful supply of local canned and baked goods, fresh produce, field crops, flowers, shrubs, trees and wreaths. Call for dates and location. (828)733-3642.

8 **Riverwalk** – Newland, the highest county seat this side of the Rockies, boasts a level 1.1 mile trail that easily ambles along the Toe River in the middle of this bustling little town.
In downtown Newland, turn R off of Hwy 194 onto Ash St.

9 **Waterfalls Park** – Jake Owens and Junior Sluder had a beautiful idea when they started the park now run by the town Volunteer Fire Department. An easy to moderate trail starting at the falls takes you back to a serene spring.
On Hwy 194 in Newland across from the Ingle's.

Side trip...

10 **Gardens of the Blue Ridge** 9056 WILDFLOWER LN – If you'd like to see a top quality display of native wildflowers that you can also purchase, visit North Carolina's oldest licensed nursery. Although this is a working garden and not a display garden, you can tour a variety of nature's beauty ranging from the vivid hues of the Celandine Poppy and Blackberry Lily to the delicate fronds and petals of the Cinnamon Fern and Vasey's Trillium. Mon–Fri 8am–4pm & Sat 8am–12noon. (828)733-8894. www.gardensoftheblueridge.com
At Pineola, bear R on Hwy 181 S. Take L on Pittman Gap Rd, .25 mi to R on Wildflower Ln.

...Meanwhile, back on the trail

LINVILLE

11 **Linville Cottage Bed and Breakfast** 154 RUFFIN ST – A white picket fence surrounds this lovely third generation 1908 home that features four upstairs rooms, a cottage out back, and the not-to-be-missed Grandfather Suite with its own private garden. Delight

The Road Goes On Forever

Side trips, tidbits, adventures, and treasure hunts

SPOT IT

It's somewhere on this loop. Can you find it?

your senses wandering through the English perennial beds and old remedy herbs in the gardens behind the house. In all likelihood, a number of fragrant herbs will enhance your breakfast. (877)797-1885.

From Newland, take Hwy 181 to Linville. Just before intersection with Hwy 105, turn L on Ruffin St. Cottage is on R.

Breathtaking views from the summit of Grandfather Mountain. Be sure to pack a wind-breaker.

12 **Grandfather Mountain** US 221 & BLUE RIDGE PARKWAY – The U.N. has recognized this environmentally significant mountain as an International Biosphere Reserve, a place where man and nature exist in harmony. Ancient black cliffs, colorful rhododendron, native animals and spectacular views from the highest swinging footbridge in America. Open daily except Thanksgiving & Christmas days. Winter 8am–5pm. Spring & Fall 8am–6pm. Summer 8am–7pm. (800)468-7325. www.grandfather.com

Turn L back onto Hwy 181 and cross through intersection with Hwy 105. Continue on Hwy 221 approximately 2 mi. Entrance will be on your R.

BANNER ELK

13 **The Banner Elk Inn** 407 MAIN ST E – Amidst the forest greens and dark woodsy furnishings of the historic inn, you will find a mesh of Old World charm and Southern warmth. The gardens are full of lupines, candytuft, hosta and tiger lilies playing hide and seek from season to season. Guests will enjoy one of five cozy rooms and a lavish breakfast. Across the street is the well-groomed Tate-Evans Park, providing a nice break for a walk or picnic. (828)898-6223.

Hwy 105 to L onto 184. Through Sugar Mountain take R onto 194 N (Main St). Inn is .4 mi on L.

14 **Banner Elk Stables** 796 SHOEMAKER RD – You can see just a little bit more of the High Country when perched atop a quarter horse or palomino. Scenic views await you and your mount on the beautiful flanks of Beech Mountain. Open daily year-round 10am–5:30pm.

Want to perk up your salad and your garden?

Try growing an edible flower among your vegetable delights. For an easy to care for and great tasting flower treat, try nasturtiums, also known as Indian cress. All parts of the plant are edible as long as it is not treated with chemicals. Best of all, nasturtiums grow best when left alone!

The last ride starts at 4pm. Call ahead in winter months for riding conditions. (828)898-5424.

From the Banner Elk stoplight travel 1 mi on Hwy 194 N. Turn L on Shomaker Rd. Go 1 mi to end of road.

Side trip...

ELK PARK

15 Antique Station and Serendipitea 115 MAIN ST – What was once one of the first gas stations in Elk Park is now a charming stop full of garden antiques, quaint birdhouses and obscure treasures, such as tiny walnut baskets. For a cup of tea with whimsy, step into the Serendipitea shop where you can role-play with the hat of your choice while enjoying a bite of cake or quiche. If you're lucky, you'll catch Nancy Collins at the Autoharp or violin, or perhaps in a storytelling mood. Mon–Sat, 10am–5pm & Sun 1pm–5pm. (828)737-9070.

Take 194 S. Turn R on Hwy 19E (N) to Elk Park. Parallel to Hwy 19E on Main St.

You might want to take your freshly caught mountain trout home and cook it yourself. DON'T FORGET the rosemary in your herb garden. There is no better match for trout than fresh rosemary.

Filet your fish and add rosemary stalks inside the filets, grill and enjoy. You won't believe what a good cook you can be!

...Meanwhile back on the trail

16 Grandfather Mountain Nursery & Garden Center 11468 HWY 105 S – Under the nose of Grandfather, you will find this hillside garden of maximum and native rhododendrons, azaleas, native wildflowers, vegetables and fruits. Apr–Oct Mon–Sat 9am–6pm & Sun 1pm–5pm. Other times by appointment. (828)963-7931.

At Banner Elk at intersection of Hwys 105 and 184 (at Tynecastle), take Hwy 105 N for 2.5 mi. Nursery will be on L.

17 Grandfather Trout Pond and Gem Mine 10767 NC HWY 105 – Grab a rod and reel and throw in a line to catch a dinner of fresh mountain trout. You can grill it on-site and enjoy it at one of the picnic tables. Or, have your trout smoked and save it for a palatial picnic. If the three stocked ponds don't interest you, there are 14 kinds of gems waiting to be discovered at the

KEEP WHAT YOU CATCH

The Road Goes On Forever

Side trips, tidbits, adventures, and treasure hunts

For a rug deodorizer, use a mixture of crushed rosemary, ground cloves and baking soda. Sprinkle on your carpet, leave for an hour, then vacuum it up.

flume. The Follow Your Bliss shop will polish your gems for a fee, custom design your gems into jewelry and mail them to you. Open daily year-round except Christmas. Summer 9:30am–6:30pm. Fall–Dec 10am–5pm. Jan–Mar 12noon–5pm. (828)963-5098.

Heading towards Boone on Hwy 105 N, turn R across from entrance to Seven Devils.

Make sure to stop by the Carlton Gallery for unique garden art and sculpture, like the spectacular piece below.

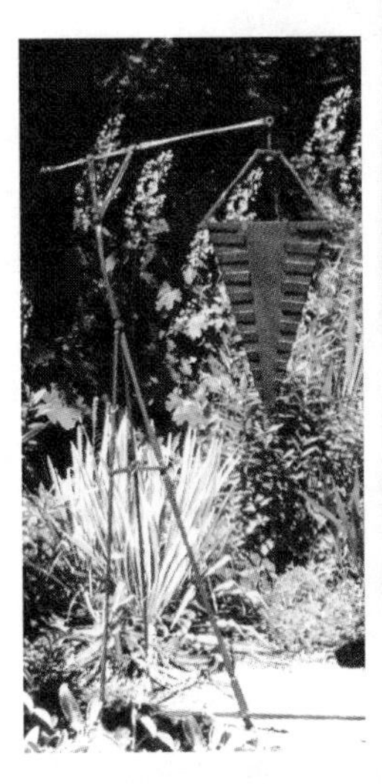

18 **Carlton Gallery** 140 ALDRIDGE RD – Regardless of how tired you may be, the mesmerizing wind sculptures outside this art gallery will lift your spirits. A perennial garden full of wind and stable sculptures lends its magic to the bubbling creek beneath it making this a merry stop along your trail. A fairy-tale bridge crosses the creek to the adjoining gallery of fine art, woven works, sculpture, jewelry, pottery and contemporary crafts. Mon–Sat 10am–5pm, Sun 11am–5pm. Winter hours may vary in inclement weather, so call ahead. (828)963-4288.

Continue on Hwy 105 N about .25 mi past entrance to Seven Devils on L. Turn R on Aldridge Rd at Creekside Galleries.

VALLE CRUCIS

19 **The Ham Shoppe** 124 BROADSTONE RD – If you want to grab lunch before venturing into that bit of heaven known as Valle Crucis, make this your stop. It sits at the intersection of Hwy 105 N and Broadstone Road. While it is famous with the locals for its ham biscuits, vegetarians will find plenty of choices as well. Watch out for birds trying to fly in to roost in the birdhouses, bouquets and floral swags lovingly produced by Susan Musilli of Mountain Flower. (828)963-7756. www.mountainflower.com The Ham Shoppe is open Mon–Sun 8:30am–5pm. Call ahead for a ready-made picnic. (828)963-6310.

20 **Mast Farm Inn and Restaurant** 2543 BROADSTONE RD – When you see the romantic beauty and ageless comfort of this three-story farmhouse, you'll wish it were home. When you walk in, you'll feel like it is.

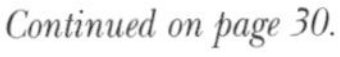
Continued on page 30.

Guidebook Symbols

Kid Friendly Site
1 Farm · 1 Trail · 1 Lodging · 1 Special Attraction
1 Garden · 1 Festival · 1 Restaurant · 1 Garden Art

Over the river and through the woods... to visit Western NC counties between Thanksgiving and Christmas for a "choose and cut" Fraser fir. Many families make annual treks to one of 400 tree farms to hand-pick their own "natural treasure", cut-to-order right out of the field. In 1999, over six-million trees were harvested from 14 NC mountain counties and shipped all over the U.S. and beyond.

Though white pine and blue spruce are also offered, 90 percent of all plantation trees are Fraser firs. Why? This native NC species, named for 18th century Scottish botanist and Appalachian explorer John Fraser, is the country's favorite holiday tree. With an elegant, pyramid shape and a deep evergreen color, it's been the official tree at the White House eight times since 1973. Fraser firs are wonderfully aromatic, hold their needles unusually well, and possess strong upright branches with soft, touchable foliage.

Fir cultivation requirements are beautifully met by high mountain terrain. Steep slopes, inhospitable to other crops, provide excellent drainage. Cool climate and generous rainfall produce sturdy, steady growth and high needle retention. Farms of every size, selling from several dozen trees to hundreds of thousands per year, can be seen peppering the mountainsides in all stages of development.

A typical seven-foot Christmas tree matures in seven to 12 years, seed to harvest. Three years old when planted into hillside fields, the young trees are first sheared when three feet high. This branch-promoting process continues over the years, as does regular pest control and fertilization.

Unlike their plastic substitutes, real trees give back to the environment. Over 50 million Christmas trees are grown in NC on 25,000 acres, enough to supply the population of greater Charlotte with plenty of oxygen. And, for every tree cut, at least one more is planted.

As one grower says, "Let your children come to see where their Christmas trees lived when they were babies." Some families stay for a weekend or more, enjoying cozy B&B's, unique craft galleries and traditional holiday festivities. Summer travelers, check out "Christmas in July" in Ashe County. For brochures, maps and "choose and cut" dates, call the NC Christmas Tree Association in Boone, NC at (800) 562-8789. Or, check out the website at www.ncchristmastrees.com

The Road Goes On Forever

Side trips, tidbits, adventures, and treasure hunts

Don't forget to recycle your Christmas tree. Add peanut butter and birdseed to the branches for a birdfeeder, chip it for mulch, or use to help control erosion.

Choose & Cut Christmas Tree Farms

Watauga:

Big Ridge Tree Farm..........................(828)963-5151
Bordeaux's Fraser Firs......................(828)265-0037
Clawson's Choose and Cut
....(828)264-3162
Cornett-Deal Christmas Tree Farm
....(828)297-1136
Cozy Nook Farm..............................(828)264-2346
Denver and Ann Taylor Nursery
....(828)963-5782
Dotson's Nursery............................ (828)963-4464
Ewing's Fraser Fir Farm...................(828)297-2856
Garry Henson Farms......................(828)264-0809
Gary and Lynda Brown...................(828)264-2800
High Country Nursery....................(828)264-9123
J & D Tree Farms..............................(828)262-1845
Long Ridge Farms.............................(828)297-4373
Payne Christmas Tree and Horse Farm
....(828)297-2255
Raymond Farthing Nursery............(828)297-2646
Walker Farm.......................................(828)264-0931
What Fir!..(828)297-4646

Ashe:

Arrington Tree Farm.........................(336)877-1854
Bards Nursery...................................(336)246-9439
Dixon's Tree Farm.............(336)982-2173 or 3685
Jack's Trees..(336)877-2115
Lee's Trees...(336)246-7936
Lyalls Nursery.....................................(336)246-7516
Mountain Memories Christmas Trees
.... (336)246-7037 or 877-1571
Rambling Springs Ranch...................(336)982-2276
Shady Rest Tree Farm
....(336)877-1908 or 982-2031
Terry Sheets..(336)982-2562
Tim Sexton..(336)982-9293
Top of the Mountain Christmas Trees
....(336)982-3507
Wayland's Nursery............................(336)246-7729

Alleghany:

Bickerstaff Trees, Inc.........(336)372-8866 or 4884
City Limit Trees
.....................................(336)372-6188 or 851-0267
Claude Edwards Tree Farm
....(336)372-4322 or 1711
Crazy Fox Tree Patch......................(336)372-2162
Discount Tree Farm..........................(336)372-8242
Edwards Choose & Cut..................(336)657-3463
Joines Christmas Trees.....................(336)372-4847
Jones Tree Farm.........(336)359-8299 or 657-1720
Lawrence Trees.................................(336)372-8589
Lil' Grandfather Mountain Christmas Tree Farm
....(336)359-8817 or 2537
Maines Tree Farm............................. (336)363-2901
Old Quarry Farm.............................(336)657-3556
Pine Shadows Farm...........(336)363-2890 or 2436
Ritchie's Trees 'N' Trim.....................(336)363-3229
Roberts Tree Farm...........................(336)657-8587
Sam Miller Trees............................... (336)359-2365

Avery:

Bentley Tree Farms............................(828)733-0453
Brook Hollow Nursery.................... (828)733-9161
C & G Nursery, Inc...........................(828)733-4850
Cartner Christmas Tree Farm........ (828)733-2391
Franklin Tree Farms..........................(828)765-2518
Ginger Hollow Nursery...................(828)733-3366
Haw Mountain Nursery.................. (828)733-9298
Milltimber Creek Farms..................(828)733-0718
Raymond Farthing Nursery............(828)297-2646
Red Barn Choose and Cut.............(828)733-5025
River Tree Farm................................(828)898-5762
Sam's Nursery...................................(828)733-3353
Smith, T E...(828)898-9574
Sugar Grove Nursery.......................(828)733-5272
Sugar Plum Farms.............................(888)257-0019
Three Oaks Nursery.........................(828)733-2662
Twin Pines Nursery...........................(828)733-0776
Vaughan's Blue Ridge Nursery
....(828)733-0330 or 5150

Guidebook Symbols
Kid Friendly Site
Farm · Trail · Lodging · Special Attraction
Garden · Festival · Restaurant · Garden Art

You could sit all day and admire the peaceful gardens at the Mast Farm Inn and Restaurant...

Nine rooms with their own flavor of comfort sit atop of the renowned restaurant below serving New Southern Cuisine. Originally constructed in the 1800's, the outbuildings have been beautifully renovated on the inside to become four private cottages—each of them a haven of hospitable warmth. With the scenic old barn and nearby organic gardens of flowers and vegetables, you'll be tempted to take a brush to the palette and muse indefinitely. (828)963-5857. www.mastfarminn.com

Turn L off Hwy 105 N onto Broadstone Rd (SR 1112). Travel 2.5 mi to Inn on L.

21 Altavista Gallery/B&B 2839 BROADSTONE RD – Beauty comes in many forms at this historic B&B. Perennial flower beds encircle the house in a halo of glorious hues while inside, a fine art gallery of garden scenes and plaques offers another serene setting. Don't miss the mountain views from the rockers and swing on the front porch before a stroll to the Watauga River. Mon–Sat 11am–5pm & Sun by appt. Jan–Mar Mon, Thu & Sat 11am–5pm. (828)963-5247. www.altavistagallery.com

Gallery is just down Broadstone Rd on L.

...or you could buckle your seat belt and see what that new car can do on some of the curviest back roads you can imagine. You'll have your car begging for mercy.

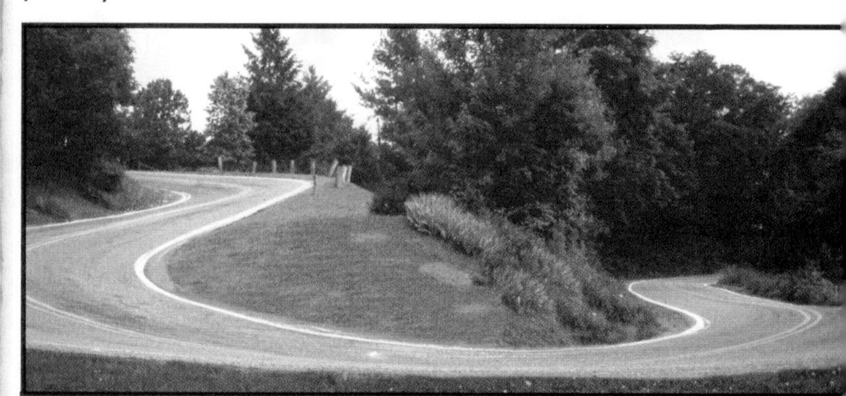

The Road Goes On Forever

Side trips, tidbits, adventures, and treasure hunts

22 Mast General Store Annex/Candy Barrel
2918 BROADSTONE RD – Aside from the fact that there is a slew of fine shopping here, consider cruising to the rear of the store for a bite at the Creekside Deli with a fine view of the Watauga River valley. After eating, you may want to burn a few calories strolling around the leisurely Valle Crucis Park which parallels the river. Or, just enjoy your picnic at one of the tables. Nature provides an extra bargain with the great bird watching. How is it there are people fortunate enough to live here all year long? Mon–Sat 10am–6pm & Sun 1pm–6pm. Winter hours vary. (828)963-6511.
Turn R off Broadstone Rd onto two-lane gravel road.

At the Inn at the Taylor House, you don't have to steal their beautiful garden ideas. They'll gladly show you how to achieve the same look in your own garden.

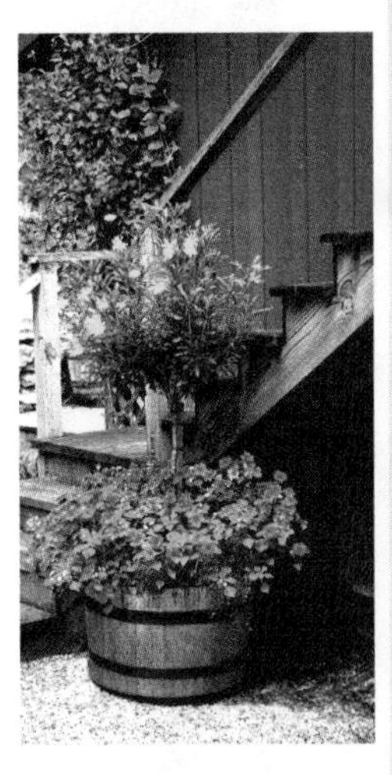

23 Inn at the Taylor House 4584 HWY 194 – This 1910 farmhouse is full of charm, whimsy and roosters—the French symbol of hospitality. Lucky guests of the 10-room inn and Red Cottage enjoy a fresh, gourmet breakfast before wandering about the extensive herb garden and lush landscape. The on-site Milk House Gift Shop features temptations such as white picket fence coat racks and miniature moss-covered twig chairs. Ask about floral workshops and cooking classes. Oh, and the resident calico cat is available for photos. Paris never had it so good. Mon–Sun 9am–6pm. (828)963-5581. www.highsouth.com/Taylorhouse
Just past the Annex, turn L onto Hwy 194 S. Travel approximately .75 mi to Inn on R.

24 Valle Crucis Conference Center
146 SLOLES WAY – Nature and spirituality meet here at the true "Valley of the Cross" where Clarks Creek and Crab Orchard Creek flow toward each other to form a St. Andrews Cross. This is the site of the 1842 Episcopal Mission and now year-round retreat for non-profit groups. Across Hwy 194, the Center maintains a cross-country walking/running trail and two three-circuit labyrinths for the community. Also,

Guidebook Symbols Kid Friendly Site
1 Farm | 1 Trail | 1 Lodging | 1 Special Attraction
1 Garden | 1 Festival | 1 Restaurant | 1 Garden Art

Alpacas were first imported into the United States in 1984 and quickly spread into Canada. Today there are just fewer than 10,000 alpacas in North America. Alpacas and their cousin, the llama, have been domesticated for about 6,000 years. Providing the food, fuel, clothing and transportation for the ancient Inca civilization, alpacas are today still considered a cherished treasure by the peoples of the Altiplano regions of Southern Peru, Bolivia and Chile.

from the Center there is a .5 mile walk back to Crabtree Orchard Falls where local Boy Scouts have labored over handrails and platform steps to make the ascent easier. Vegetables from the garden show up on the dinner table, and a crop of sorghum cane transforms into the heady sweet smell of wood smoke and molasses in October. This is truly God's country. (828)963-4453. www.highsouth.com/vallecrucis

On 194 S, 1.2 mi on R just past the Inn.

25 **Valle Crucis Fair** – Look for Norman Rockwell at this annual fall event held in a hay field near the Conference Center. Celebrate the harvest season with locals by enjoying over 130 food and craft vendors and entertainment. You can even learn how to make apple butter and apple cider. Third Saturday every October. Call the Holy Cross Church for info. (828)963-4609.

Past Conference Center on L just before Dutch Creek Rd.

26 **Fireweed Alpaca Ranch** 1702 DUTCH CREEK RD – Did we take a wrong turn and end up in Peru or perhaps France? Animal husbandry takes on a European approach at

this mountaintop ranch. Teri Phipps and David Schieferstein allow their exotic livestock to live underneath their home in the walk-out basement making access to these cute critters easy, educational and entertaining. Do you know why alpaca fleece is warmer than sheep's? You'll find out in the Fireweed Fibers Natural Clothing Store. Expect to leave your heart behind with Baby Zack. Open Sun & Mon 1pm–4pm and by appointment. (828)963-2766. www.fireweed-ranch.com

Head back towards Valle Crucis on Hwy 194 N, turn R on Dutch Creek Rd. Ranch is .2 mi on your R.

27 **Mast General Store** 3565 HIGHWAY 194 – Just because you can find your way in, doesn't mean you can find your way out—at least not in a hurry. Your quest to find the gardening section will be overrun with an enticing eclectic array of merchandise sidetracking you from

The Road Goes On Forever

Side trips, tidbits, adventures, and treasure hunts

your true mission. A Valle Crucis landmark. Sit a spell on the back porch and enjoy a nickel cup of coffee to take it all in. Mon–Sat 7am–6:30pm & Sun 1pm–6pm. Winter hours vary. (828)963-6511. www.mastgeneralstore.com

Take Hwy 194 N to Valle Crucis Elementary School. Store on R.

BETHEL

Side trip...

28 Cornett-Deal Christmas Tree Farm 142 TANNENBAUM LN – In Mountain Dale Valley, family names endure as much as evergreens in ice storms. Diane Cornett's great-grandfather first settled in the area in 1915. Today, she carries on the legacy of the family name through her Fraser fir tree farm. Unusual handmade ornaments may be found in the craft shop

Originally a German tradition, the Christmas tree did not make it to the United States until the 1800s. It was introduced into Williamsburg, Virginia by Charles Minnegerode, a German immigrant.

along with fresh wreaths and warm apple cider. Nestled just above the trees is the Songbird Cabin with magnificent views of Beech Mountain, the back of Seven Devils and on clear days, the well-known profile of The Grandfather. Opens Fri after Thanksgiving & every Sat 8am–5pm & Sun 1pm–5pm until Christmas. Cabin open year-round. (828)297-1136. www.songbirdcabin.com

From Valle Crucis take 194 N 1.1 mi to L on Mast Gap Rd. Continue for 3.2 mi to Hwy 321. Turn L and continue 6.1 mi to R on Bethel Rd. After 3.2 mi turn L on Mountain Dale Rd. Travel 2.5 mi and turn L onto Tannebaum Ln.

29 Beaverhorn Elk Ranch 377 BEAVERHORN RANCH RD – North Carolina has joined the Eastern states of Kentucky and Tennessee in

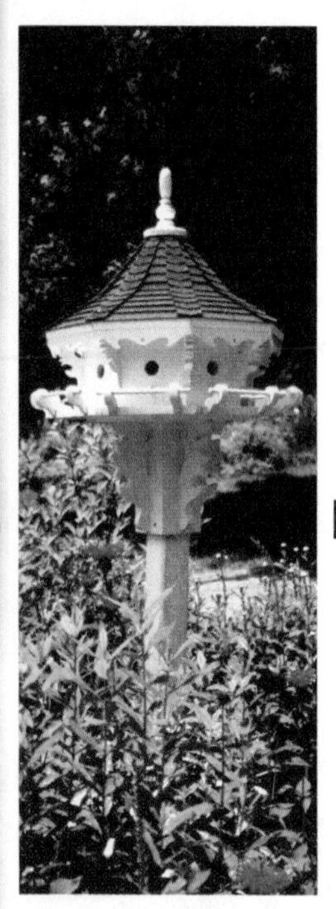

The four-diamond rating doesn't only apply to the human guests of the Lovill Inn in downtown Boone. It's also where discriminating birds stay.

releasing elk into the wild, but Pete and Joey Perdue have their own herd that you can view. From late-May through June, you can see the baby elk, and from September-October you can hear the hauntingly beautiful tones of bulls bugling. Discover the journey of harvested antlers to the Orient where they are processed for pharmaceuticals. Mon & Thu 10am–12noon & 2pm–4pm. (828)297-1193.

Turn L on Mtn Dale Rd and travel about 2 mi as road becomes Beaver Dam Rd. Turn R on Beaverhorn Ranch Rd.

...Meanwhile back on the trail

COVE CREEK

30 **Farm Heritage Days** 207 DALE ADAMS RD – It's a Who's Who of the Watauga farming community. If you want to see it all in one scenic stop, this is the one to make. Christmas trees and bees, apples and ornamentals, herbs and emus, elk and alpacas, the High Country sky is the limit. Third Saturday in September from 10am–5pm. (828)297-2200.

From 194 in Valle Crucis take 194 to L on Mast Gap Rd. Turn L and immediately turn R onto Old Hwy 421. Festival is held on the L in the park in front of Cove Creek School.

VILAS

31 **Payne Christmas Tree & Horse Farm** 959 SHERWOOD RD – You'll be impressed with this tidy Wildlife Demonstration Farm from the moment you drive through the stand of pines at the driveway entrance. When walking among the Fraser firs, you're likely to send a covey of wild turkeys squawking skyward. Appaloosa horses graze in the lush green valley below the Christmas trees, which makes it hard to resist a ride or at least the gift of an apple. Open Thanksgiving–Christmas. Fri–Sun 9am–5pm & Mon–Thu by appointment. (828)297-2255.

From Cove Creek, continue N on Old 421 for .5 mi to Sherwood Rd. Turn R on Sherwood Rd. Farm is .3 mi on R.

ZIONSVILLE

32 **Shady Grove Gardens** 904 WILL ISAACS RD – Susan Wright is ready to take you on a

The Road Goes On Forever

Side trips, tidbits, adventures, and treasure hunts

Both the onion and asparagus are members of the lily family.

pleasant path through the trees to two acres of over 300 perennials. On Sundays in July, you can pick your choice of daylilies and she'll dig them up for you. Flowering shrubs, viburnums, hydrangeas and cut flowers provide fireworks of color and fragrance. Mid-Apr–Oct Sat & Sun 1pm–5pm & Mon 9am–5pm. (828)297-4098.

Continue on Sherwood Rd, take L on Hwy 421N for 2.7 mi. Turn R on Will Isaacs Rd, 1 mi on L.

Pass through the arbor and into 11 acres of quiet woods at the Lovill House.

BOONE

33 **Lovill House** 404 OLD BRISTOL RD – This historic B&B wears the tiara of a four-diamond rating due to impeccable, well-appointed rooms complete with wormy chestnut arches, pine and maple floors, and a tasty gourmet breakfast. It's the grounds, however, that will really astound you. Although within the city limits, this country home features 11 acres of beauty to stroll through, complete with a bubbling stream, pristine waterfall, lovely old barn, and a colorful explosion of perennials. Innkeepers Anne and Scott will arrange mountain bike and rafting trips too. (828)264-4204. www.lovillhouseinn.com

From the junction of Hwy 421 and 321W of Boone, drive 5 mi. Turn L onto 3rd Old Bristol Rd. Inn will be on L.

34 **Sculpture Gardens at ASU Visual Arts Center** 733 RIVER ST – Contemplate outdoor sculpture from ASU's permanent collection or the annual Rosen Competition as you stroll through this state university campus. Pieces reflect the gamut of styles and materials. Art located throughout Appalachian State University Campus. For more information visit the Turchin Center for Visual Art or call (828)262-3017.

35 **Angelica's** 506 WEST KING ST – Somewhere on earth at this very

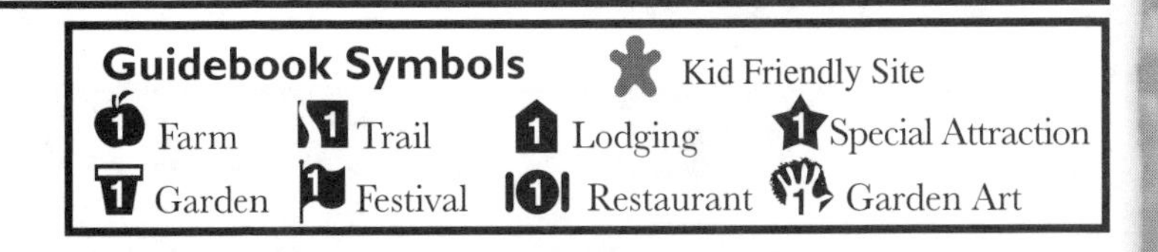

moment, someone is probably making a pilgrimage to this organic vegetarian restaurant and juice bar to partake of the tomato roasted garlic soup. Nova and Mike Nelson create exciting entrees and appetizers using organic produce from their own farm. In keeping with their pledge to the environment, they compost all the 600 lbs. or so of weekly food scraps to naturally replenish the soil at their nearby farm. Mon–Sat 11am–9pm & Sun 11am–5pm. (828)265-0809.

On Hwy 421(King St) in downtown Boone.

36 What Fir! 6671 JUNALUSKA RD – The innovative name is only the beginning. On this all-walkable 40-acre Christmas tree farm, you'll find beautiful ponds and mountain scenery to explore before venturing to choose and cut your own tree. The gift shop is full of local crafts such as birdhouses, baskets and The Alpaca Corner–a showcase of sweaters, head bands, hats, scarves and little finger puppets made from this soft wool. On some December weekends, you might even find several alpacas ready for photos (compliments of Fireweed Ranch). A box of holiday costumes delights the kids and, no doubt, amuses the alpacas. Watch how wreaths and table-top decorations are made. Opens one weekend before Thanksgiving–one week before Christmas 9am–5pm. (828)297-4646. www.whatfirtreefarm.com

From the New Market Center at Hwy 421/221 and Hwy 194, turn N on 194 and go 1.7 mi to Howard's Creek Rd. Turn L and go 6.5 mi where road turns to Junaluska Rd. Continue 1 mi and turn R at sign.

37 Daniel Boone Native Gardens 651 HORN IN THE WEST DR – Native flora of the region is featured in this 10-acre garden sponsored by the Garden Club of NC. Rare and endangered species may be seen amongst the bog garden,

Daniel Boone Native Gardens

Next door to "Horn in the West", this sanctuary for native plants is a living field guide on three acres. It was conceived in 1957 with the twin goals of education and conservation. The informal design now spreads over a triangular plot generously provided by the city of Boone.

Curving paths invite an easy, graceful amble through several distinct habitats - including a fern garden, twining vine arbor and **(cont'd)**

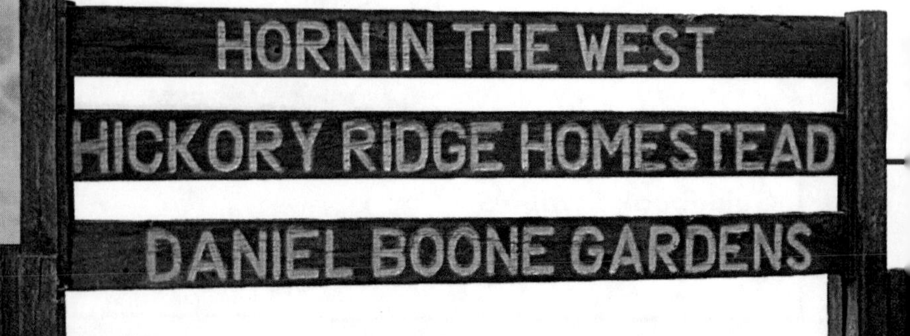

arbor and meditation garden. Admission is $2pp. Open May 1–mid-Oct. (828)264-6390. The self-guided Boone Area Home and Garden Tour which is held annually on the second Saturday in July from 10am–4pm begins at this location. (828)264-7270.

From King St, turn R on Blowing Rock Rd. After 2 blocks, turn L on Horn in the West Dr and follow to end.

38 **Hickory Ridge Homestead Museum** HORN IN THE WEST DR – While you're at the Native Gardens, don't miss a chance to visit this recreated Appalachian homestead just next door. If you're lucky you may visit on a day when the museum sponsors natural dye demonstrations. In late October, you can find the perfect apple here at the annual apple festival. Group tours available. June–Aug Tues–Sun 5pm–8pm. Aug–Oct Sat–Sun 5pm–8pm (828)264-9089.

Next door to the legendary Horn in the West Theatre.

39 **Watauga County Farmer's Market** HORN IN THE WEST DR – For almost 30 years this farmer's market has brought locally grown produce and plants, as well as local crafts, out of the hills and into the parking lot of the Horn in the West. Visitors and locals alike can enjoy the bounty of this region, be it from the earth or the hand. Open Sat mornings May–Oct and also on Wed mornings July–Aug. (828)297-3017.

40 **Appalachian Cultural Museum** UNIVERSITY HALL DR – Whether it's the weather that is sending you indoors or a quest for knowledge, the Appalachian Cultural Museum fits the bill. Reflecting Appalachian life through both permanent and temporary exhibits, the museum educates guests about the history and culture of the area, offering something for all ages. Tue–Sat 10am–5pm & Sun 1pm–5pm. Group tours available. (828)262-3117.

Take 221-321 S (Blowing Rock Rd) toward Blowing Rock. Past Staples, L onto University Hall Dr.

the most recent addition, a bog garden. Dedicated in 1992 and created by volunteers, the small bog hosts an incomparable selection of rare and unusual species.

Wildflowers, ferns, shrubs and

flowering trees are well-marked and plentiful. Most plants, from the common to the endangered, have been gathered or donated by gardeners from across the state.

Supported by the NC Garden Clubs and individual contributions of money, materials and sweat equity, this charming garden opens its gates (wrought by Daniel Boone VI) from May through October, weather permitting.

Do you want a garden around your bird feeder? Add millet seed to the mix and let the birds do the work for you. They are messy eaters, and the dropped seed will create a small garden around the feeder next year.

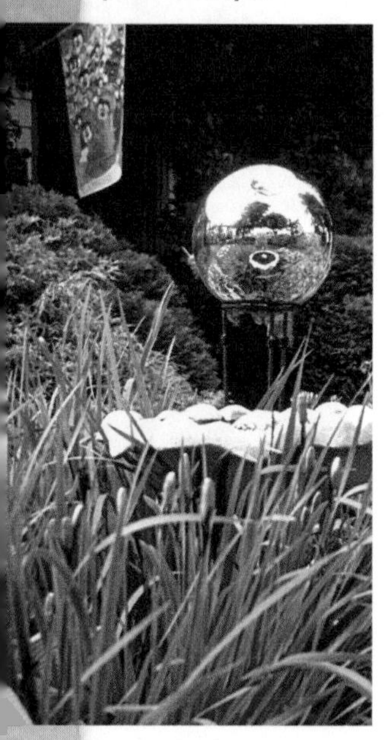

41 **The Arbor** 4416 HWY 105 S – A unique store so full of nature that a flying squirrel has made the back porch his home. A creative variety of locally made willow and mountain twig furniture, birdhouses and arbors will have you looking in all directions at once. You'll also appreciate the hand-painted slates, potter benches, garden angels and when in season, ivy and perennials. From the back porch you can gaze down upon Laurel Creek as it rushes over mossy stones on its way past Flintlock Campground behind the store. There's a rustic trail down to the water if you've time to while away in a tranquil spot. Apr–Oct Mon–Sat 10am–5pm. Nov–Mar Wed–Sat 10am–5pm. (828)963-7475. www.thearbor.net

At the junction of Hwys 105 and 321, take 105 S for 3 mi. Store is on R.

BLOWING ROCK

42 **Inn at Yonahlossee** 226 OAKLEY GREEN – A popular girls' camp with the Cherokee name for "Trail of the Bear" is now a 300-acre resort bordering Moses Cone Memorial Park. Pristine views can be had for a song from any of the private cottages, homes and Inn rooms. World-class facilities include The Equestrian Center, indoor and outdoor tennis courts, fitness center and indoor pool. There are miles of bridle trails, walking trails, autumn leaves to examine and river rocks to admire. Yeah, you'll sing all right. Open daily year-round 8am–6pm. (828)962-1986. www.yonahlossee.com

From Hwy 105 S, turn L on Poplar Grove Rd. Travel 3.8 mi to Shull's Mill Rd. Inn is on R. (From BRP, exit at Mile Post 294.5. This is the 221/Blowing Rock exit. Bear R and follow Shull's Mill Rd for 2.5 mi.)

43 **The Gamekeeper** 3005 SHULLS MILL RD – Tucked into the mountainside across the road from the Yonahlossee Inn, you'll find a woodsy restaurant featuring Modern Mountain Cuisine in a warm atmosphere. Stone fireplace and intimate bar provide comfort while inhaling aromas from the hickory-wood-fired grill. Limited outdoor dining. May–Oct Mon–Sat

About one million acres of land are used for growing Christmas trees. Each acre provides the daily oxygen requirements of 18 people.

6pm–10pm. Nov–Apr Fri–Sat 6pm–10pm. (828)963-7400.

Continue on Shull's Mill Rd. Entrance is .2 mi on L.

44 **Hebron Falls Trail** If your soul needs to be soothed by the sound of a waterfall, take this 30-minute non-strenuous walk. Beautiful in all seasons but especially impressive with ice sculptures in the winter months.

Continue further on Shull's Mill Rd. for .5 mi to gravel Old Turnpike Rd on R. Follow through residential area. Continue for 1.3 mi around several curves to a distinct U leading up mountain. Wide area at U curve for parking. Trail entrance across from U.

45 **NC Mountains to Sea Trail** A white pine forest with ferns and wildflowers surround you on an easy and scenic piece of the statewide trail. The one-hour well-graded trail takes you through country walked and loved by the Cherokee and pioneers alike. Non-strenuous.

From Shull's Mill Rd, go .3 mi past Old Turnpike Rd. Continue to a row of maple trees on the R side of the road with steps leading up the L bank. Park on the shoulder near the large trees. You'll see a wooden pasture fence emerging at the end of the trees. Use the provided wooden entry into the pasture.

46 **Trout Lake** Just before Shull's Mill intersects the Parkway access, turn onto a narrow one-way paved road leading into the woods. Follow this road all the way to the parking lot. The trail is level with beautiful flowers and rhododendron and leads around the lake.

To get to 221 toward Blowing Rock take L out of parking lot.

Dry, south-facing slopes have extremely acidic soils that support evergreens such as mountain laurel and pines, as well as oaks, huckleberries, blueberries, and hickories.

Moist, north-facing slopes support mixed evergreen and hardwood growths generally dominated by hemlock, tulip poplar, and maple.

Species-rich cove hardwood forests dominate lower slopes and creek drainages. The sheltered sites support a wide range of flowering understory trees, showy ferns and wildflowers, and dense stands of rhododendron.

The clearest way into the universe is through a forest wilderness.
-- John Muir

If your kids are "trailhopping" with you, check out the very first theme park in North Carolina, Tweetsie Railroad! The western-themed park offers a ride back in time via a wild west town and an old steam engine locomotive.
Open first weekend in May–mid-May Fri-Sun. Mid-May-–mid-Aug daily. Mid-Aug–Oct Fri–Sun. 9am-6pm.
(800) 526-5740.
The park is located on Highway 321 in Blowing Rock.

47 Glen Burney Trail and Cannon Memorial Gardens Skirting the New Year's Creek, this ancient 1.5 mile trail descends about 800 feet below Blowing Rock providing breathtaking vistas of two waterfalls, the Glen Burney and the Glen Mary. Steep grade.

From Main St in Blowing Rock turn R onto Laurel Ln. You will see a sign directing you to Cannon Memorial Gardens. Take R at stop sign. Trail and Gardens will be on your L.

48 Speckled Trout & Oyster Bar Café Magic happens when David Bartlett smokes fresh local rainbow trout with hickory and apples. It disappears. Enjoy trout smoked as an appetizer or panfried as an entrée. Either way, you can't miss. Open daily 9am–3pm & 5pm–9pm. (828)295-9819.

On the corner of Main St and Hwy 221 S.

49 The Village Café MAIN ST – If you want to start your day off right, you would be well advised to begin with breakfast or brunch at this popular, seasonal café. Customers may choose between dining amongst tassel ferns, rhododendrons and pagoda trout lilies in the courtyard or in one of the two cabins, which are both listed on the National Register of Historic Places. Regulars know that on the weekends reservations aren't just recommended; they are necessary. Open daily mid-Apr–Nov 8am–3pm except Wed. Closed Dec–mid-Apr. (828)295-3769.

Access off Main St on L.

The Village Café offers a quiet refuge from the busy main street of Blowing Rock. Tucked back behind Main Street you can lunch in a luscious garden and then hit the shopping streets after you have rejuvenated yourself.

50 Crippens Country Inn and Restaurant 239 SUNSET DR – Ever tasted a sage fritter? You're in for a treat. The herb gardens compliment Chef James Welch's culinary creations while the English gardens of peonies, phlox, hyacinths, red honeysuckle, Japanese iris and lilac could inspire you to write a sonnet. Don't miss the blueberries in mid-summer. This elegant country inn features eight rooms and a cozy chestnut-walled cottage. Restaurant is open:

The Road Goes On Forever

Side trips, tidbits, adventures, and treasure hunts

Don't rake your leaves, just mow them on your lawn and you've got a natural fertilizer for your lawn.

mid-June–Oct Mon–Sun 6pm–close & Nov–mid-June Thu–Sat 6pm–close. (828)295-3487. www.crippens.com

Off of Main St on Sunset Dr.

FLEETWOOD

51 **Creation Herbal Products** 13765C HWY 221 – Anna Carter and Mike Hulbert have the distinct honor of having produced the first NC Goodness Grows! product to be exported to Japan. The warehouse where they make natural herb and plant-based soaps, bath, beauty and medicinal products is an interesting educational experience. Take a bar with you for the end of the trail. Mon–Fri 10am–4pm. (828)262-0006. www.creationsoap.com

From Blowing Rock, take the BRP to Mile Post 276.4. Take Hwy 421 to Deep Gap. At Deep Gap, turn L off Hwy 421 onto Hwy 221 N. Travel 1 mi to last driveway on L in Watauga County next to church.

52 **River Farm Inn** 179 RIVER RUN BRIDGE RD – Do you remember your mother saying, "Don't act like you were raised in a barn!" She wasn't talking about this one. An 1880's reconstructed dairy barn provides two suites, French Country and Victorian, with luxurious amenities and inviting grounds along the New River to explore. Hillside trails lead through 125 acres of woods reminiscent of Walden. Or, take an easy seven-mile bike ride into historic Todd. There is also a carriage-house suite and a log cabin for families. (336)877-1728.

Continue on Hwy 221 N for about 5 mi Turn L onto Railroad Grade Rd, just past the fire department and elementary school. Follow for 3.5 mi along the river to bridge on L.

GLENDALE SPRINGS

53 **Glendale Springs Inn and Restaurant** 7414 HWY 16 – Amanda Smith knows her flowers—all 245 varieties of them. Delicate specimens like Bleeding Heart and Rosehips add to the overall Victorian feel of this lovely inn. Follow the

Red Rose Vinegar
1 cup red rose petals
8 cups wine vinegar

Wash the dried rose petals and dry. Macerate in the vinegar for 10 days. Stir each day. Strain into sterilized bottles.

Nature never breaks her own laws.
-- Leonardo da Vinci

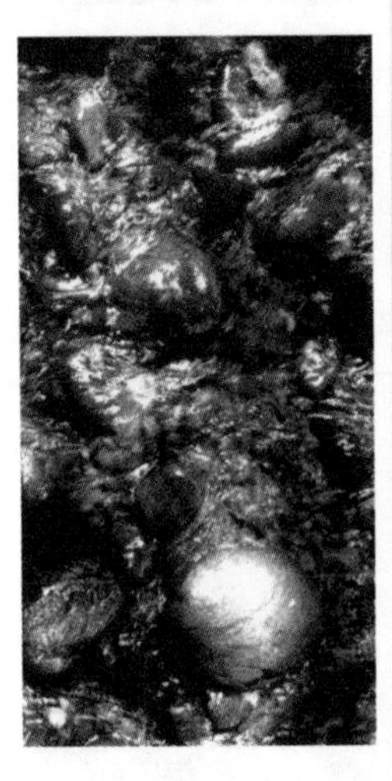

Guidebook Symbols

Kid Friendly Site

1 Farm · 1 Trail · 1 Lodging · 1 Special Attraction

1 Garden · 1 Festival · 1 Restaurant · 1 Garden Art

wrap-around porch from one end to the other and you'll be convinced you've entered a more romantic era. Under the grapevine arbor leading to the herb garden is the perfect spot to pledge eternal love to your beloved. Superb restaurant and beautiful rooms. Call Bill Clinton for a reference. Restaurant open Mon–Sat 11am–2pm & 5pm–9pm. Sun brunch 11am–2pm. Closed Wed. (336)982-2103. www.appnetsite.com/glendalesprings.htm

From Hwy 221 turn S for .5 mi and turn L on SR 1169. Travel about 5 mi and turn L on SR 1003 (Idlewild Rd.) Travel 4.5 mi and turn R on Hwy 163 and proceed 1.4 mi to Hwy 16 N. Turn L and travel 2 mi to Glendale Springs. Inn is on L

54 **Holy Trinity Episcopal Church** For artistic and mystical inspiration, be sure to pay homage to Ben Long's Last Supper fresco in this quaint church. The tranquil grounds are a good place to stop and reflect on a bench or enjoy a peasant lunch at a picnic table. Open daily year-round and 24 hours a day.

On Hwy 16 from BRP exit at Mile Post 259.

Holy Trinity Church, inside and out.

Special attraction:

55 **Greenhouse Crafts** 248 JW LUKE RD – There once was an old greenhouse behind this retail shop, hence the name. Unusual collection of garden accessories such as wormy chestnut flower vases, shepherd's crook stakes, hand painted flower pots and iron garden edging. Enjoy the gardens outside as Michael Bell strikes enchanting chords on the dulcimer. Mon–Sun 10am–5pm. (336)982-6666.

Across from Church of the Frescoes.

LAUREL SPRINGS

56 **Sam Miller Trees and Meadow Ridge Campground** Enjoy breathtaking views of the Blue Ridge Parkway while picking out a Christmas tree for your family. Call ahead for tours. Open Nov 18–Dec 24 Mon–Sun 9am–5pm. (336)359-2365.

Access the BRP at Mile Post 259 in Glendale Springs. Take Hwy18 N exit towards Laurel Springs turn L and go under BRP. Continue .2 mi. Farm will be on L.

The Road Goes On Forever

Side trips, tidbits, adventures, and treasure hunts

The only Zen you find on the tops of mountains is the Zen you bring up there.
– Robert Pirsig

57 **Tucker Farms** 300 CRANBERRY CREEK CABIN – This is where the trail leads to trout. Stay in this two-bedroom rustic cabin with 1.5 mile frontage of Cranberry Creek, a favorite haunt of local rainbow trout. Fraser fir and tobacco farming co-exist amicably with this retreat featuring 250 acres of trails marked for birdwatching. Open Apr–Dec Mon–Sat 8am–5pm & Sun 1pm–5pm. (336)982-3442.

At Laurel Springs, turn L off Hwy 18 N onto Hwy 88. Travel 2 mi to R on Upper Cranberry Creek Rd. After 1 mi, cross creek and turn R on private Cranberry Creek Trail, .25 mi to cabin.

Don't forget your birding books if you plan on staying at the Tucker Farms Cabin.

58 **Burgiss Farm** 294 ELK KNOB RD – 55 F° is the temperature of the earth. Know that before you get here and Tom Burgiss will give you a sample of the wine he makes on-site at Grapestompers. You can see wine being made and purchase a how-to kit to take home. Next door, the Burgiss Barn shakes it up every Saturday night from 7pm–11pm with bluegrass and old-time mountain music. Admission is $5pp. Anything that can be cooked on a barbecue pit is available. Two-bedroom B&B available to one party at a time. You can't leave this farm without a smile on your face. 800)233-1505. www.grapestompers.com

Take 18 E toward Sparta .9 mi. Turn R on Elk Knob Rd. Burgiss Barn will be on R.

If you want to see some trails and prefer biking to hiking, bring your mountain bike along for the trip. WNC has many trails just for bike enthusiasts. If you don't have a bike, but you want to ride the trails, Buffalo Bob's will be happy to rent you one...or two!

BLUE RIDGE PARKWAY

59 **Buffalo Bob's** MILE POST 232 – This eclectic store offers Blue Ridge Parkway sightseers a needed snack break. If dinner is more what you had in mind, you better bait a rod and head toward the trout pond. Bike rentals and two cabins are also available. Wed–Sat 11am–8pm & Sun 1pm–8pm. (336)372-2433.

Off BRP at Mile Post 232 on L.

60 **Inn of the Red Thread** 110 MOUNTAIN HEARTH DR – Innkeepers Diane Lasley & Shelly Wilson adopted the name from an

Guidebook Symbols

Kid Friendly Site · Farm · Trail · Lodging · Special Attraction · Garden · Festival · Restaurant · Garden Art

Rose and Honey Syrup

1/2 cup dried rosebuds
1/2 cup distilled water
2 lbs. honey

Put the roses into a bowl and pour the boiling distilled water over them. Let the rose tea infuse for 5 hours. Strain the liquor off into a saucepan, then stir in the honey. Bring slowly to a boil and simmer until it is a thick syrup. Pour into sterilized bottles, seal and label.

Perfect for pancakes!

ancient Chinese legend. A rustic and restful B&B with cozy amenities and a labyrinth for meditation walks. Bubbling creek, ponds, trails and wildlife will work their wonders on your blood pressure. Nutty grain pancakes are a favorite at breakfast. Inviting lodge restaurant open to public on Friday nights. Corporate, educational and spiritual retreats offered. (336)372-8743. www.innoftheredthread.com
From the BRP, turn R onto Vestal Rd just before Mile Post 231. Turn R again onto Mountain Hearth Dr.

61 **Pine Shadows Farm** 111 CAMP BUTLER RD – You can feel the heart of this forest green farmhouse beating in rhythm with nature amidst the surrounding stands of Christmas trees. Wheel-thrown and slab-built pottery by Robin and Daniel at Carter Pots on-site. Call ahead for hours. Trees sold Thanksgiving–second weekend in Dec. (336)363-2436.
Turn R on Vestal Rd to R on Rash Rd. Travel 1 mi to R on Cherry Lane Rd. At intersection with Hwy 21, turn R (S) and travel .8 mi to Camp Butler Rd. Farm is on L.

ENNICE/SPARTA

62 **The Little Farm** 1385 BIG OAK RD – True to its name, Frances Huber's petting farm is indeed the place for little folks and children at heart. Miniature goats, sheep, horses, cows and potbellied pigs share the views with "Oreo Cookie cows." What's not allowed here: living vicariously through your children…be here now! Tue–Sat 10am–5pm. Call for groups of 15 or more. (336)657-3013. www.thelittlefarm.com
Take Hwy 21 N towards Sparta, travel approximately. 4.5 mi to R on Foxridge Rd just past Macedona Rd which is on L. Take R onto Barrett Rd. At .3 mi turn R onto Big Oak Rd. Farm is 7 mi on R.

Gooseberry pie. Enough said!

63 **Senator's House** 360 MAIN ST – Have you ever had fresh gooseberry pie? If not, don't postpone joy. The fine restaurant in this historic house offers delicious renditions of local produce. Thu–Sat 6pm–10pm. (336)372-7500.
Downtown Sparta.

The Road Goes On Forever
Side trips, tidbits, adventures, and treasure hunts

64 **Bald Knob Farmhouse** 50 BALD KNOB RD. – If you have a big group traveling together, just rent this whole four-bedroom house with everything you need except food. Dwarf nandinas and jonquils celebrate life under the black walnuts and invite you to the party by way of the walking trails. Past hay rakes and mowers, you've four miles to walk to the New River. (336)372-4191.

Take Hwy 18 N out of Sparta for 4 mi to Francis Motors on R. Turn L on Pleasant Home Rd. Go 1 mi to Bald Knob Rd on L.

Gardening Wisdom:

When planting under trees, dig individual planting holes for each plant. Add compost to each hole before adding plants. You'll find that both your tree and your plants will thrive.

65 **Red Roof Farms** 200 RED ROOF LN – Miniature horses will grab your heart in a big way at this 200-acre farm on Bald Knob Mountain. Hiking trails crisscross the rolling green hills and up through the trees on the ridge with views you can't put a price on. Ducks vacillate happily in their perfect world of three trout ponds. You can choose between four two-bedroom cottages that come complete with breakfast and an infusion of serenity. Take a bottle of the spring water with you when you leave…reluctantly. (336)372-8785.

From Pleasant Home Rd turn L onto Vox Rd. Farm is third driveway on L.

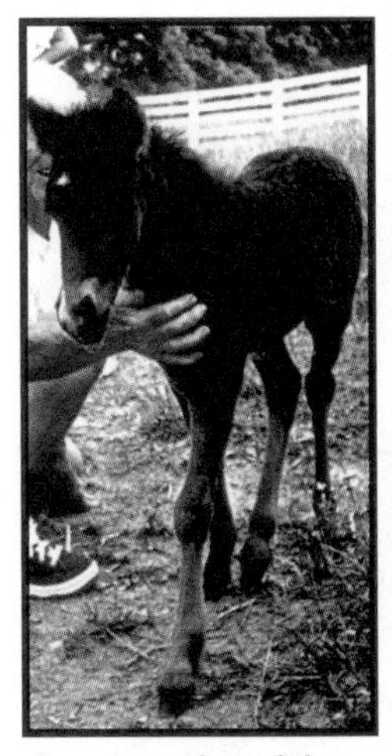

A new member of the Red Roof Farms family.

PINEY CREEK

66 **Mangum Pottery** TURKEY HOLLOW LN – Gardens of whimsy will playfully call to you as you make your way to the pottery studio. This quiet mountain studio boasts a serene pond and a pottery-filled garden. Apr–Dec Thu–Sat 10am–4pm. Call for appointment Jan–Mar. (336)372-5291.

From Sparta, take Hwy 221 for about 5 mi. Turn R onto Walnut Branch Rd. Travel .8 mi and turn R onto Stratford Rd. Continue for .7 mi and take R on Halsey. Travel 1.3 mi and then L onto Turkey Hollow Ln. Continue to top of the hill. Studio is on L.

Fun pottery in a whimsical garden - what a combination!

Don't forget to stock up on cheese and crackers at the New River General Store for a tasty road-trip snack.

67 **New River General Store** US 221 – For three generations, folks around these parts have enjoyed the old-time country store with hoop cheese, hand-ground coffee, country hams, mountain honey and molasses, as well as a sundry of groceries, toys and housewares. Take a stroll on the banks of the New River or rent a canoe or kayak. Camping and fishing supplies also in stock. Mon–Sun 8:30am–6pm. (336)982-9192.

Continue back on Hwy 113 to R on Hwy 221. Travel 3.4 mi and cross the New River. Store will be immediately on your R.

SHATLEY SPRINGS

68 **Shatley Springs Inn Restaurant** SHATLEY SPRINGS RD – OK, we'll tell you that you need to visit this spot for the water. And, you're going to need a big glass of it to wash down the country style meal you'll consume. Serving breakfast, lunch and dinner including family style. Open Mon–Sun 7am–9pm. (336)982-2236.

Take Hwy 221 to intersection with Hwy 16. Turn R on 16 N and travel 1.3 mi to sign on L.

For a refreshing summer beverage, try this recipe for Lavender Lemonade

1 1/2 cups sugar
5 cups water
12 stems fresh lavender
2 1/4 cups lemon juice

Boil 2 1/2 cups of water with sugar. Add lavender stems and remove from heat. Place lid on the pot and let cool. When cool, add 2 1/2 cups water and the lemon juice. Strain out the lavender. Serve with crushed ice and garnish with lavender blossoms.

CRUMPLER/GRASSY CREEK

69 **River House Inn & Restaurant** 1896 OLD FIELD CREEK RD – "Take me to the river"... and then take me here and leave me. Four miles of staircase trails ramble in and among the wooded bluffs behind this unique B&B. What appears to be old outbuildings in need of new paint, transform into luxurious suites and cabins on the inside. Eight guest rooms in the inn enjoy the heavenly fragrant ambience that wafts from below in the five-star restaurant. The 500-year-old sycamore down by the New River deserves at least honorable mention. Open year-round. (336)982-2109. www.riverhousenc.com

Travel 3.2 mi on Hwy 16 N to L onto Old Field Creek Rd. (SR 1539) just past the bridge. Turn R at stop sign travel about .5 mi to Inn on R.

The Road Goes On Forever

Side trips, tidbits, adventures, and treasure hunts

Lavender is one of the most commonly used fragrant herbs. It is very easy to grow and can even survive in exceptionally dry conditions.

JEFFERSON

70 **Summit Support Services** 406 COURT ST – You can buy daylilies and other plants here but there's no price on the good feeling you'll have when you leave. This cottage industry of craft items, herbs, bulbs, perennials and baked goods supports Homefolks, a group home for adults with developmental disabilities. Mon–Fri 9am–3pm. (336)246-4491.

Recently moved to 406 Court St off of Main St in Jefferson across from the post office

71 **High Country Greenhouses** 1990 HWY 88 – Hydroponic tomatoes, annuals, geraniums, poinsettias, aquatic plants, koi, fruits, vegetables, bedding plants, herbs, perennials, trees and shrubs live happily ever after in the greenhouses surrounding a fairy tale cottage and goldfish pond. Open year-round Mon–Sat 8am–5pm & May 1–July 1 Sun 8am–5pm. (336)246-4030.

Take Business 221 to NC 88 towards Warrensville. Go 2 mi and greenhouse is on R.

72 **Mt. Jefferson State Natural Area** 1481 MT. JEFFERSON STATE PARK ROAD – On a clear day, you can see much of Ashe and Alleghany Counties from here. The .3 mile Summit Trail is an easy ascent through a cove forest of red maples, yellow birch and basswood. Deer, red-tailed hawks, and red squirrels locally known as "boomers" enjoy life in this botanical paradise. Open daily Nov–Feb 9am–5pm, Mar & Oct 9am–6pm, Apr, May & Sept 9am–7pm, & June–Aug 9am–8pm. (336)246-9653.

Hwy 221 Bypass to SR 1152 (Mt. Jefferson State Park Rd) Continue to top of mountain.

WEST JEFFERSON

73 **Smoky Mountain Barbecue** 1008 S JEFFERSON AVE – They "will serve no swine before its time" referring to the pork's 20-hour roasting period or maybe customers with bad manners. Since the early 1900's, salt, brown sugar, fresh mountain air and time have been the only ingredients

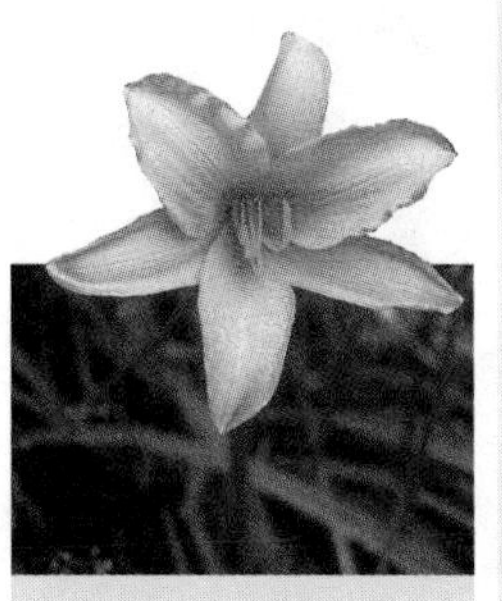

If you want your garden bright and colorful all summer try adding these 10 annuals to the mix. They bloom all summer!

Annual Baby's Breath
Brazilian Vervain
Cleome
Feverfew
'Flamingo Feather' Wheat Celosia
Flowering Tobacco
Heliotrope
Mealycup Sage
Snapdragon
Sweet Alyssum

No, you didn't miss this barn along the trail. It's one of folk artist Don Stevenson's hand sculpted replica birdhouses. Stop at his studio in Morganton. (Page 176 Site 20.)

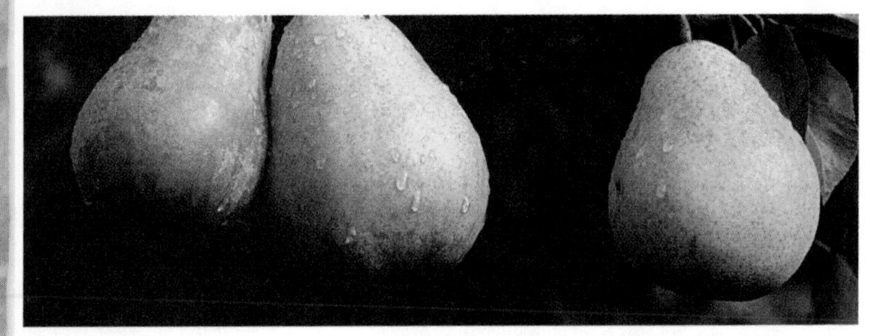

If you want pears, or apples, to appear whole in your fruit display but be cored and ready to eat, core them from the bottom. Take the corer and insert it at the bottom of the fruit to just below the stem, but not through the stem.

Buying local foods from farmers allows you to directly support family farms, rural communities and the environment.

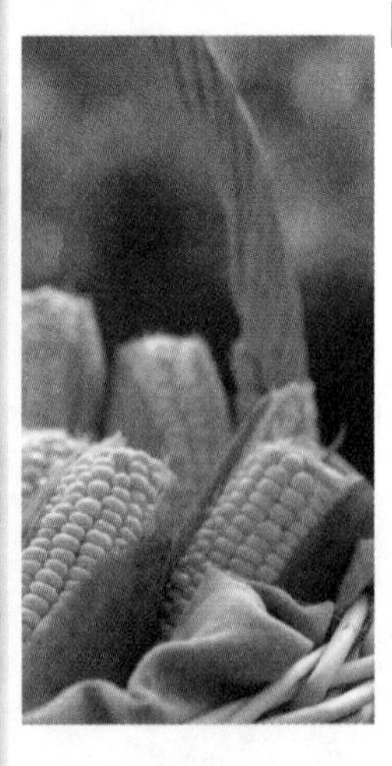

that A.B. Vannoy Ham Company has used for its curing process a few blocks away. Call for tours of ham company. Restaurant open Mon–Thu 10:30am–9pm. Fri–Sat 10:30am–10pm. Closed Sun. (336)246-6818.

From Jefferson take 321 Business into W Jefferson. 3 mi on R.

74 **The Tobin Farm Inns** TOBIN FARM RD – Pastures of apple and pear trees, miles of marked trails with streams and waterfalls, and a spring-fed pond full of ducks are amenities of the two-bedroom renovated barn and two-bedroom cabin built around a tree. (336)877-1302. www.TobinFarmInns.com

Continue S on Hwy 221 past the intersection with Hwy 194. Turn L on Nettle Knob Rd and travel 2.7 mi to Tobin Farm Rd. Barn is on R.

Side trip...

LANSING

75 **Miller Century Farm** 324 MILLER DR – A microcosm of Blue Ridge heritage, this fifth generation farm has seen the production of corn, molasses, wheat and cattle. A walking trail goes up 3700' with views of Mt. Jefferson and Mt. Rogers. The rich soil once tilled by antique farm tools and still fed by seven springs, now reaps a bounty of prize-winning vegetables in the greenhouse. Primitive camping available. Open year-round. Call ahead for tours. (336)384-2332.

At Lansing, take Little Horse Creek Rd to L on Long Branch Rd to end. Turn R on Monroe Miller Rd. Turn L up driveway at second trailer. Pick up the trail again back on Hwy 194 S of West Jefferson.

The Road Goes On Forever

Side trips, tidbits, adventures, and treasure hunts

In the 1800's, cornmeal was often used with soap to wash the dirt from farmers hands. Cornmeal helped loosen the dirt and was said to stop the hands from chapping.

...Meanwhile, back on the trail

TODD

76 **Todd General Store** Where chickens, galax and ginseng were once taken in trade for sugar, salt and other necessities not found on the farm, you will find the hub of this once-booming logging town. Established in 1914, the store still pays homage to a time when life was simple and genuine. Honey, hams, candy, feed, groceries and Ashe County cheese seem timeless icons of glory days long past but not forgotten in the glowing embers of the pot-bellied stove, the heart of this historic site and community. Open year-round. Mon–Sat 8am–7pm & Sun 12:30pm– 5pm. Winter hours Mon–Sat 8am–6pm & Sun 12:30pm–5pm. (336)877-1067.

Continue on NC Scenic Highway 194 S from West Jefferson for approximately 7 mi to Todd. Store is on the L.

Did you know that apples have been on the planet for over 2-1/2 million years?

Remnants have been found in a Stone Age village in Switzerland, and ancient Greeks and Romans grew several varieties.

If you want to cultivate your own apples, plant your tree in early spring while the tree is dormant.

77 **RRR Tree Farm** HWY 194 – If you're passing through in December, ride a hay wagon with Red Alderman through his beautiful Christmas tree farm. You'll hear the story of how he came to produce Wounded Warrior, a homeopathic pharmaceutical while searching out the perfect tree. Lodging packages available. Open weekends one week before Thanksgiving–two weeks after. Visit website for hotels in the Boone area that provide directions with reservations. (336)385-6624. www.rrrtreefarm.com.

78 **Moretz Mountain Orchard** 2820 BIG HILL RD – Located near historic Todd, this orchard boasts over 90 varieties of apples including antique varieties like Virginia Beauties and Wolf River as well as Honey Crisp and Pristines. Owner Bill Moretz has also started a Paulownia Plantation adjoining the orchard. These timber trees have gigantic leaves that can reach up to three-feet in diameter. Pick your own apples daily. Sep–Oct Sat–Sun 1pm–6pm. Call for tours. (828)264-3424.

Continue through Todd to R on Big Hill Rd. (100 ft past the General Store). 3 mi on L. Look for three buildings right off the road.

Guidebook Symbols

Kid Friendly Site

Farm · Trail · Lodging · Special Attraction

Garden · Festival · Restaurant · Garden Art

Grandfather Mountain

A mountain to write home about. A place of pilgrimage, long before its summit sported a swinging bridge. "Climbed to the summit . . . and with my companion and guide sang the hymn of the Marseillaise, and cried: 'Long live America and the Republic of the French! Long live Liberty,'" plantsman Andre Michaux wrote of his visit to Grandfather Mountain in 1794. "I couldn't hold in, and began to jump about and sing and glory in it all," American naturalist John Muir noted a century later.

Grandfather Mountain still inspires intense emotions. Hike through Grandfather's cool, moist spruce-fir forest, skirting gray-green boulders clasped in sinewy embrace by the roots of yellow birches. Wind among the snaky limbs of rhododendron and high-bush blueberry to a rocky outcrop. Wilson's and Harper's Creek spill down the mountainside below you, concealed by an infinity of trees. Croaking, coal-black ravens surf air currents overhead, as torn scraps of cloud sweep up the ridge and over Grandfather's rocky spine. The air's sharp. The sky's blue. Tiny leaves of cliff-hugging sand myrtle shine.

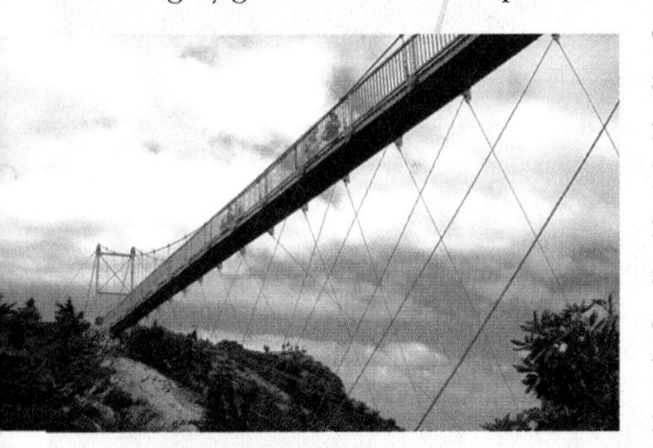

No wonder you—like Michaux and Muir before you—feel exhilarated. You're in a special place. The Southern Appalachians—of which Grandfather Mountain is a part—are, biologically speaking, the richest temperate forest on earth, home to more than 200 species of wildflowers, 400 mosses and liverworts, 200 hardwoods, 14 varieties of conifers, and 2,000 kinds of mushrooms and fungi. Grandfather alone supports 16 distinct habitat types—and more than 40 rare

and endangered plant and animal species. Many wear names far more flamboyant than they are: Rock Gnome Lichen, Trailing Wolfsbane, Wretched Sedge, Bent Avens, the North Carolina Funnelweb Tarantula (a minute spider, only recently discovered on the mountain), Heller's Blazing Star, the Virginia Big-eared Bat, Weller's Salamander, Roan Rattlesnakeroot.

Mountain owner Hugh Morton began donating a series of conservation easements to the Nature Conservancy in 1991; almost 3,000 of Grandfather's 5,000 acres eventually will be protected. In 1992, the mountain was designated an International Biosphere Reserve. It's one of 352 such sites worldwide—the first privately owned property in the program.

That's just the latest recognition of Grandfather Mountain's species richness. For almost 300 years, naturalists have found their way here, many to collect new plants for the gardens of European royalty. Among the mountain's early visitors: Mark Catesby, author and illustrator of the first detailed natural history of the region; Philadelphia botanist William Bartram; Scotsman John Fraser (for whom the Fraser fir is named); and Harvard's Asa Gray, the father of American botany, who discovered the exquisite (and endangered) lily that bears his name on an expedition in 1841.

Secrets of the natural world have been discovered here, and keep on revealing themselves, to university scientists and researchers—and to the likes of you and me, when we glimpse our first peregrine falcon hurtling through the skies, or peer into the speckled throat of a red-orange lily in bloom.

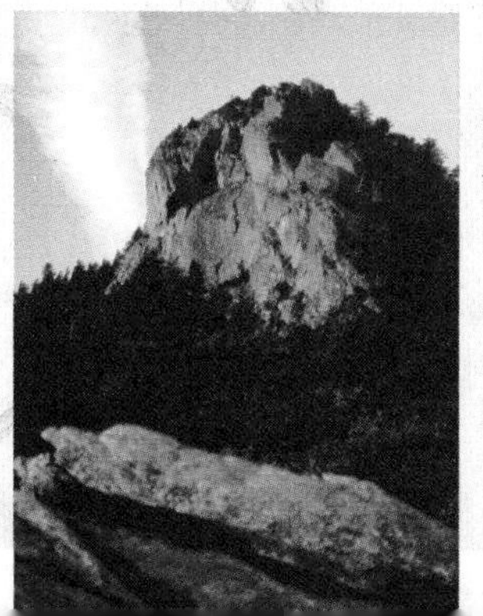

Jewels & Gems Meander

Weathered barns wear Virgin's bower. A doe shepherds her twin spotted fawns. Sunflowers keep step with shoulder-high tobacco. ✧ Forget cruise control. Downshift your traveling speed. Here, journey and destination are indistinguishable. ✧ Scramble over Doggett Mountain. A patchwork of fertile valleys and furrowed hills commands your attention—in its panoramas and intimate details. Around the bend from a white frame church with his and her outhouses, secluded rental cabins flank a restored farmhouse. An airy garden emporium is planted securely on an old foundation. New and old are happily juxtaposed. ✧ Unpack a picnic at Max Patch. Swallows carve the skies above a waving grass sea dotted with Queen Anne's lace, St. John's wort, purple self-heal, and creamy butter-and-eggs. ✧ Like handspun yarn dropping from a spindle, valleys widen, then taper through rocky ravines. At Hot Springs, gracious Victorian homes bespeak an earlier grand era. Climb out of the French Broad valley and descend to the college town of Mars Hill. Farmers, herb growers, purveyors of goat cheese and handmade soaps spread their wares in a weekend Farmer's Market. ✧ Watch a novice cook at a roadside café and learn the art of crimping crust. Hungry patrons queue up for a slice of hot-from-the-oven cherry pie. Appetite sated, tour Jarvis Japanese Gardens where former tobacco farmers tend plate-sized lotus flowers and 500-year-old bonsai. ✧ Friendly folk on front porches lift languid hands in greeting. Clotheslines

Japanese Iris in the afternoon sun...you'll mistake the blooms for sapphires, they're so beautiful.

Oh, the treasures to find.

sag with jeans and overalls. Life-size wooden figures and a lop-eared hound dally by a Beelog storefront. ✧ Play kissy-face with Joseph the llama. Stroke fuzzy bunnies' fur. Circle the Burnsville square, then brake at a produce stand for succulent Gingergold nectarines and a dozen double-yoked eggs. ✧ Cows graze the valley floor beneath brooding Black Mountains. Slip into a permacultural paradise of Chinese medicinals, Old World perennials and uncommon conifers. Pick blueberries on an organic farm. ✧ Scarlet dahlias nod around enduring cottages of artfully selected river rock. Dusty rose joe-pye weed and raggedy native sunflowers play a constant refrain on country roads. Christmas trees and grazing sheep texture hillsides. Family cemeteries face the rising sun. ✧ Descend mammoth flagstones to a shady glen where generations of Dellinger's milled Cane Creek Community's corn. Cross a footlog. Peer under the millrace. Watch the wheel turn. Picturesque Bakersville, crafted of studios, creekwalk park and county courthouse, is gateway to the Roan. Quilted on this mountaintop are fragrant spruce-fir forests, lush grassy balds and God's own 600-acre rhododendron garden. ✧ Come down out of the clouds and make tracks for Spruce Pine. Follow a coal train 'til it crests the Blue Ridge. Hop onto the Parkway to catch a moonrise above an orchard's terraced slopes. And, before you go, reflect that amid these water-carved mountains, families still fashion farmsteads, harvest half-runners, build barns, spin dreams, and send down deep roots. ✧

Jewels & Gems Meander

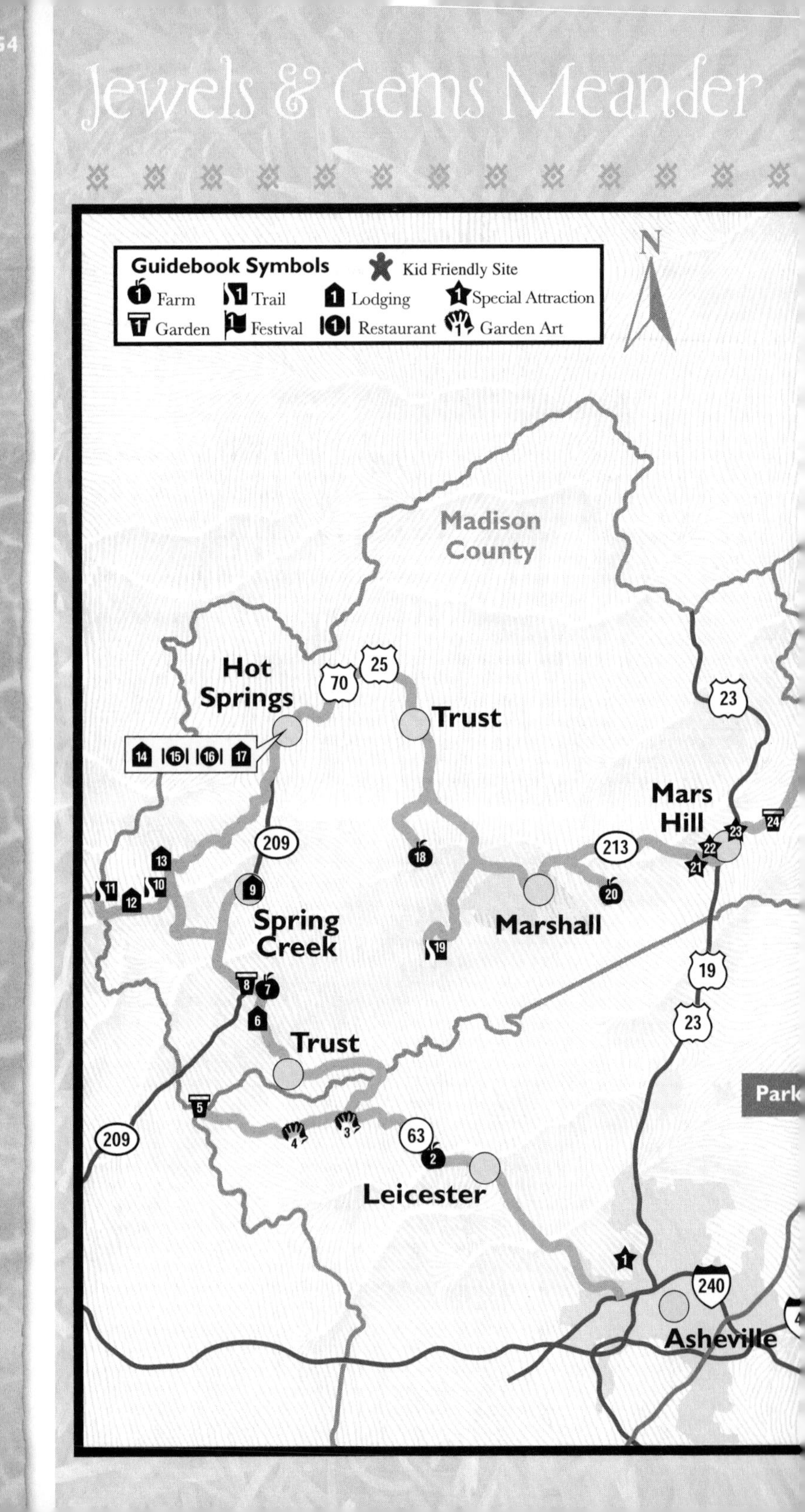

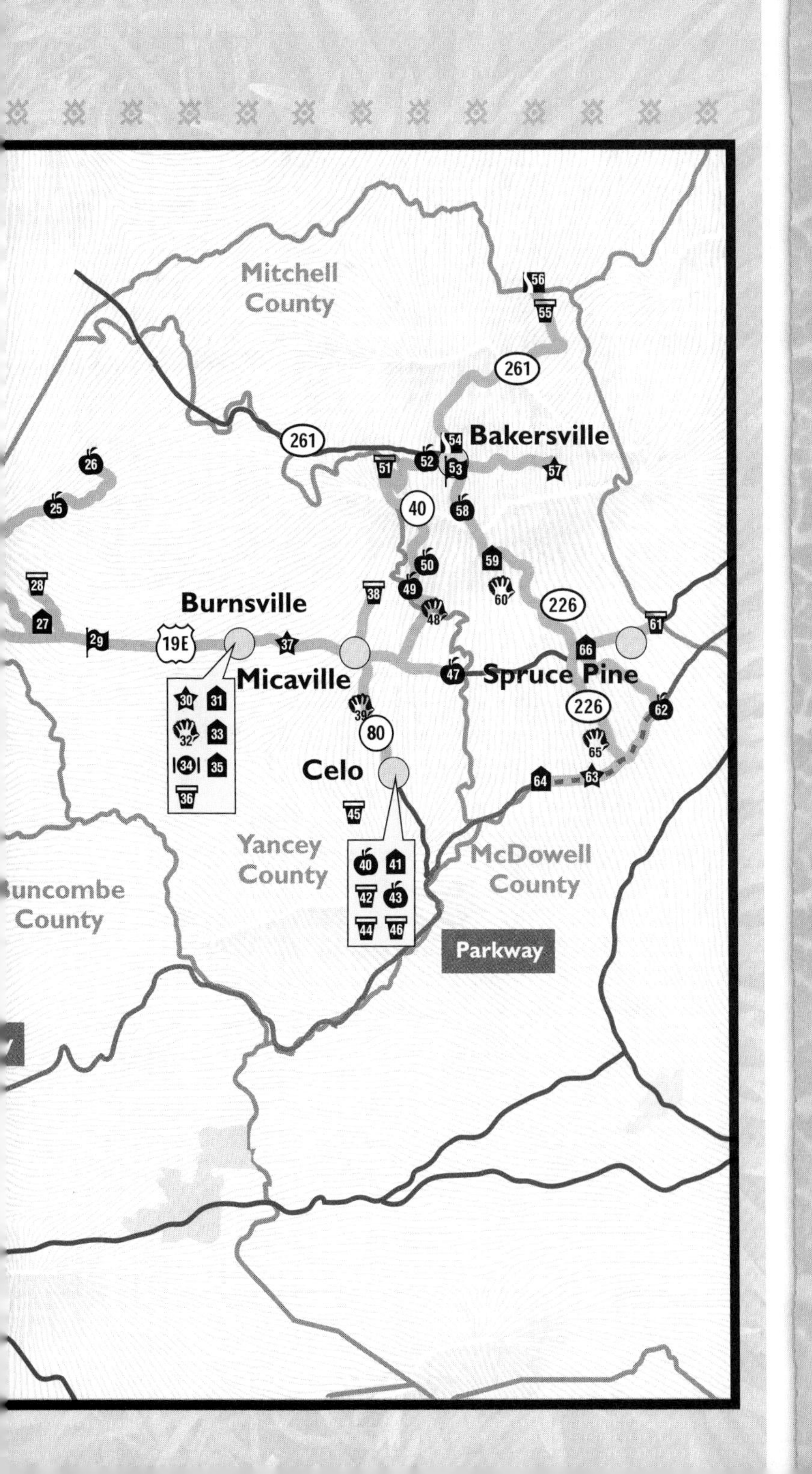

Mitchell County
Bakersville
Burnsville
Micaville
Spruce Pine
Celo
Yancey County
McDowell County
Buncombe County
Parkway
261
40
226
19E
80

Hardy beauties, tough as the land supporting them, rhododendrons claim acid-rich mountain ridges. In spring, deciduous azaleas offer rounded clouds of spicy pink (R. roseum) and upright displays ranging from apricot to vermillion (R. canlendulaceum). Swamp azaleas (R. viscosum) cling to riverbanks, scenting mists with candid sweetness.

Magnificent rose-purple Catawbas (R. catawbiense), namesake of violet-hued Rhodonite garnet, crowd Roan Mountain's massive natural rhododendron garden. In June, pineapple-sized trusses top leathery evergreen foliage. Growing up to 40' high, Great Rhododendrons (R. maximum) debut in July, white to shell-pink clusters blooming deep in moist forests.

Rhododendrons' shallow roots meander across rough terrain, seeking nourishment from decomposing rock and vegetation. A hike through the dense undergrowth reveals why gnarled thickets are called "rhododendron hells", while the "flowering heaven's" grow atop this tenacious offspring of the heath family.

The Road Goes On Forever
Side trips, tidbits, adventures, and treasure hunts

What fruit has its seeds on the outside? Strawberries, of course!

LEICESTER

1 King Bio Pharmaceuticals 3 WESTSIDE DR – Dr. Frank King Jr. wants you to begin your journey with a stop by his natural medicine facility where you can take a manufacturing tour of homeopathic products and new breakthroughs in homeopathic medicines. At his home-on-the-range nearby, Dr. King raises the awareness of a symbol of America's heritage by raising 350 head of American bison. Facility is open for tours on Tue & Thu at 10am. Call for other times. (828)236-1659.

From Hwy 240 in Asheville, take Patton Ave W to K-Mart. Make R on Louisiana Rd. At top of hill, take L at the first light onto Hazel Mill. At stop sign, go straight to Westside to first facility on R. Keep to R to enter front of building.

When frost threatens, get out the large cartons, sheets, and blankets to cover vulnerable plants. In the fall, the soil is usually much warmer than in the spring, so cover the plants in late afternoon before the earth chills to take advantage of the warm soil.

2 Reynolds Farms 60 TURKEY CREEK RD – If you don't know what an M&M sandwich is, this is a good place to find out. Surrounded by 70 acres of tomatoes, eight acres of cantaloupes and three acres of strawberries, this 150-year-old farmhouse is even on the National Register of Historic Places. Cows graze on the rolling hills but take heed! Gary Larson was probably right. Once your car is out of view, who's to say that the cows don't stroll around on their back legs for a better view of the pastoral scenery? Open May 1 –June 15 (strawberries) & June 15 –Oct (tomatoes). Mon–Sat 8am–5pm. Closed Sun. (828)683-2195.

Return to Patton Ave and turn R. Take R onto Leicester Hwy and travel approximately 10 mi to R on Turkey Creek Rd. Go .3 mi to farm on L.

3 The Jones Pottery 209 BIG SANDY MUSH RD – In a large anagama-style kiln fired by wood, whimsy and will, Matthew Jones produces items for the garden such as bird feeders and houses, Japanese bells and other large garden accents, planters featuring unique brushwork and traditional glazes, and vases and pitchers for flower arrangements. Apr–June & Sep–Oct

Add soda cans turned upside down to the bottom of big pots to cut down on the weight and the amount of potting soil.

Thu–Sat 9am–5pm. Call for July & Aug hours. (828)683-2705. www.jonespottery.com

Turn R on Hwy 63 and continue approximately 1.5 mi to L on N Turkey Creek Rd. Travel approximately 2 mi and bear R on Earley's Mountain Rd for another 3 mi to R at home with board fence. Road changes name to Big Sandy Mush Rd. If you cross Hog Eye Rd, you've gone too far.

4 **Friendswood Brooms** 8 WILLOW CREEK RD – Harry Potter, and perhaps even the Wicked Witch of the West, might just visit what was once Waldrup's General Store back in 1890. The old store now serves as the studio for area master broom makers, Ralph and Marlow Gates. Both functional and artistic, these brooms will, you know it's coming, sweep you off your feet! Open Tue & Thu 10am–2pm. But, call before visiting just to verify. (828)683-9521. www.friendswoodbrooms.com

Continue up Big Sandy Mush Rd for approximately 1 mi. Turn L on Willow Creek Rd. Studio is on L

5 **Sandy Mush Herb Nursery** 316 SURRET COVE RD – From Incarnata to Primula to Angel Trumpets to Foxtail Lily, you will find what you're looking for, and more, at this remote flora and fauna paradise. Unusual trees such as Acer Griseum and Stewartia stand watch over Kate and Fairman's own hybrid Trinity Purple Bee Balm, Cocoa-mint Rose scented geranium, Dancing Waters Rosemary, and Backwall Thyme to name but a few. A butterfly herb garden awaits a stroll-through as does an aromatic tour of the 80 varieties of scented geraniums in one of the greenhouses by way of the five water gardens. Open Thu–Sat, but call first. (828)683-2014.

While this nursery is very much worth the time to get to it, it is a very remote site on top of the mountain so be forewarned. Continue up Big Sandy Mush Rd for 2.5 more mi and continue on dirt road for .9 mi and then .75 mi on the paved driveway. Nursery is on L.

What is a tomato?

Well, it depends on who you ask. According to botanists, North America's favorite vegetable is actually a fruit. However, in 1893, the US Supreme Court overruled Mother Nature and declared that, although botanically speaking tomatoes are fruit, they would be called vegetables because they're served with the main meal.

The Road Goes On Forever

Side trips, tidbits, adventures, and treasure hunts

The average American eats 13 pounds of tomatoes a year, plus an additional 20 pounds a year in the form of ketchup, salsa, soup, and BBQ sauce.

SPRING CREEK

Stone's Throw Farm 500 MOUNTAIN VIEW RD – If an escape is what you're after, here's the emergency exit. A 76-acre farm and forest ensure that you have all the space you need to unwind. Admire the horses from the front porch of your fully furnished, nestled-in-a-cove cabin; hike the trails behind the barn or the old wagon road. (828)622-9510.

Continue back down Big Sandy Mush Rd for 4.6 mi to L on Sandy Mush Creek Rd. Travel 2.5 mi to L on Hwy 63. Go 7.7 mi on Hwy 63 to sign on L. Travel .5 mi down Mountain View Rd to farm.

Briar Rose Farm 91 DUCKETT TOP TOWER RD – To see the wide variety of activities that take place on a working farm, stop here to visit Tom and Judie. They have long-wool sheep for spinning, goats for making cheese and soap, Belted Galloway cattle, free-range chicken, a lumber mill, and landscaping boulders for sale. Call for appointment. (828)622-7329.

1.5 mi N on 63 and far is on the R.

Herb of Grace Farm 1951 NC 63 HWY – From the moment you step through the "door outdoors", the magic of this nursery, garden and retail shop will move you. Discover many rare and hard-to-find plant varieties to enjoy here or to introduce into your own garden. The shop is fashioned after one you may find in France and features luxurious treats for you and your home. Relax with a cup of tea and the music of the lazy creek. Wed–Sat 10am–6pm & Sun 12noon–5pm. (828)622-7319. www.theherbofgrace.com

Just around the corner on the R.

Continue N on 63 for 1.7 mi to intersection with 209 in Trust. Turn R to continue N on 209. Note mileage.

Mountain Valley View Cabins 225 MOUNTAIN VALLEY DR – Perch on top of a mountain ridge to witness

Cut down on mowing and add color to your landscape with these groundcovers:

Astilbe,
Creeping Jacob's Ladder,
Crested Iris,
Green and Gold,
Hardy Ice Plant,
Heartleaf Bergenia,
Perennial Sweet Pea,
Plumbago or Leadwort,
Showy Evening Primrose

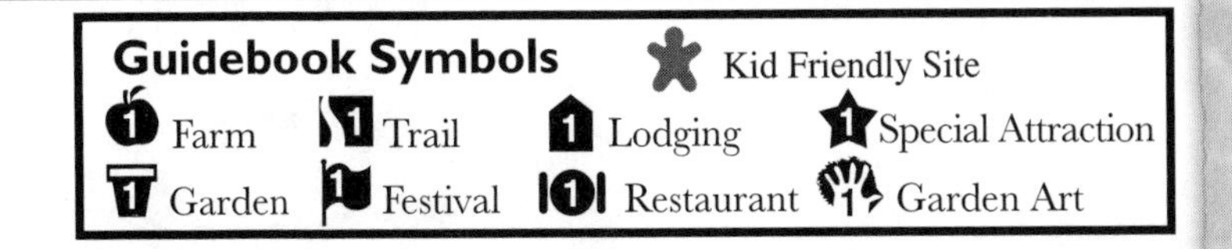

incredible views from your own private cabin. Fully furnished and roomy, use your cabin as "home base" for exploring the area or stay close by and enjoy the stream, the fishing pond, and the barbecue grill. (888)808-8812. www.ncmountainview.com

Continue 3.1 mi N of Trust on Hwy 209 to L on Freedom Ln. Sign will be on R. Continue to L on Mtn Valley Dr.

10 **Little Creek Outfitters** 767 LITTLE CREEK RD – Ride through the quiet mountain meadows and shady forest glades on a horse that's suited for your level of riding skill. Various rides are available for your personal adventure, including half-day, full-day, sunrise, sunset, overnight, and fly-fishing trips. Call for appointment. (828)622-7606 or (828) 622-9686. www.littlecreekoutfitters.com

Backtrack on Hwy 209 S for 1.5 mi to R on Caldwell Corner Rd. Go 2 mi to T-intersection. Turn R onto Meadow Fork and go 1.7 mi to L on Little Creek towards Max Patch. Go .3 mi and bear L on Little Creek Rd. Travel 2.7 mi up gravel road to stables on R.

11 **Max Patch** – Take your watch off and leave it in the car. Get a blanket, a bottle of wine, some cheese and good bread then head up to the top of this mountain bald. Because of the unique treeless terrain, your sight is completely unobstructed for a 360-degree view. The blue skies of Max Parrish will deepen into lavender hues of twilight before transforming into brilliant star-studded black velvet. Astrology 101 for kids. Possible time portal for lovers. The Appalachian Trail runs over the top and connects to many other trails for you to hike. There are no facilities here, so prepare accordingly.

Continue up Little Creek for .9 mi. Turn R at intersection onto Max Patch Rd. Continue 1.6 mi to parking lot.

12 **Max Patch Cabins** POPULAR GAP RD – What better way to end your day of cloud watching and star gazing at Max

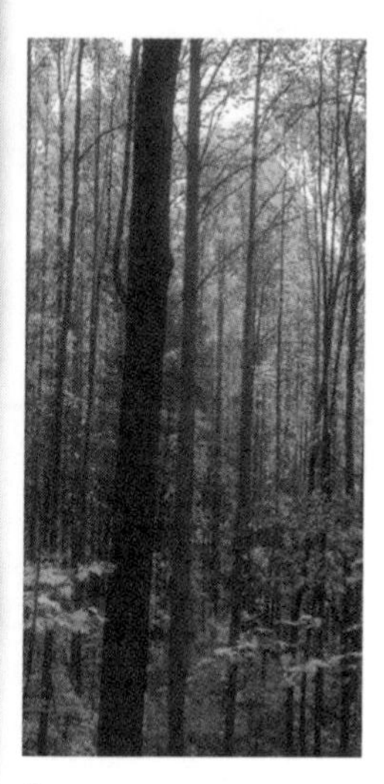

Trees

I think that I shall never see
A poem lovely as a tree.
Poems were made by fools like me.
But only God can make a tree.

Joyce Kilmer

My father considered a walk among the mountains as the equivalent of churchgoing.

-- Aldous Huxley

The Road Goes On Forever

Side trips, tidbits, adventures, and treasure hunts

Patch than to retire to one of these cozy cabins snuggled into the mountain. Available for nightly or weekly rentals. Horse boarding included in rental fee if needed. (828)627-2716.

From the top of Max Patch, turn L out of the parking lot and return down the mountain for 1.6 mi to Little Creek Rd and then L on Little Creek for .9 mi. Turn L on Popular Gap Rd and immediately turn L again at entrance. Cabins adjacent to Little Creek Outfitters.

13 **Conklin's Cabin** 1147 DEERFIELD DR – If you want to get away from it all, this is the place you've been looking for but couldn't find. This private cabin that sleeps four is within walking distance of the Appalachian Trail and Max Patch. After your walk, a melodious stream will lull you to sleep. (828)622-9618. www.ncvalley.com

Return to Meadowfork Rd and turn L. Travel approximately 1.3 mi through a left-hand steep curve. Turn L on Panther Branch Rd and go 1.3 mi past first Deerfield Dr sign. Go through privacy gate and immediately bear to the L for .1 mi. Cabin is at first drive on R.

HOT SPRINGS

Turn L onto Meadowfork Rd and travel to intersection with Hwy 209 N. Continue N on 209 to Hot Springs. If you're interested in a picnic spot or a campground, you'll pass the Rocky Bluff Recreation Area on the way.

14 **Duckett House** 433 LANCE AVE – Breathe easier from a rocking chair on the huge wrap-around porch of this historic inn; or maybe in front of the private fireplace in your room, or on a creek-side stroll. The flower and vegetable gardens are a sight to behold, and they also contribute to the home-cooked vegetarian meals. (828)622-7621. www.duckettehouseinn.com

Just inside the town limits on the R.

15 **Smoky Mountain Diner** 70 LANCE AVE – If these folks can handle Appalachian Trail hiker appetites, chances are pretty good that you'll leave here satiated. Trail burgers with onion straws, iron skillet-cooked trout, turnip greens,

Get rid of bugs in the garden without using chemicals. Use small cans (like those from cat food or tuna) and fill with a mixture of beer and sugar. Place the cans near plants throughout the garden. Bugs like the sweet smell and take a swim!

It's another one of Don Stevenson's hand-sculpted replica birdhouses. Don't forget to stop by Don's studio in Morganton. (Page 176 Site 20)

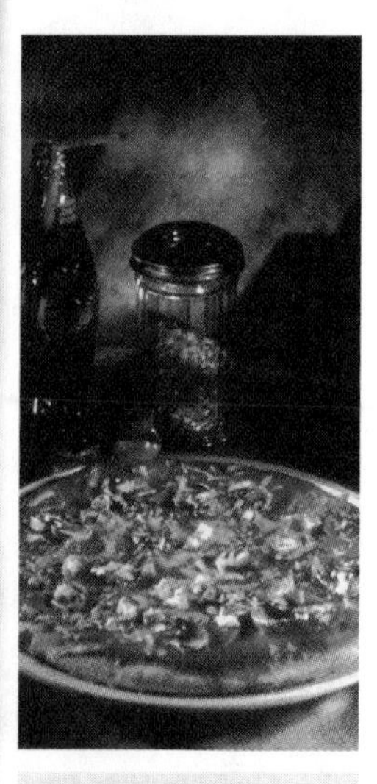

Make your own Gardener's Soap

Buy any soap mold of your choice to make your own soap in whatever shape you like.

2 tablespoons of cornmeal
1 bar of glycerine soap
1/2 teaspoon of your favorite fragrance oil

Melt the glycerine soap in a pot on the stove or in the microwave. Mix in cornmeal and oil. Stir briskly. Pour soap into mold. Allow to cool and set in the mold.

fried okra, fried apples and green beans cooked by GRITS (Girls Raised in the South). Open daily year-round. Mon–Fri 6am–9pm. Sat 7am–9pm. Sun 7am–3pm. (828)622-7571.

Continue on Lance Ave for about .3 mi. Restaurant is on L.

16 **Bridge Street Café and Inn** 145 BRIDGE ST – The best view of Spring Creek is from the covered deck at this restaurant serving creative Mediterranean and vegetarian renditions of local organic produce. Catch the breeze under the ceiling fan on the deck as you enjoy homemade soup and salad, pizza from a wood-burning oven, or an Italian dessert. Mar–Oct Thu & Sun 5:30pm–9pm. Fri & Sat 5:30pm–10pm. Sun brunch 11am–2pm. (828)622-0002. www.bridgestreetcafe.com

Continue down Lance Ave to intersection with Bridge St.

17 **Mountain Magnolia Inn & Retreat** 204 LAWSON ST – This 130-year-old Victorian home has been restored so beautifully that it was featured in *This Old House* magazine. The extensive gardens are the perfect complement to the grounds of this mountain top bed & breakfast. Dinner is available to guests and non-guests on Fri & Sat nights. (828)622-3543. www.mountainmagnoliainn.com

Go .1 mi. L at sign.

Continue through Hot Springs to the intersection of 209 and 25/70. Continue on 25/70 to Hwy 208 and turn R toward Marshall. Travel 5.2 mi to Walnut. Go about .3 mi and turn R at Walnut.

MARSHALL

18 **Eagle Feather Organic Farm** 300 INDIGO BUNTING LN – A designated Native Botanical Sanctuary and home of the NC Ginseng and Goldenseal Company, you'll find these and many more rare, endangered and threatened plants growing in a natural forest environment. Learn to identify plants or purchase some to plant and nurture on your property. Slippery

The Road Goes On Forever

Side trips, tidbits, adventures, and treasure hunts

elm and black walnut also for sale. Tours and workshops available. Check website for schedule and call for appointments. Sat 2pm–5pm & Sun 1pm–4pm. (828)649-3536. www.ncgoldenseal.com

As you turn R in Walnut there will be a church on the L and the Walnut Cash & Carry on the R. Go 2.1 mi on Johnson Branch Rd and cross the French Broad River. Take an immediate L onto Anderson Branch Rd and go 1.4 mi. Turn L at Indigo Bunting Ln. Go .3 mi on gravel road to R-turn opposite white mobile home. Farm is at end of road about .1 mi.

19 **Sandy Bottom Trail Rides** 1459 CANEY FORK RD – This horseback-riding operation gives you a real taste for Appalachian farm life. Weave through herds of cattle and goats on your way to visit a garnet mine or to climb a ridge that offers 360-degree views. Choices range from two-hour to overnight trips. Ride in a covered wagon or set out just before sunset. Open daily. Call for appointment. (828)649-9745. www.sandybottomtrailrides.com

Return to Hwy 25/70 and travel 3.4 mi from Walnut toward Marshall. Turn R on Little Pine Rd and travel 3.8 mi. Make a L on Caney Fork for 1 mi.

20 **Nowhere Branch Angora Goats** 555 WILL GREEN RD – Queen Anne's lace dots the hills, creating a white maze for herding dogs to frolic during breaks from the goats. Situated on a serene mountaintop, this working farm boasts 50-70 Angora goats. There is also a small dye garden and spinning demonstrations. Registered angora goats, mohair fleeces, fine wool-kid mohair blend yarn. Blueberries, winter squash, tomatillos, and other vegetables. Mon & Tue 1pm–6pm or by appointment. Closed Sep 15–Oct. (828)689-9622.

Take Little Pine Rd back to Hwy 25/70. Travel 3 mi to take Hwy 213 toward Mars Hill. Travel on Hwy 213 toward Mars Hill for 1.7 mi. Turn R onto Silver Mill Rd. Turn R at Laurel Branch Church. Pass Sexton Church, cross Bull Creek and continue to L on Will Green Rd. Travel up dirt road staying L to top of ridge.

Return to Hwy 213 towards Mars Hill for approximately 6 mi to downtown. Hwy 213 will become Main St.

Blueberry Vinegar

3 cups blueberries
9 cups white wine vinegar

Wash and mash blueberries in a colander over a bowl and put the fruit and juice into a large jar.

Pour the vinegar over and macerate for 8 days, stirring every day.

Strain and bottle into sterilized bottles, seal and label.

Use old Christmas tree branches to mulch under berry plants to keep them weed-free.

Guidebook Symbols

Kid Friendly Site
Farm · Trail · Lodging · Special Attraction
Garden · Festival · Restaurant · Garden Art

Benefits of Using Native Plants

Native plants are hardy and should withstand regional weather extremes when properly sited and planted.

They promote wise stewardship of the land and the conservation of our natural resources.

They provide food and shelter for native wildlife.

They restore regional landscapes and inspire pride in communities.

They prevent future invasive plant introductions.

MARS HILL

21 **Rural Life Museum** CORNER OF COLLEGE ST AND US 213 – The pre-industrial and industrial periods in the Southern Appalachian region are captured in the rural life artifacts preserved and exhibited within a lovely ivy-entwined native stone building on the Mars Hill College campus. Free. Guided tours by appointment. Open during the school year Mon–Fri 2pm–4pm. (828)689-1424.

Museum is located in the Montague Building at the corner of College St and US 213.

22 **Saturday Farmer's Market** HWY 213 ON MARS HILL COLLEGE CAMPUS – Spring, summer, and fall unveil all sorts of temptations at this locally supported market: produce, cut flowers, bedding plants, medicinal plants, honey, eggs, pickles, preserves, baked goods, crafts, soaps and more. Sat 8am–1pm. (828)689-4586.

Across from the college tennis courts on R.

23 **TJ's Mountain Market** 607 CARL ELLER RD (HWY 213) – A statue of St. Francis of Assisi goes together with peace lilies like peas and carrots. You'll find those here as well amongst the ferns, bedding plants, flowers, and other vegetables and fruits. Apr–Dec Mon–Sat 8am–7pm. (828)689-VEGE (8343).

Continue E through town 1 mi. Market will be on L beside Pizza Roma.

Continue through town heading E 1.5 mi. Exit onto Hwy 19/23 N. Travel 2 mi. Continue on 19E towards Burnsville.

24 **Jarvis Landscaping and Japanese Garden** OLD MILL RD – Checked the airfare to Japan lately? An economical and alternative route is to visit the exquisite and lovingly created gardens of landscapers Jack Jarvis and Randy Doan. Lotus-flowered water gardens and unusual trees such as the Manchurian weeping cherry embrace the central pièce de résistance, a gated bonsai garden featuring a 500-year-old

The Road Goes On Forever

Side trips, tidbits, adventures, and treasure hunts

SPOT IT

It's somewhere on this loop. Can you find it?

Ponderosa pine among many other of the miniature elders. Sat 9am–6pm & Sun 2pm–6pm. (828)689-3859.

Travel 1.5 mi on 19E. Turn R onto Old Mill. Cross one-lane bridge at .3 mi and continue .2 mi on gravel road. Turn R and go .1 mi. On the R.

WEST BURNSVILLE

Side trip...

25 **Wellspring Farm** RIDDLE BRANCH RD – A thrill for all your senses, this working farm has a wonderful collection of experiences. You'll find llamas, angora rabbits, chickens, and sheep that call this farm home. The integral parts of life here include spinning the fiber from the animals, making soap, and cultivating herbs and organic vegetables. All are available in the retail shop. Wed–Sat 10am–4pm or by appointment. (828)682-0458. www.wellspringfarm.com

Continue 6.6 mi E on 19E, turning L onto Schronce Creek which becomes Bald Mtn Rd at top of mountain. Take that 7.6 mi and turn L onto Riddle Branch (S.R. 1405). First drive on R at green mailbox and then veer R.

If you are collecting flowers and other plants to press and preserve, make sure you do your collecting in dry weather. It helps to preserve the color because the flower or plant will dry faster.

26 **White Oak Farm** LITTLE CREEK RD – Showier than a farm, yet more than a garden, it's a flower farm! Filled with 20-year-old perennials, this mountain top Eden is where many dried flower arrangements and wreaths are born. Tour the drying room to see where the rest of the magic happens. Farm hours Fri & Sat 10am–5pm, but call ahead. The retail business is The Cottage Gate at 202 E Main St in Burnsville. (828)682-7226.

Return to Bald Mountain Rd. Turn L traveling 3.4 mi to stop sign. Turn L onto Little Creek and go 1 mi to steep gravel drive on R. Continue .8 mi up driveway to farm.

Take Bald Mtn Rd (Schronce Creek) back to 19E.

Meanwhile, back on the trail...

27 **The Panes Residential Spa Retreat** OFF OF HWY 19E – Pamper yourself inside and out with a visit to this secluded retreat. Massage, skin treatments, and even an outdoor, gazebo-style, garden-surrounded hot tub. You can stay in the main house or rent the restored log cabin. Both

"Pride in Tobacco" is a common front-bumper slogan in these mountains where local farmers are proud of their thriving Burley Type 31. Individual as the farms that host them, ventilated tobacco barns are a real piece of regional architecture. The balance of humidity and temperature flowing through these barn vents produces a superior-grade cigarette tobacco.

Coastal tobacco is harvested by machines and flu-cured by applied heat but mountain-grown tobacco is carefully harvested by hand and air-cured. The mature stalks are cut, "studded" onto tobacco stakes, and left to wilt in the field. Hung in the barns to cure, the farmer later "works it off" the sticks, separating the tobacco into grades determined by color and texture. After baling, the finished product is delivered to Asheville. Described as "luxury farming at its best", the farmer is guaranteed to sell every pound he has produced at a good price.

Anyone can grow tobacco, but to sell it a farmer must have access to an allotment. This system was established around the time of the Depression to stabilize the economics of tobacco in the state. Passing from generation to generation via inheritance, the right to sell tobacco can also be purchased or leased to other growers within county lines.

A few years ago, the fungal diseases Blue Mold and Black Shank were the biggest enemies of local growers. Now there's a larger problem looming on the horizon. The economic implications of lawsuits at the tobacco-company level are trickling down to producers. Agricultural agencies are seeking alternatives for farmers whose families have grown tobacco for generations. But for now, Burley 31 - standing proud in triangular plots perched on rocky hillsides or flourishing in neat fields stretching across acres of rich bottom land - is king of the road.

The Road Goes On Forever

Side trips, tidbits, adventures, and treasure hunts

boast natural lighting through antique stained glass windows. Appointments Mon–Sat 9am–9pm. (828)682-4157. www.thepanes.com

From the intersection of Schronce Creek and 19E continue on 19E for .2 mi and turn L at sign. Drive .5 mi where gravel becomes paved. Continue to house.

28 **Edgewood Gardens** LICKSKILLET RD – Guaranteed to shock you with the variety of hosta plants that exist, you must visit this spectacular garden and laboratory. New "breeds" are born here and thrive in the naturally shaded and moist mountain terrain. Learn about the science of tissue culturing, just enjoy the rich beauty here, or take some plants home with you. Fri–Sat 8am–4:30pm & Sun 2pm–5pm. (828)682-4174. www.gardensights.com/missvitro

Return to 19E. L to go E. Turn L onto Lickskillet Rd at 1 mi. Travel 1.6 mi. L onto gravel. Stay on main road for .5 mi. L at fork. Cross a stream. At pavement bear R. Continue up hill. Turn L into drive.

29 **Hillbilly Farm Days** OLD HWY 19 E – If you're in the area the last weekend of September, here's an agricultural event you'll want to catch. Features tractor pulls, apple butter and cider pressing, antique tractor engines, horse plowing, lawn and garden tools, cornmeal grinding, food, music and the fine, but dying, art of making molasses. (828)682-7125.

Return to Hwy 19E towards Burnsville for approximately 1mi to L at large sign. Take short access road to merge with Old Hwy 19. Event is held behind the Cane River Middle School and across the street from Prices Creek General Store.

DOWNTOWN BURNSVILLE

30 **Saturday Farmer's Market** HWY 19 E – A loyal and friendly assortment of people bring veggies, flowers, plants, baked good, jellies and jams, cheese, eggs, herbs, and more to this easily accessible market. Support them in their efforts to continue a wonderful mountain tradition. Open Apr–Oct Sat mornings. (828)682-3096.

Return to 19E towards Burnsville for several miles to L on Cherry St. Turn R on Main St and go .01 mi to R at sign into parking lot across from post office.

Plant these flowers in your garden to draw butterflies: Snapdragons, Butterfly Bush, Gayfeather, Pansies, Morning Glories, and Zinnias.

Farms provide needed habitats for birds and increase the amount of green space in our communities.

There is nothing useless in nature;

not even uselessness itself.

– Montaigne

31 **Terrell House** 109 ROBERTSON ST – This historic inn offers the best of both worlds; walking-distance convenience to downtown and a luxurious garden sanctuary that lets you retreat. A colonial style B&B, you'll find fine furnishings, yet won't feel like you have to take your shoes off to go inside. (828)682-4505.

Continue E on Main St for .2 mi to L on Robertson St. Inn is located .1 mi on L.

32 **Sisters Three and Me** 507 W MAIN ST – You may not see the sisters but you're sure to see the locust post and rhododendron furniture. Handmade baskets of smoke vine (sarsaparilla) vie for attention propped against a delightful assortment of birdhouses and feeders. All of that before you get in the front door! Inside you'll find antiques collected from five generations of the Shehan family including barn wood furniture. Open Apr–mid-Dec Mon–Sat 9am–5pm. (828)682-7980.

Back to Main St and turn L. Travel .1 mi to shop on R.

33 **The Nu-Wray Inn** TOWN SQUARE – An 1833 B&B boasts a brick courtyard surrounded by azaleas and wisteria. Enter this secret garden through the trellis of an outer courtyard. It features gloxinia, coneflowers, trumpet vines, daylilies, and an angel fountain that provides a choice gossip spot for robins. Breakfast under the grape arbor as you listen to the mingled melody of the songbirds. Dinner 5:30pm–8pm except Sun. Lunch 11:30am–12:30pm Sun & Mon. (800)368-9729.

Just off the town square on the R.

34 **The Garden Deli** 107 TOWN SQUARE – For anyone who has ever enjoyed eating under a tree, this is a mandatory stop. An enormous willow tree provides shade and atmosphere while you enjoy a bowl of freshly-made soup, a salad or sandwich. Indoor seating provides a birds-eye view of local landscapes painted by artists of the Burnsville area. Open year-round. Mon–Sat 11am–2pm. (828)682-3946.

Across the street and Town Square from The Nu-Wray Inn.

The Road Goes On Forever

Side trips, tidbits, adventures, and treasure hunts

Run wilted lettuce under cold water, shake it dry, wrap it in paper towels and place in your refrigerator over night. The next day it will have perked right up.

35 **Wray House B&B** 2 S. MAIN ST – This 1902 Federal-style B&B features a cloistered courtyard garden, Charleston style, with a 75-year-old cherry tree, grape arbor, and old plantings of peony, roses, rhododendron, boxwood and Begonia Grandis. Five rooms and a cottage along with a full breakfast, gourmet dinners by reservation and afternoon tea in the garden by advance reservation. (828)682-0445. www.wrayhouse.com

Bear R on S Main St after Town Square and then R again. B&B is just behind the library.

Protecting your garden tools is very important. Fill a bucket with sand. Then pour a can of motor oil over the sand. When you come in from the garden plunge the tool into the sand a few times. Not only will the sand clean the excess dirt from the tool but the oil will coat the tool so that it won't rust. And, as always, tools should be kept in a dry location.

36 **The Cottage Gate** 202 E MAIN ST – A delightful treasure, this gardening shop with a retail nursery, gardens, and labyrinth offers specialty items you can't resist, many locally crafted. Soothing water fountains, dried flower crafts, cutting gardens, and assorted gardening related items will surely tempt you. Mar–Dec Tue–Sat 11am–6pm. Jan–Feb Fri–Sat 11am–6pm. (828)678-9209.

Two blocks E of Town Square on the R.

37 **The Bow-Legged Scarecrow** HWY 19 E – The great name is only the beginning. Fresh produce abounds in this tidy operation. They place an emphasis on organic and local products, so you'll enjoy the best the mountains have to offer. Mon–Sat 10am–6pm. Closed Sun & month of Jan. (828)678-9671.

Continue E on Main St for .7 mi to intersection with 19E. Turn L and go .7 mi to stand on R.

MICAVILLE

38 **Mountain View Daylily Garden** DOUBLE ISLAND RD – Ooh, a solid acre of hundreds of varieties of daylilies, well-marked for purchase or just curiosity. Stop by if you're looking for gardening inspiration from one of the large display beds, or if you want to pick up that rare lily you've been hunting for. Mon, Tue & Fri

Guidebook Symbols

Kid Friendly Site
1 Farm · 1 Trail · 1 Lodging · 1 Special Attraction
1 Garden · 1 Festival · 1 Restaurant · 1 Garden Art

Greetings
A little violet
opened its eye
Right in the face
of the bright
Smiling sky.
It came out from
hiding with just
this to say:

"I am happy
to greet you.
Good morning Day!"

-- Cynthia DeFord Adams

9am–6pm. Wed, Thu & Sat 9am–4pm. (828)675-5136.

Continue E on 19E for 2.7 mi to R on 80S. Travel .2 mi to L on Double Island. Continue for 3.5 mi to garden on R.

39 **Craven Handbuilt Porcelain** 2250 HWY 80S – Ian and Jo Lydia partner to create a fine, but approachable porcelain line that will add charm to any home. Their studio and gallery is perched on the side of a mountain that offers a dramatic view in the distance and a lovingly cared for flower and herb garden at your feet. Open Wed–Sat 10am–4pm. Mon & Tue by appointment. (800)764-2402.

Return to 80S. Follow 80S signs thru Micaville and travel 2.2 mi to studio on R.

CELO AREA

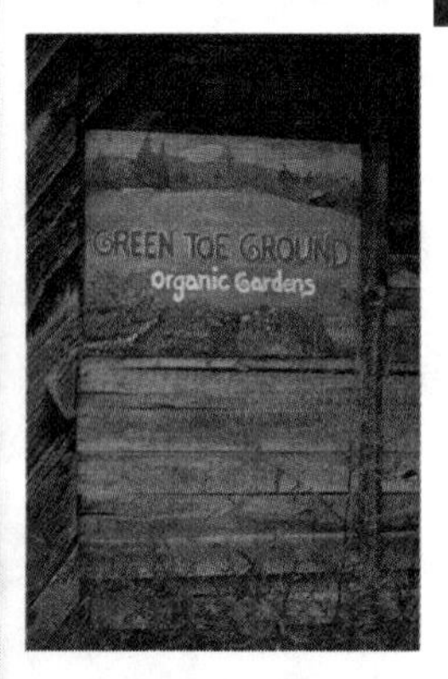

40 **Green Toe Ground Organics** 582 GRINDSTAFF RD – No vampires to be had at this organic farm where both softneck and hardneck garlic are grown in addition to cut flowers and herbs, salad mix and heirloom vegetables. A honeybee operation buzzes industriously next to the laid-back South Toe River while the scent of tuberoses will make you reel on the bank. May–Oct Tue–Sat 8am–4pm. Closed Sun–Mon. (828)675-0895.

Continue on 80S for 1.9 mi to L on Browns Creek Rd at Celo. Go .5 mi to R across one-lane bridge. Travel 1 mi on Grindstaff Rd to parking area at barn on L.

41 **Celo Inn** 1 SEVEN MILE RIDGE RD – Stay here if you want an experience that will leave you well grounded through communion with nature. Just yards off the Toe River, enjoy the creek, the flower and vegetable gardens, and the rustic comfort that Randy and Nancy offer you at a very reasonable rate. (828)675-5132.

Continue S down Grindstaff Rd for 1.7 mi to L on Hwy 80. Turn abruptly L onto Seven Mile Ridge Rd. Inn is immediately on L.

42 **Beverly Hills Nursery** 288 HALLS CHAPEL RD – No, this is not a spa/greenhouse combo although you'll feel you've been treated royally by the knowledgeable staff regarding unusual

---

The Road Goes On Forever
Side trips, tidbits, adventures, and treasure hunts

Daffodils for Southern Gardens:
April Beauty
Campernelle daffodil
Trumpet narcissus

landscape plants such as dwarf conifers, woody shrubs and perennials. May–Nov Mon–Fri 9am–3pm. Call ahead to verify. (828)675-4756.

From Seven Mile Ridge Rd, cross the bridge and turn L immediately at T-intersection onto Halls Chapel Rd. Go .2 mi to nursery on R.

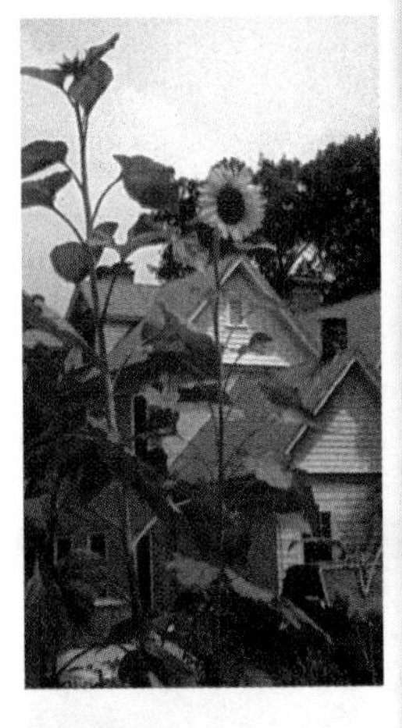

43 **Mountain Farm** 861 HALLS CHAPEL RD – Pick your own organic blueberries after you stroll through beautiful gardens set with a breathtaking view of the Black Mountains. Pack a picnic to eat on the grounds or to go up the road to a bank on the Toe River. Open during summer. Fri–Sun 10am–sunset. (828)675-4856.

Continue on Halls Chapel for .7 mi to L at farm sign.

44 **Arthur Morgan Elementary School** 1901 HANNAH BRANCH RD – Gardens are planted, weeded, cared for, and harvested by 7th, 8th, and 9th grade students who show the promise of having very green thumbs by the time they are old enough to have gardens of their own. You'll find flowers, vegetables, and fruit trees on the grounds of this innovative boarding school. Mon–Fri 8am–4pm. (828)675-4262.

Return to T-intersection and continue on gravel road for 1 mi. School is on L.

Arthur Morgan Middle School

45 **Mountain Gardens** 3020 WHITEOAK CREEK RD – Wander through the wooded setting of these hillside gardens that contain Oriental and medicinal herbs, available for your education and your purchase. Marvel at the extensive library that is likely to answer any question you may have about the uses for these herbs. Call ahead for workshop and tour information. Mon–Sat 11am–5pm or by appointment. (828)675-5664. www.gardens.webjump.com

Return to 80S. Turn L to go S. Travel .3 mi to turn R onto Whiteoak Creek. Follow signs for 2 mi. Gardens will be on R.

46 **Mt. Mitchell Nursery & Decorative Evergreens** 4810 HWY 80 S – You'll be amazed by the numerous varieties of native shrubs, evergreens and zone-qualified perennials and

The Humble Bee

Wiser far than human seer,
Yellow-breeched philosopher!
Seeing only what is fair,
Sipping only what is sweet,
Thou dost mock at fate and care.
Leave the chaff, and take the wheat.

Ralph Waldo Emerson

annuals planted in the beautiful display gardens and ponds. Take a peek inside the greenhouses and see why Elaine and Ted are such big exporters of local evergreens and forest products to the Netherlands and Japan. Tue–Wed & Fri–Sat 9:30am–4:30pm. (828)675-0480.

Continue S down Hwy 80 for .3 mi from the intersection with Whiteoak Creek Rd. Nursery is on R.

Mountain Plums. Sweet, juicy and just picked from the trees at Shady Lane Farm.

BAKERSVILLE

47 **Shady Lane Farm** ARBUCKLE RD – Just like his father before him, David Duncan surveys his farm with an appreciative eye and a walk full of pride. And, well he should. Together with his mother, Savannah Duncan, he runs the family's 50-acre farm, 20 percent of it stocked with Stamen apple orchards of Red and Golden Delicious, Rome Beauty, Granny Smith, and Jonathan varieties as well as old-time varieties such as Virginia Beauty and Sheepnose plums too! Cows moo, the spring gurgles, the willow tree whispers its secrets to the wind, as apple fans pick and choose their favorites from the bins at the apple house. A beautiful assortment of lilies, roses and dahlias nod in the breeze that they're happy to be here too. Mid-Sep–Thanksgiving Mon–Sat 8am–dark. (828)675-9232.

Return to 19E via Hwy 80 N. Turn R on 19E and go 1.5 mi. Turn L on Arbuckle Rd and go .2 mi to second house on L.

Fast compost: Throughout the day, place fruit and vegetable scraps in a blender. At the end of the day, add water, puree the scraps and add the mixture to the compost pile.

48 **Energy Exchange** NC 80 N – Bet you didn't think you'd find thriving greenhouses on a landfill site, but you will here. This innovative program takes the naturally odorless methane gas created by the decomposing trash underground and directs it to burners that heat several greenhouses, a pottery kiln, and glass-blowing equipment. A wonderful representation of creative environmentalism and community development. Call ahead for appointment. (828)675-5541. www.energyxchange.org

Return to 19E. Turn R onto 19E and travel .3 mi to turn R onto 80 N. Travel 2.3 mi to the entrance on L.

The Road Goes On Forever

Side trips, tidbits, adventures, and treasure hunts

SPOT IT

It's somewhere on this loop. Can you find it?

49 **Laurel Oaks Farm** NC 80 N – On this picturesque working sheep farm you can stay in the cozy chalet or the large log cabin. Or, just stop by for a tour to visit the 50-plus sheep, the llama, and the Great Pyrenees guard dog. Kick back to fish in one of the ponds or in the Toe River. If you've any interest in wool-spinning, Yvonne is a wonderful demonstrator. Call ahead for appointment. (828)688-2652. www.laurel-oaks.com

Return to 80N and turn L. Travel 3.2 mi to farm on L.

50 **Murdock Farm** 7159 NC 80 N – A wonderful collection of native bedding plants and perennials grow organically on these grounds. Choose a plant that is potted or still in the field. Many flowers are dried for wreaths in the fall. An artist's studio and gallery are also part of the experience to enjoy on this farm. Thu–Sun 1pm–sunset. (828)688-1030.

Continue on 80N .2 mi. On R before cemetery.

51 **River Gardens** TOECANE RD – You can't turn around without being surrounded by gardens full to the brim with blooms. Stroll through at your leisure or hunt for the perfect plant for that sunny spot in your own garden. Cut flowers and bouquets are a wonderful way to take home with you the joy of this riverside garden. Sun & Mon 10am–6pm. (828)675-9140.

Continue on 80N. Turn L at 5 mi onto Mine Creek to follow 80N. Go 2 mi and turn L onto Hwy 226 going N. Travel .1 mi to L onto Toecane Rd. Travel 1 mi and turn R across the river. As you cross bridge, turn L at T-intersection. Travel 2.1 mi to gardens on L.

52 **Oak Moon Farm** 452 ROAN VIEW DR – At this homestead dairy goat farm, you are sure to be entertained by the goat "family." This farm produces fresh and aged cheeses for you to purchase, or

Presprout your perennials in a yogurt cup lined with a coffee filter. When the seeds sprout, move them to individual pots. Use a pencil to make a hole for each sprout in the potting soil. Use tweezers to move each sprout from the yogurt cup to a pot.

Too much sun means stress, pests, and diseases for rhododendrons and azaleas, so keep them shaded.

learn how to make your own with a one-day apprenticeship. Open house during Spring and Holiday Toe River Studio Tours. Call for special events. (828)688-4683.

Return to Hwy 226 heading toward Bakersville. Just before blinking light in town, turn R onto Baker Ln. Cross the bridge and make the second R onto Ridgeview. Make a deep curve to L at church. Farm is next R.

Rhododendron Festival DOWNTOWN BAKERSVILLE – The spectacular blooming season of the Catawba Rhododendron provides great cause to celebrate in this small town. Mid-June brings admirers to the area to enjoy crafts, local fare, music and more. Call the Mitchell County Chamber of Commerce. (800)227-3912. www.mitchell-county.com

Return to Hwy 226 and turn R to go S. R at stop sign to get to downtown.

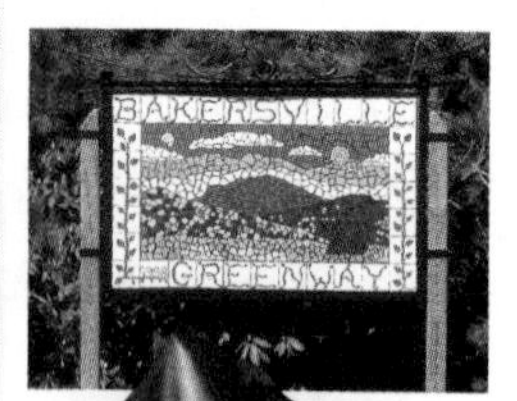

Bakersville Creekwalk CRIMSON LAUREL WAY – See the strength of a small town coming together in the completion of this community park featuring a gazebo, fishing piers, picnic tables and a creekwalk. Sunrise to sunset.

Located on Hwy 226 in downtown Bakersville.

Side trip...

55 **Daylily Farms & Nursery** 8907 NC 261 – Walking down the garden slope, you'll be amazed and impressed with the 1200 colors of this lily, hosta and perennial nursery. In June, the blooms are fabulous, the aroma, intoxicating and you'll think you've landed smack in the middle of Disney's Fantasia. With thousands of plants in more varieties than you can count, be prepared to load up your car. Some plants are pre-potted or you can have one dug up just for you. May–Aug Mon–Sun 10am–5pm. (828)688-3916.

From the stop sign at the intersection of Hwys 226 and 261, continue N on Hwy 261. Nursery is on L at 10 mi.

The Road Goes On Forever

Side trips, tidbits, adventures, and treasure hunts

Roan Mountain NC/TN STATE LINE ON HWY 261 – In mid-June on this natural bald, the 600 acres of rhododendron and flame azalea are breathtaking. As you stroll through the low-growing "rhodos", you'll delight in the seemingly unending views of pink blossoms, blue sky and blue mountains. Picnic grounds and facilities available in this area of the Pisgah National Forest. (828)682-6146.

Continue N on Hwy 261 for 3 mi. Look for sign.

To the dull mind nature is leaden.

To the illumined mind the whole world burns and sparkles with light.

– Ralph Waldo Emerson

...Meanwhile back on the trail

Dellinger Grist Mill CANE CREEK RD – Corn grinding is an art that has been faithfully continued by the Dellinger family for years. Take a tour and watch a demonstration of the restored 130-year-old mill that uses water power to stone-grind corn into cornmeal. June–Sep Third Sat 10am–5pm. Oct 15–Nov 30 Mon–Sat 10am–5pm. Or, call for appointment. (828)688-1009.

Return to the intersection of Hwy 226/261 in Bakersville. Take the next L onto Cane Creek. Mill is located 4 mi on R. Park on L.

The afternoon knows what the morning never suspected.

– Swedish Proverb

Saylor Orchard 1022 SAYLOR LAKE RD – Jim Saylor was named NC Apple Grower of the Year for 2000 for many reasons that we mere apple-eaters don't understand. But, what we do

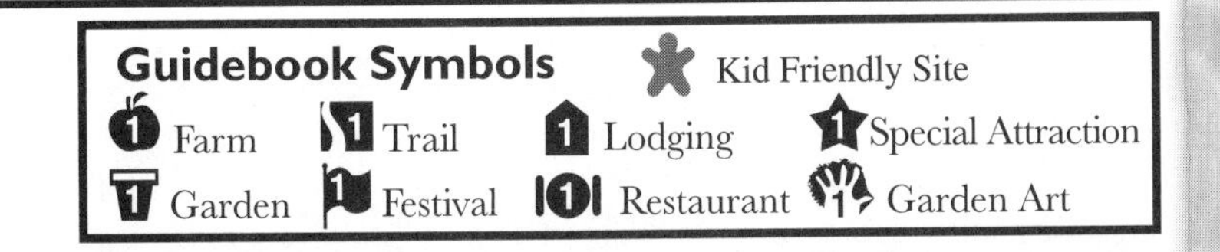

Guidebook Symbols Kid Friendly Site

Farm | Trail | Lodging | Special Attraction

Garden | Festival | Restaurant | Garden Art

Apple Mask

1 apple, cored and quartered
2 tablespoons honey
1/2 teaspoon sage

Blend together the apple, honey and sage. Refrigerate 10 minutes. Pat mixture on face. Leave mask on for 30 minutes then rinse.

know is he grows delicious apples! Set in a lush valley with a fishing pond, the orchard is a heavenly place to saunter and select your favorites. And, you certainly don't want to miss the cider. Sep–Nov Mon–Sat 8am–6pm. Or, call for appointment. (877)688-4411. http://hometown.aol.com/jimsaylor/Index.html

Return to stop light. Turn L to head S on Hwy 226. Orchard on L at 1.5 mi.

59 **Cabin in the Laurel** 163 CABIN IN THE LAUREL RD – Anticipate sweet dreams among the rhododendron. A 200-year-old cabin was renovated in the early 1900's and will accommodate several people. A small rustic log cabin offers an indoor camping experience. Both offer spectacular views. (888)701-4083. www.cabininthelaurel.com

Continue S on Hwy 226 for 3.2 mi to R on Wing Rd. Travel .5 mi to sign on L.

60 **Penland School of Crafts** PENLAND SCHOOL RD – One-, two-, and eight-week classes in books and paper, clay, drawing, glass, iron, metals, photography, printmaking, textiles and wood are offered amongst the garden grounds. The excellent work of world-renowned Penland instructors, resident artists and students is available for sale in the Gallery. Classes run mid-Mar–mid-Nov. Tuition varies. The Gallery is open mid-Apr–early Dec Tue–Sat 10am–12noon & 1pm–5pm. Sun 12noon–5pm. Closed Mon. (828)765-6211. www.penland.org

Return to Hwy 226 S and travel approximately 3 mi to R at produce stand onto Penland Rd. Go 1 mi to R on Penland School Rd. Travel 1.2 mi to school on R.

The Road Goes On Forever

Side trips, tidbits, adventures, and treasure hunts

Make-Ahead Potting Mix for Plants in Pots
1 part topsoil
1 part peat moss
1 part vermiculite
Add compost for fertilizer.

SPRUCE PINE

61 Mayland Community College 200 MAYLAND DR – The campus of this college offers convenient access to its greenhouses, wildflower trails, and continuing education classes. Check the schedule to see if your visit coincides with a weekend horticulture class. Mon–Sat sunrise to sunset. (828)765-7351. www.mayland.cc.nc.us

Continue S on Hwy 226 for 2.7 mi from Penland Rd to intersection with 19E. Turn L onto 19E and travel approximately 4.5 mi to campus on L. (This is 3.2 mi past the light at Altapass Rd.)

62 Orchard at Altapass ORCHARD RD – More fun than Johnny Appleseed could hope for, this is a must-stop for everyone. See the feature article on page 80 to get more details on all the orchard has to offer: apple picking and cider, hay rides, live mountain music, butterfly garden, monarch butterfly fostering, wetlands garden, hiking trails, homemade fudge, and local crafts. Open May–Nov. Mon–Sat 10am–6pm & Sun 12noon– 6pm. (888)765-9455. www.altapassorchard.com

Retrace 19E 3.2 mi to turn L onto Altapass Rd. After 4.5 mi, turn R onto the BRP heading S. Orchard at Altapass is on the L at .7 mi.

63 Big Lynn Lodge 226A N – If not for a fire in 1965, Big Lynn, a massive Linden tree here before the arrival of Columbus, might still be standing. Known locally as the "Marrying Tree", Big Lynn stood on the county line of Mitchell and McDowell counties offering couples escape from the legal jurisdiction of one county for the other if the families did not approve of the match. Two sprouts from the original tree stand sentinel for the lodge, cottages and restaurant. (800)654-5232.

Travel 3 mi on BRP to intersection with 226A. Continue 1.3 mi on 226A S to Lodge on L.

Fresh herbs added to apple jelly make aromatic jellies to enhance the flavorful apple.

***Apple Mint Jelly:** Add one bunch of mint to the apple while it is cooking. Look at the color after the juice is strained. Add a few drops of green food coloring if it is not as colorful as you'd like.*

***Apple Rosemary Jelly:** Add several sprigs to the apple while it is cooking. Add green food coloring and a sprig of rosemary in the jars before pouring the jelly in.*

Guidebook Symbols

Kid Friendly Site
Farm | Trail | Lodging | Special Attraction
Garden | Festival | Restaurant | Garden Art

Interested in how to make soap? Try these books:

The Handmade Soap Book by Melinda Coss and Emma Peios, Storey Books, 1998

The Soap Book: Simple Herbal Recipes by Sandy Maine, Interweave Press, 1995

The Soapmaker's Companion by Susan Miller Cavitch, Storey Books, 1997

Photo courtesy of The Switzerland Inn

64 **The Switzerland Inn** LITTLE SWITZERLAND – Save the airfare overseas with the vista from these 12 acres of misty blue mountains and deep green valleys. Easy access to horseback riding, gem mining, and trout fishing as well as hikes to the top of Mt. Mitchell, the highest peak in the East. Lodge, chalets and restaurant. (800)654-4026.

Continue 1.3 mi on 226A S to Inn on R.

65 **Blue Ridge Soap Shed** 179 MEADOW VIEW RD – Indulge your senses in the delights of 50 recipes of handmade soap. Watch them make specialties like goat's milk, glycerine, old fashioned, seasonal, hand repairing, scents for men (Stud Bubbles), sensitive skin, bug repelling, and more. Native plants are used to provide many of the scents you'll find in this retail shop: mint, wildflower, lavender, magnolia, apple, and many more creative combinations. Open daily 10am–5pm. (828)765-6001. www.soapshed.com

Head back on 226A N toward Spruce Pine for .6 mi to 226 N. Turn L on 226 N. Turn L onto Meadow View at .6 mi. Travel .2 mi and turn L. Shop is on L.

Dig into the rich story of geology at the newly renovated North Carolina Minerals Museum. You'll discover the history of minerals and mining in the Spruce Pine area and find out how quartz is used for telescopes and most of the computer chips in the US. Open year-round 9am-5pm weather permitting. Closed during lunch in the winter months. Located at Mile Post 330.9 at the intersection of the Blue Ridge Parkway and Route 226 from Spruce Pine. (828) 765-2761.

66 **Richmond Inn** 51 PINE AVE – Located in a scenic mountain setting, the half-century old Inn is shaded by towering white pines and landscaped with native dogwoods, mountain laurel and rhododendron. Combining convenience and serenity, you'll find comfort and beauty to help you create new memories. And, you'll find yourself wanting to "write home" about the gourmet breakfast. (877)765-6993. www.richmond-inn.com

At Hwy 226, turn L. Go N for 4.4 mi, across 19E and bridge. R at light on Oak St. At .3 mi, turn L on Walnut at sign. Follow signs for L on Opal and L on Pine. Inn is on R.

The Road Goes On Forever

Side trips, tidbits, adventures, and treasure hunts

Time is the longest distance between two places.

-- Tennessee Williams

The Vision

It is our vision now
To tend our mountains as the shepherd tends
His animals. As he defends
Against marauders, accidents, disease,
Let us protect the soil, rivers, trees,
And the long skyline bright with sun or snow.

Let us return once more
To proven ways that made us friends with nature,
Among all creatures the caring creature,
And plant upon the generous mountain side
The corn and roses that justify our pride
In what we have recovered of ancient lore.

Then may our peaceful farms
Mantle gently the shoulders of the hills
Where the massive cumulus spills
The treasure of its rain and where the moon
In the October night as cool as bone
Silvers the apples in the trees' dark arms.

Fred Chappell
Poet Laureate, State of North Carolina, 1999–2003

The Orchard at Altapass

"Watch your heads! Don't bruise our apples," Bill Carson jokes, as the hay wagon jounces along beneath limbs laden with King Luscious and Virginia Beauties ripening in the summer sun at the Orchard at Altapass. Strains of "Your Cheatin' Heart" drift from the apple house, mingling with the sound of a coal train trundling along the track that skirts the Orchard's lower boundary. Swallowtails sail from butterfly bush to joe-pye weed in the Orchard's butterfly garden, as Bill spins tales he's gleaned from local folks since he traded a corporate job for the pains and pleasures of apple-growing.

Bill's justifiably proud of the 3,000 old-variety apple trees that he, his wife Judy and his sister Kit Trubey have rejuvenated along the verdant terraces stair-stepping down the mountainside below the Blue Ridge Parkway near Spruce Pine. Descend the Orchard's gravel entrance road and you engage in a species of time travel, to join a celebration of the days when apples—fried, dried, pied, sauced, jellied and jacked—were as vital to mountain families as corn, potatoes and beans. When apple butter bubbled in iron pots. When neighbors gathered on front porches to make music and swap the tales that Bill now tells: of Overmountain Men trudging along the Orchard road toward the Battle of Kings Mountain; of Charlie McKinney, his 48 children—and four (simultaneous) wives; of the 1916 flood,

that swept away hillsides, houses and the Orchard's first apple trees.

Step inside the apple house. It's chock full of handmade baskets, books, T-shirts and homemade preserves. Bins brim with Grimes Goldens and ruddy Stayman Winesaps. Join the cloggers, two-steppers and waltzers as the band segues from "Rocky Top" to "I'll Fly Away." Let a sliver of walnut fudge melt on your tongue while you marvel at a monarch butterfly emerging from its chrysalis in Judy's nature center, between the ice cream counter and the lawn chairs drawn up to the dance floor. There's Bill, demonstrating his expertise at "the Altapass shuffle," another talent he's unearthed since rooting himself in the Blue Ridge.

The Orchard is far smaller today than in the 1930s, when it was Altapass community's largest industry and paid better wages than railroad jobs. In its heyday, the Orchard shipped 125,000 bushels a season, from 32,000 trees cloaking 600 acres. Then, in the 1940s, the Parkway sliced it in two and appropriated much of its acreage. By 1995, when Bill, Judy and Kit saved its remaining 276 acres from development, the surviving trees were in sad shape; the apple house stood cavernous and dark. Thanks to their patience, perseverance and vision, lights shine again in the apple house; the trees hang heavy with fruit.

Arbors & Orchards

Mossy terracotta meets ivy-covered brick on a city street. In an airy barn's hay-filled manger, ewes-in-waiting embody peaceful patience. Lush emerald lawns set off sumptuous B&B's. On this rural-urban adventure, pockets of pleasure await at every bend of the road. In the trailhead town of Black Mountain, follow your nose to a local bakery for a fresh treat. Stroll streets of awning-clad storefronts and gardeners' galleries. Welcoming inns and handsome houses settle around the business district like a warm shawl. At Warren Wilson College, a working farm engages students, where the Cherokee once planted squash and corn. Entering Asheville, stop at the Biltmore Estate. Creamy Lenten roses bow their heads in raised bed islands. A sea of spring flowering bulbs floods the grounds of a grand chateau. Tour Montford Historic District. Cascading phlox in a hundred shades of lavender spills across stacked rock walls. Crisp picket fences, trellises and mythic statuary grace grounds of stately Queen Anne homes turned B&B's. Wander Wall Street to Lexington Avenue. Taste harmony in a bowl or poems on a plate at inspired in-town eateries. Discover exotic floral interiors next door to an alley garden. From Weaverville to Barnardsville and back, sycamore-lined creeks meander through lush pastures in mountain-rimmed valleys. Grape vines twine between forked trunks of venerable apple trees on a farm whose fruitful pleasures only begin with berries—crimson, black, yellow and blue. Red and white cattle

You could eat your way across the map. Everything from apples to potato candy. If you don't know what potato candy is, ask around. You're sure to find some at a roadside stand.

Oh, the fruit of the trees!

munch dandelion-studded fields. A miniature stallion peers over his shoulder, protecting his short shaggy herd. Nurseries offer myriad choices of thyme: coconut, Wedgewood, lemon, silver and French. Approach agriculture on a larger scale in Henderson County's broad expanses of sod farms, tilled fields and apple orchards. Banks of Easter and Stargazer lilies perfume a rosy retail outlet. Do you prefer Bridal White or American Beauty? You'll find those and dozens more to delight your eyes. Walk around Johnson Farm, a legacy of self-reliance bestowed upon Henderson school children by a pair of bachelor brothers. On Hendersonville's main thoroughfare, flower-filled islands are interplanted with parking spaces. Garden shops and galleries mix and mingle amid ivy-covered conifers in Flat Rock. At Carl Sandburg's sturdy farm, wife Lillian bred superior dairy goats. Hike Connemara's hill to visit Tapestry, Thea, Thistle and twin Toggenburg kids tended by home-schooled children. A red-tailed hawk tips a wing above Cloud Nine. Edneyville's orchards and produce stands with hillsides gauzy in spring's rush to color: soft magenta redbuds; azaleas in clean shell pink and powdery violet; the draped lace of dogwoods, and splashes of incandescent green. Slide into Hickory Nut Gorge. May apples unfurl umbrella leaves; sparkling water leaps Rocky Broad boulders. Tilted rock seeps are mossed and ferny, furred and feathered with emergent life. It's time to go. Cross the Eastern Continental Divide, then wind back to Black Mountain.

Arbors & Orchards

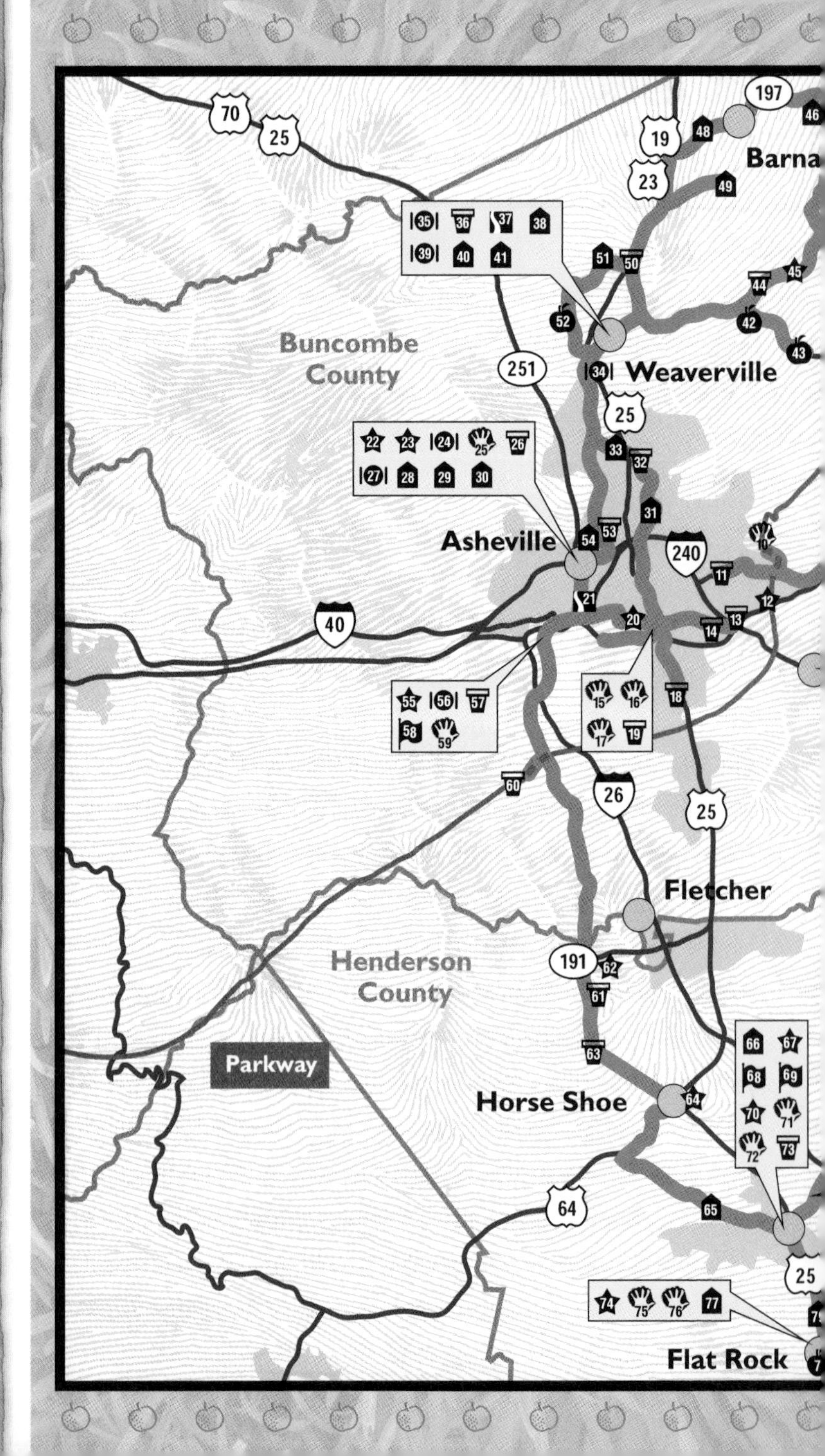

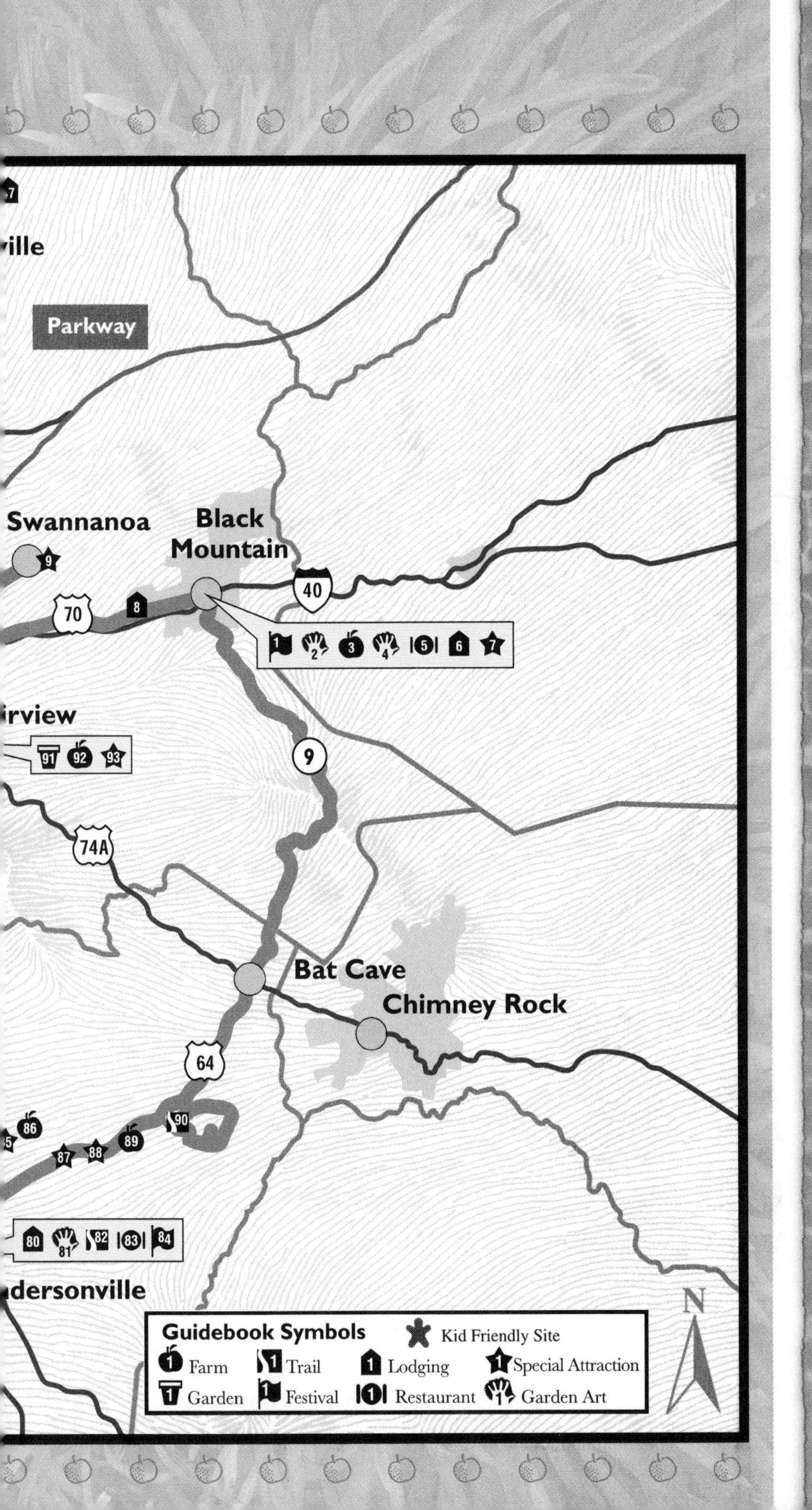
ille
Parkway
Swannanoa
Black Mountain
40
70
8
9
irview
74A
Bat Cave
Chimney Rock
64
86
87
88
89
90
80
81
82
83
84
dersonville
N
Guidebook Symbols
Kid Friendly Site
Farm
Trail
Lodging
Special Attraction
Garden
Festival
Restaurant
Garden Art

BLACK MOUNTAIN

1 **Sourwood Festival** If you find yourself on the trail in August, be certain to take in this annual street festival featuring live bee demonstrations, arts, crafts, games, food and local and regional music. Call for exact dates and times. (800)669-2301.

On Sutton Ave by the Old Depot at the railroad tracks and Black Mountain Ave.

2 **Black Mountain Iron Works** 120 BROADWAY ST – Memories of the 1960's whiz by among yard whimsies, such as iron butterflies and steely-eyed people that you can, nevertheless, see straight through. Dan Howachyn shares his creative space with local artists to display garden benches, fountains, and clay birdfeeders. Check out the blown glass iris stems of Belle Mead Hot Glass Studio and the exquisite hand painted leaves and cattails on Teri Godfrey's ceramic sinks. And, on summer weekends, forge and anvil demonstrations are common. June–Oct Mon–Fri 12noon–6pm & Sun 12noon–5pm. Closes at 5pm during the winter. (828)669-1001.

Turn L at Broadway St. Studio on L.

3 **Valley Garden Market** 661 OLD TOLL RD – This is the stop for home-baked, home-created and home-grown items such as chocolate chip cookies, quilts and elephant garlic. May–Oct Sat 9am–11am.

In the parking lot of Town Hall.

4 **Black Mountain Gallery** 112 CHERRY ST – Marshall and Eddie Hollifield are currently pursuing a listing in the *Guinness Book of World Records* for the largest turned wooden bowl, but you won't need that to appreciate trees from the inside out with these ingenious wood turners. Mon–Sat 10am–5pm & Sun 1pm–5pm. (828)669-1874.

Turn L onto State St. Take next L onto Cherry St. Gallery on R.

The Road Goes On Forever

Side trips, tidbits, adventures, and treasure hunts

Cool as a cucumber? The inside of a cucumber on the vine measures as much as 20 degrees cooler than the outside air on a warm day.

5 Black Mountain Bakery 102 CHURCH ST – Follow your nose to the fragrances wafting out of this shop where bagels, baguettes and quick breads are baked daily with stone-ground, unbleached organic flours. The cinnamon rolls may hold you hostage. Tue–Sat 8am–4pm. Lunch served from 11am–2pm. (828)669-1626.

Turn back onto State St. Turn R onto Church St. Bakery is on R.

6 The Red Rocker Inn 136 N. DOUGHERTY ST – Check out this whimsical inn for a gracious Southern breakfast, whether or not you're staying overnight. Grounds are minimal, but lovely, and you might need to make a few laps after breakfast while readjusting your belt. Or, enjoy the Southern tradition of family-style dining on the garden porch at dinner. Reservations required for both meals if you are not a guest at the inn. (828)669-5991.

Take R off of State St (Hwy 70) onto Dougherty St. Inn is on R.

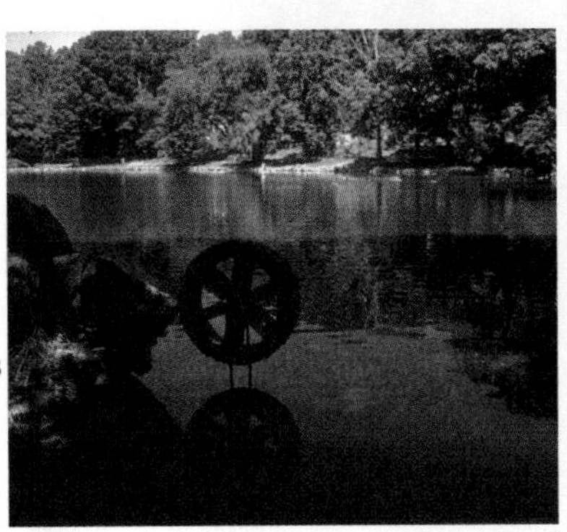

7 Lake Tomahawk This public park does not offer any interpretive plant signs but does provide a beautiful setting to breathe deep and muse while strolling around the tranquil lake. Yellow evening primroses bloom at twilight from late May–first of July. Dr. John Wilson, who lives next door, knows the secret behind the flowers. He'll be there watering them or you can call him at (828)669-2841. Open year-round.

From State St, turn R onto Gragmont. Bear R onto Rhododendron Ave. Park is on L.

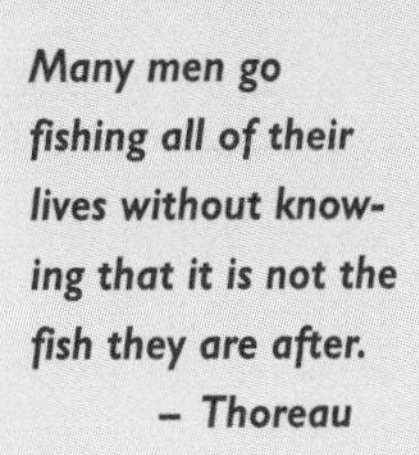

Many men go fishing all of their lives without knowing that it is not the fish they are after.
– Thoreau

8 Black Mountain Inn 718 W OLD HWY 70 – The most historic inn in Black Mountain boasts overnight stays by Hemingway and Steinbeck, in addition to rose gardens and groves of rhododendron and fruit trees on the three acres surrounding the lodge. (800)735-6128.

1 mi W of town on Old Hwy 70.

SWANNANOA

Warren Wilson College 701 WARREN WILSON RD – Heritage runs deep (literally), with an archaeological dig site of a Cherokee Native American village circa 1400 AD. Appropriately located behind the dig site are gardens of heritage plants planted by the students every year. Included in the seven-acre certified organic garden are vegetables, soft fruits, cut flowers, culinary and medicinal herbs. Produce market open mid-May–Aug Tue & Fri 11am–1pm. From late Aug–late Oct/early Nov, the market hours on Fri run later. Grounds open year-round 8am–5pm. (828)298-3325.

Off US 70 between Asheville and Swannanoa. 1.3 mi. north on R. .02 mi to greenhouse on R.

For a low-cost but high-powered fertilizer, use dried alfalfa normally used to feed horses and other livestock. Just spread a liberal amount of alfalfa on the ground and till it in.

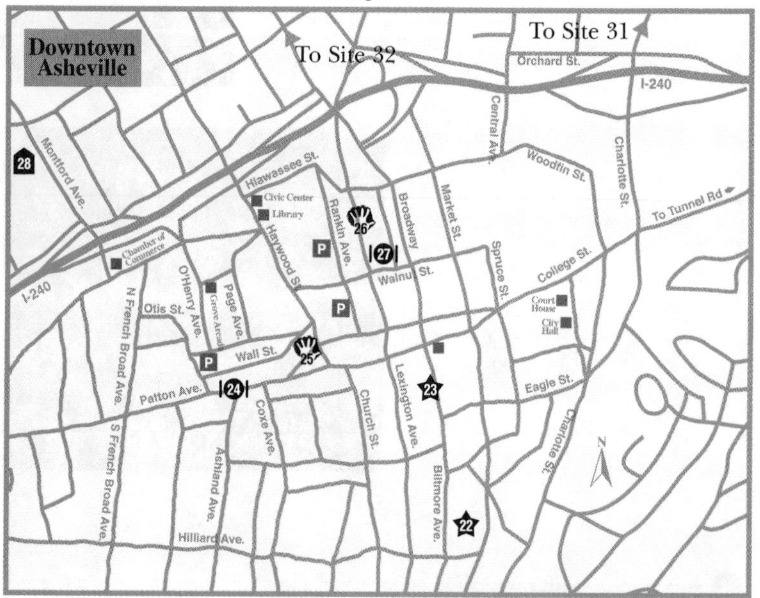

ASHEVILLE

Folk Art Center BLUE RIDGE PARKWAY MILE POST 382 – Through a cooperative agreement with the National Park Service, the Southern Highland Craft Guild operates the Center for exhibition and retail sales of regional,

---

The Road Goes On Forever

Side trips, tidbits, adventures, and treasure hunts

Join the gardening craze! It's the number one hobby in the United States.

traditional and contemporary crafts. The Center features the 100-year-old Allanstand Craft Shop, three galleries and a craft library. Visitors can experience craft-making through the frequent demonstrations held at the Center. Open daily Jan–Mar 9am–5pm & Apr–Dec 9am–6pm. Closed Christmas, Thanksgiving and New Year's Day. (828)298-7928.

Turn off Hwy 70 (Tunnel Rd) onto BRP N. Follow signs to Mile Post 382.

Barefoot Gardens 22 OVERBROOK PL – You don't need to go barefoot to feel the earth under your feet. It's evident in the organic gardens, home orchard, flowers, wild garden, bamboo, herbs, and forest garden that surround this lovely home. A beneficial insect habitat, dynamic accumulators, small pond, array of animals and garden art enhance this island of permaculture in the land of suburbia. Guided educational tour for $5 pp. Mon–Tue 9am–4:30pm. (828)298-0426.

Take BRP back to Tunnel Rd (Hwy 70) and exit R. Travel 1.8 mi. to L on Overbrook Rd (opposite State Police/driver's license office). Go uphill, turn R at T-intersection onto Overbrook Place. Last house on L.

WNC Nature Center 75 GASHES CREEK RD – Take a walk on the wild side in 40 acres of rhododendron and rambling trails to view native animals of the Southern Appalachian Mountains. Red and gray wolves, mountain lions, predator birds and farm animals live peacefully in this nature sanctuary with educational and interactive exhibits. Admission pp: Adults $5; Seniors $4 & Children $3 (3-14 yrs old). Open daily year-round 10am–5pm. Closed during winter holidays. (828)298-5600. www.wncnaturecenter.org

On Tunnel Rd (Hwy 70) travel E to R on Swannanoa River Rd (Hwy 181). Turn L on Azalea and then R onto Gashes Creek. Cross the bridge and L up the hill.

Nature uses as little as possible of anything.
– Kepler

MANNA Food Bank Demonstration Garden 627 SWANNANOA RIVER RD – A garden for the greater good…the produce raised here goes to soup kitchens and food

Butterflies are welcome visitors to any garden. But, did you know that the average life span of an adult butterfly is only about one month?

pantries that feed hungry families in the area. It was created as both an educational and a demonstration garden. A master gardener on site Tuesdays 9am–12noon to answer questions, and interpretive literature is available. Before you hit the trail again be sure to enjoy a stroll through the butterfly gardens. Mon–Fri 8am–4pm. (828)299-3663.

Take Azalea Rd to L on Swannanoa River Rd (Hwy 181). Travel .5 mi to MANNA offices and garden on L.

14 **B.B. Barns** 831 FAIRVIEW RD – Owners Barney Bryant and Ned Gibson will assure you that every plant, tree and shrub in their nursery and greenhouses is hand-picked. That loving attention to detail spills over into their retail shop with its potting benches, statuary, supplies and gifts of every variety for the garden and for the gardener. Call about schedules for free gardening workshops and seminars. Mon–Sat 9am–6pm. (828)274-7301.

Continue on Swannanoa River Rd (Hwy 181) to L on Fairview Rd. Cross Hwy 240 just past Home Depot on L.

Pick up a few geraniums for your vegetable garden. They are a natural insect deterrent.

15 **Common Ground and Screen Door** 115 FAIRVIEW RD – You'll not find a better collection of gardening books anywhere in these parts and at 40-75 percent off the retail price no less. Add to that the eclectic variety of garden art to wander through after you open "the screen door" and you'll find botanical bliss. Numerous booths by a creative gardening community will entice with offerings such as dried flower fairies, garden sachets, topiaries, iron leaf screens and tin watering pots. Mon–Sat 10am–6pm & Sun 1pm–5pm. (828)277-DOOR.

Continue on Fairview through residential area for approximately 1.5 mi. Common Ground will be on your L.

16 **Biltmore Cast Stone** 6 FAIRVIEW RD – Bird feeders and baths, sundials and fountains, planters and statuary are all handmade on site at this manufacturing and retail outlet for garden and home products made from resin

A rose is a rose is a rose.
– Gertrude Stein

and marble dust, and concrete. Personalized signs and rocks are also available. Jan–Mar Mon–Sat 10am–5pm. Apr–Dec Mon–Fri 9:30am–5:30pm & Sat 10am–5pm. (800)743-7415. www.biltmorecaststone.com

Down the hill and on the right across the railroad tracks.

17 **New Morning Gallery** 7 BOSTON WAY – You know you've stumbled into garden art extraordinaire when you find yourself amongst welded sculptures of cats on motorcycles, Jim Millar's bronze calla lily fountains and Andy Brinkley's brass and copper interpretation of a frog mowing. Beautiful wicker rocking chairs from Wisconsin. You'll be knocked out by the award-winning gardens surrounding the gallery. Jan–Mar Mon–Sat 10am–6pm & Sun 12noon–5pm. Apr–Dec Mon–Sat 10am–7pm & Sun 12noon–5pm. (828)274-2831. www.newmorninggallerync.com

Turn R off of Fairview onto Sweeten Creek Rd. Turn L into Biltmore Village for parking.

18 **The Gardens of the French Broad River Garden Club** 1000 HENDERSONVILLE RD – Considered Asheville's "secret gardens", the French Broad River Garden Club presents eight distinct gardens named Kitchen, Cherokee, The Arbor, Fragrant, Industrial, Medicinal, Biblical and Wall. Nestled amongst 19th century cabins, these gardens can be enjoyed with a short stroll or intensive exploration. Open during daylight hours. For more information write to: French Broad River Garden Club Foundation, 1000 Hendersonville Rd, Asheville, NC 28803.

Travel S on Hwy 25 (Hendersonville Rd) for 2.1 mi. Turn L onto Deanwood Circle (street is called Busbee on R). Gardens are on R.

19 **The Gardener's Cottage** 34 ALL SOULS CRESCENT – Primroses, oak leaf ivy and hydrangeas create a palette of soft hues in this English nature shop. Twig furniture, garden accessories and vases of fresh cut flowers vie for attention. Be sure to see the mushroom tree on

Herbs and flowers for your hair:

Chamomile flowers soften hair.
Lavender stimulates hair growth.
Marigold lightens hair color.
Rosemary darkens hair color.
Parsley adds luster.

To prepare an herbal hair rinse, simply bring to 1 tablespoon of dried herb to boil in 4 cups of water. Let simmer for 30 minutes. Cool for 30 minutes. Strain and use on clean, wet hair. Leave it on for 20 - 30 minutes.

Correct handling of flowers refines the personality.
– Bokuyo Takeda

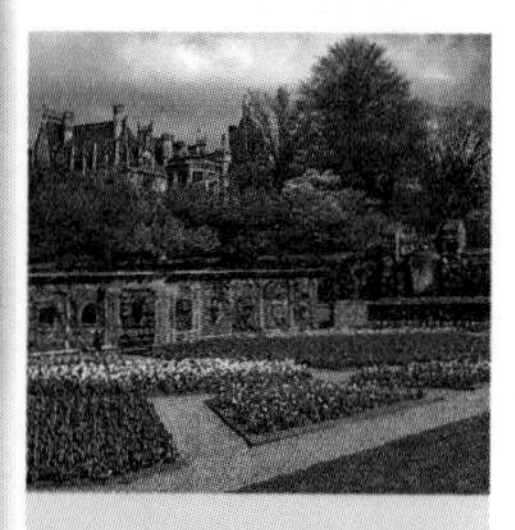

The Biltmore Estate is home to a number of impeccable gardens designed by Frederick Law Olmsted, father of American landscape architecture.
• The Azalea Gardens featuring 1,000-plus native and hybrid azaleas.
• The Spring Gardens enhanced by groves of white pine and hemlock over a sheltered valley of rhododendrons & hollies.
• The Walled Garden offering four acres of daffodils, hyacinths, tulips, dahlias, globe amaranth, zinnias, peonies, and chrysanthemums.
• The Shrub Garden with winter jasmine, vernal witch hazel, Japanese cherries, lilacs, dogwoods and azaleas.
• The Italian Garden, a Renaissance landscape with three symmetrical pools surrounded by manicured lawns and enticing paths.

the upper level. Mon–Sat 10am–5pm. (828)277-2020.

Traveling on Hwy 25 return to Biltmore Village. Turn L onto All Souls Crescent. Cottage is on L.

20 **The Biltmore Estate - House, Gardens and Winery** MCDOWELL AVE – You would have to go out of your way to miss the largest private home in America. George Vanderbilt's legacy includes a chateau tour, gardens to goggle and a winery preserving the agricultural history of the estate. West-side vineyards grow serveral varieties of vinifera grapes which French winemaker Bernard Delille transforms into the estate's award-winning wines. Guided tours of the winery, barrel tasting seminars, cooking demonstrations and wine programs available. Estate-raised beef, lamb and trout available at the Bistro. Other dining facilities available include the Bake Shop, Ice Cream Parlor and the Dining Room by reservation only. An admission fee is charged. Open daily Jan–Mar 9am–5pm & Apr–Dec 8:30am–5pm. (800) 543-2961. www.biltmore.com

Entrance just past the Gardener's Cottage on the left. Follow the signs through the gate to the Reception and Ticket Center.

21 **French Broad River Park** RIVERVIEW DR & AMBOY RD – To see the French Broad in its full glory, there's no better spot than this community park where box elders rule amidst stands of sycamore, red maple, birch and cherry trees. Box elder beetles may show up to play with your kids and adorn the sleeves of your jacket. Open dawn–dusk.

From Biltmore entrance, go straight to L on Biltmore Ave. Turn L on Meadow Rd to L across the bridge on Amboy Rd. Park is on R.

The Road Goes On Forever

Side trips, tidbits, adventures, and treasure hunts

Botanically, there is no such thing as a pumpkin. Pumpkins are certain varieties of squash, which through local traditions and use, have come to be called pumpkins.

22 **French Broad Food Co-op and Tailgate Market** 90 BILTMORE AVE – Locals show a lot of support for this health food cooperative which in turn, supports organic farmers in the community. An on-site herb garden provides welcome reprieve next to the parking lot. Summer brings the heady colors and aromas of the French Broad Tailgate Market. Co-op open Mon–Fri 9am–8pm, Sat 9am–7pm & Sun 12noon–6pm. Tailgate Market open spring-fall Sat 8am–1pm. (828)255-7650. www.fbfc.com

From Biltmore entrance, go straight to L on Biltmore Ave. Go N towards town. Co-op will be on the R.

For a tasty treat, slice a squash in half and bake with a butter, cinammon and sugar glaze. Yummy!!!

23 **Mast General Store** 15 BILTMORE AVE – Yet another branch of the Valle Crucis legend springs to life amidst the hustle and bustle at Asheville's core. Outdoor gear, footwear, and garden items create another shopping stop conveniently across the street from the marvels of Pack Place. Mon–Thu 10am–6pm, Fri–Sat 10am–8pm & Sun 1pm–6pm. (828)232-1883.

Continue on Biltmore Ave towards downtown. Store is on L.

Wall St. District

24 **The Market Place** 20 WALL ST – Seasonal menus reflect the offerings of the region at this local favorite. Indigenous ingredients trout and apples star in gourmet culinary creations like "Trout on Fire" and duck breast with apple reduction. Owner Mark Rosenstein is also the author of *In Praise of Apples*. Apr–Dec Mon–Sat 6pm–9:30pm. Jan–Mar Wed–Sat 6pm–9pm. (828)252-4162.

In addition, Mark has partnered with Eve Davis of the Hawk & Ivy B&B for seasonal workshops called, "From Gourmet Garden to Gourmet Kitchen" to delight the senses by learning kitchen gardening techniques and gourmet cooking with two experts in their fields. Call Eve at Hawk and Ivy for more information. (828)626-3486.

Wall St runs parallel to Patton Ave behind the newly renovated Pritchard Park.

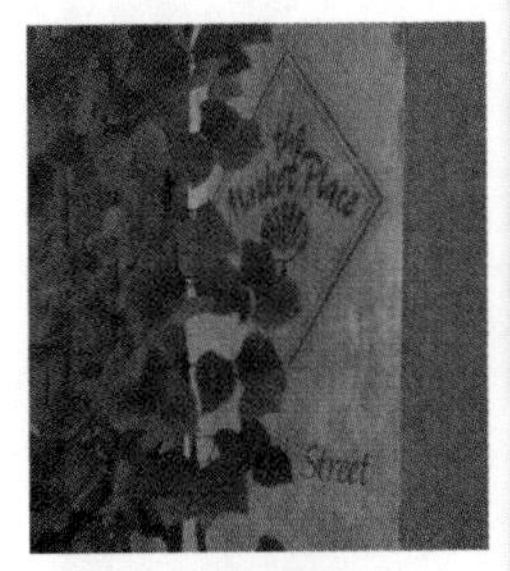

Check out DIRT, a new shop featuring home and garden décor with pottery by owner and horticulturist, Anne Kaufmann. Good stop for funky planters, bulbs, seeds, trellises and garden art. Just up from Perri Ltd at 51 N Lexington Avenue. Mon-Sat 10 am-6pm. (828) 281-DIRT(3478).

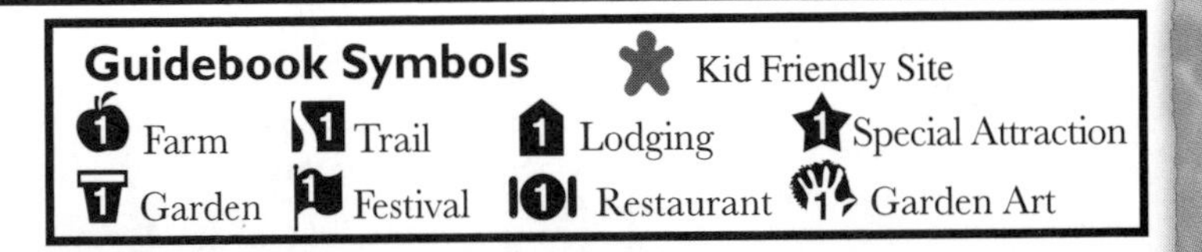

For a natural privacy fence or screen, or just to hide a not-so-attractive view, use big, bold annuals and perennials with grasses such as the following:

Annuals:
Canna
Castor Bean

Perennials:
Joe-Pye Weed
Plume Poppy
Queen of the Prairie

Ornamental Grass:
Frost Grass
Maiden Grass
Pampas Grass
Ravenna Grass

25 **Natural Selections** 10 WALL ST – If you have to kiss a few frogs in your life, make sure they're of the Leptotactylus frosti and Eleuthrodactylus species –two frogs named after University of Kansas Biology professor and natural history curator John Frost. John's nature shop is full of three-dimensional steel frogs, geckos and butterflies for your garden as well as hand carved walking sticks, stained glass butterflies and glass windchimes. Regional wildlife and scenic art mesh beautifully with the sounds of nature. Mon–Thu 10am–6pm. Fri–Sat 10am–7pm. Sun 1pm–5pm. (828)252-4336. www.naturalselections-asheville.com

26 **Perri Ltd** 65 1/2 LEXINGTON AVE – The combination of art and nature dovetails beautifully a thousand times over in Perri's floral décor studio. Old World traditions of France and Asia fuse in synchronicity with an eclectic selection of native mountain materials. He breaks all the rules in his alley garden full of obscure details such as a city rooster and outdoor chandelier. Open Mon–Sat 10am–6pm & Sun 12noon–5pm. (828)281-1197.

S Lexington St on L, just past Walnut St intersection.

27 **Max & Rosie's Café** 52 N LEXINGTON AVE – A lunch haven for vegetarians and home to many converts, this café serves sandwiches, salads and smoothies made out of fresh and mostly organic ingredients. You may want to try an "Energy Enhancer" tonic made with spinach, tomato, zucchini, cayenne and ginseng before heading back onto the trail. If a sandwich would hit the spot don't miss Rosie's tempeh reuben. Mon–Sat 11am–5pm. (828)254-5342.

Across the street from Perri Ltd.

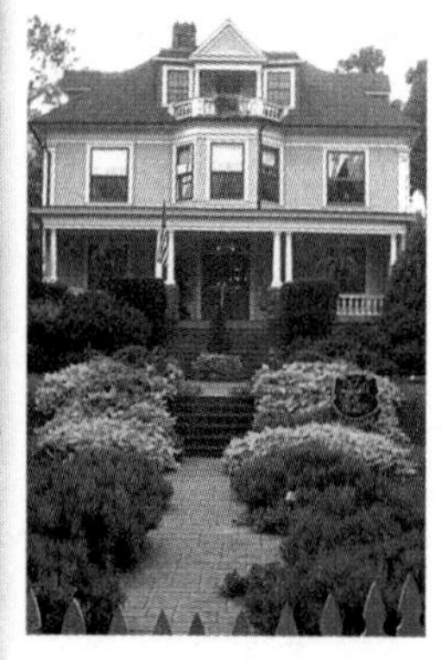

28 **The Lion and the Rose** 278 MONTFORD AVE – This Queen Anne and Georgian style B&B is the perfect setting for an afternoon cup of English tea. Annuals, perennials, and herbs abound, but the lavender lining the walkways rules the plant kingdom here. TIME/LIFE

The Road Goes On Forever
Side trips, tidbits, adventures, and treasure hunts

When cutting lavender to use in crafts, be sure you harvest the spikes before they bloom. Tie in bunches and hang upside down to dry.

even featured this Mediterranean mint in the book, *Designing and Planting Backyards.* (828)255-ROSE.

Take Lexington to R on College St to R on Haywood St. Continue on Haywood St to R at Three Brothers Restaurant on Montford Ave. Travel .6 mi. B&B is on the L.

29 **Abbington Green** 46 CUMBERLAND CIRCLE – With eight rooms named after London parks and gardens, this Richard Sharp Smith house takes you back to traditional English B&B's. Stroll around the "green." Its award-winning English gardens will make you wonder if you've been transported to somewhere near Shropshire. (828)251-2454. www.abbingtongreen.com.

From Montford Ave turn R onto W. Chestnut St, travel one block and turn L onto Cumberland Ave (at flashing signal). Bear R onto Cumberland Circle; 6th house on L.

Annual Vines for Your Garden Gate:

Balloon Vine
Chilean Glory Flower
Creeping Gloxinia
Cup-and-Saucer Vine
Cypress Vine
Flag-of-Spain
Hyacinth Bean
Moonflower
Morning Glory
Purple Bell Vine
Twining Snapdragon
Variegated Japanese Hop

30 **The WhiteGate Inn & Cottage** 173 E. CHESTNUT ST – Of the 25,000 species of orchid, 400 of them reside within the 1200-square foot greenhouse at this Victorian B&B. Ralph Coffey's prize Brassia Rex spider orchid weaves magic for on-site guests and also at the annual Western NC Orchid Show. Enjoy Frank Salvo's culinary magic with a three-course breakfast before viewing the east gardens and skyline of Asheville from the solarium. Call ahead for lectures and workshops at the inn. (828)253-2553.

Take Cumberland Circle S to E Chestnut St on L. Continue on E Chestnut St through residential area and across Merrimon Ave. Inn will be 2 blocks on R.

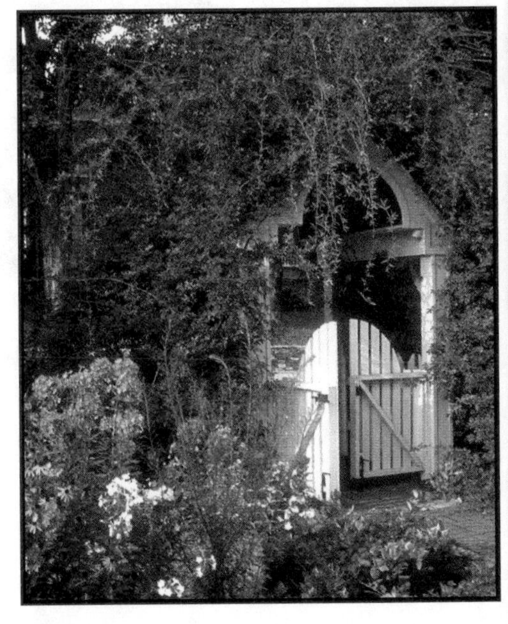

NOT TO BE MISSED! Grovewood Gallery at 111 Grovewood Road is a must for wind sculptures, steel butterfly and peacock benches, and other assorted garden art. Wander about the lovely sculpture and water gardens for inspiration and rejuvenation. Open Apr–Dec Mon–Sat 10am–6pm & Sun 10am–5pm. Jan–Mar Mon–Sat 10am–5pm & closed Sun. (828) 253-7651. Located just behind Grove Park Inn.

31 **The Grove Park Inn Resort and Spa** 290 MACON AVE – The historic grand hotel features spectacular views of the mountains and of Asheville. Walkways around the grounds encourage investigation of a newly completed, and internationally touted, health spa. After strolling the grounds during chilly weather, find your way to the gargantuan fireplaces in the lobby. Warmed appropriately, proceed on your way through the hotel to view the largest in-use collection of Arts and Crafts era furnishings. All from the nature-based decorative movement during the turn of the last century. (828)252-2711.

Continue on Charlotte St to R on Macon Ave and follow to hotel.

Don't forget to pack a picnic lunch, and bring the family dog and a Frisbee along for a fun-filled day playing by Beaver Lake.

32 **Beaver Lake Bird Sanctuary** MERRIMON AVE – This eco-filter wetland features a relaxing trail alongside cattails and willow trees, a nice wedge of nature between slices of Urbania. Funded by the NC Clean Water Management Trust Fund for the Elisha Mitchell Audubon Society.

Return to Charlotte St and turn L. Turn R on Kimberly Ave. Continue until it dead ends into Beaverdam. Turn L to intersection with Merrimon Ave (Hwy 25). Turn R and continue approximately .5 mi. Sanctuary will be on your L.

The Road Goes On Forever

Side trips, tidbits, adventures, and treasure hunts

SPOT IT

It's somewhere on this loop. Can you find it?

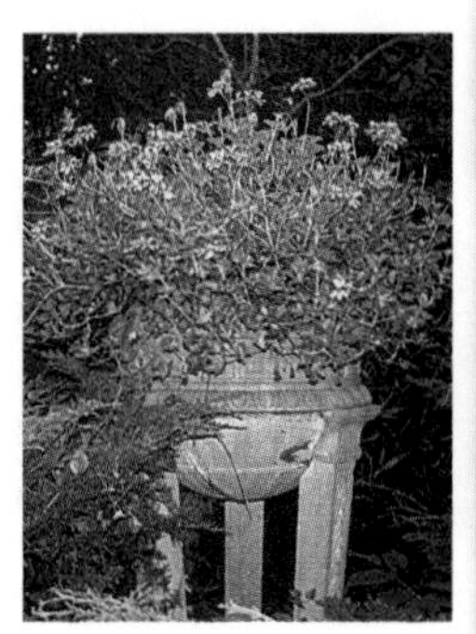

33 Old Reynolds Mansion 100 REYNOLDS HEIGHTS – The 1855 antebellum brick home of Colonel Daniel Reynolds originally sat on 1400 acres of forestland. While only four acres remain around the restored home of Fred and Helen Faber, the couple have added lovely perennial beds and a charming courtyard to complement the grounds. And yes, the ten guestroom B&B is "slightly haunted". "Who ya gonna call?" (828)254-0496.
Travel N past Beaver Lake. Turn R on Beaver Dr and L onto gravel lane.

34 Stoney Knob Café & Patio 337 MERRIMON AVE – Take a little break from trail-blazing and enjoy dining alfresco at this funky café. From the farmer's market to the table, nightly gourmet specials reflect the local flavor. Open year-round. Tue–Sat 8am–8pm & Sun 9:30am–3pm. Closed Mon. (828)645-3309.
Continue on Merrimon Ave into Weaverville for 5 mi. Café is before intersection with Reems Creek Rd on L.

WEAVERVILLE

35 Weaverville Milling Company 337 REEMS CREEK RD – It takes a certain amount of finesse to de-bone a rainbow trout in under 10 seconds, but these folks have mastered it. Locally made, home-style and continental cuisine is the rule at this old millpond operation. Nice array of mountain crafts to examine and porch dining available in the summer. Dinner only. Mon–Sun 5pm–until. Closed Wed & first three weeks of Jan. (828)645-4700.
Turn R on Reems Creek Rd. Continue for .6 mi. Restaurant is on R.

While visiting Gourmet Gardens Herb Farm, pick up some rosemary to use for tea. Some folks say rosemary tea will cure a headache and helps strengthen memory.

36 Gourmet Gardens Herb Farm and Day Dreams Inn 14 BANKS TOWN RD – An element of magic surrounds this farm where 80 varieties of scented geraniums thrive next to everlasting plants, herbal display gardens, a lily

Guidebook Symbols

Kid Friendly Site
1 Farm · 1 Trail · 1 Lodging · 1 Special Attraction
1 Garden · 1 Festival · 1 Restaurant · 1 Garden Art

pond and unusual statuary. New owner Erica Curtis has added the four guest-room B&B as the final touch. Quaint gift shop features natural wreaths, teas, herbal products and fanciful fairies. Picnicking on the grounds is welcome but watch for mad hatters and march hares. Farm and shop hours Feb-Dec Tue–Sat 9:30am–5:30pm & Sun 1pm–5pm. Closed Jan. (828)658-0766.

Turn R onto Merrimon Ave toward Weaverville. Take R onto Banks Town Rd (across from Lake Louise). Farm is on L.

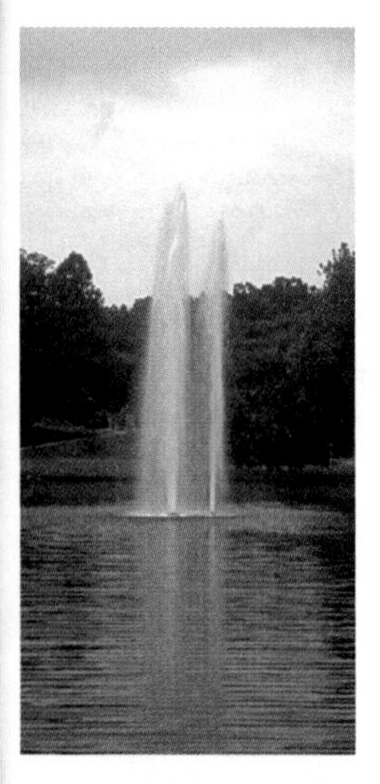

37 **Lake Louise** MERRIMON AVE – Weaverville is a town Norman Rockwell would have fallen in love with, and the romance would have started at this tranquil community park. A .9- mile walk around the lake provides views of children playing, Canadian geese a-laying, but alas, no partridges. There is, however, an old mill where Norman may well have set up his easel.

Park is across from Banks Town Rd.

38 **Dry Ridge Inn** 26 BROWN ST – A flagstone terrace leads the way to the water garden and waterfall that grace the side of this 1849 B&B. The bird sanctuary behind the house is an added delight. (828)658-3899. www.dryridgeinn.com

Continue on Merrimon Ave past lake. Brown St is just on the R.

Save a bit of clean-up time in the kitchen by putting your fresh-picked produce into a laundry basket to wash and dry it outside instead of in the kitchen sink.

39 **Sunnyside Café** 18 N MAIN ST – Head for the sunny-side of the street where Chef Jack and Patty Keeran have glorified local organic produce with such creations as the portabello stack and pecan crusted mountain trout. Don't miss the mountain apple and onion soup. Lunch Tue–Fri 11:30am–2pm. Dinner Tue–Sat 5:30pm–9pm. (828)658-2660.

Take a R on Merrimon Ave to L on Main St. Café is on L.

40 **The Secret Garden Bed & Breakfast** 56 N MAIN ST – Seclusion is assured with the dense hemlock hedge that surrounds this 1904 Low Country Charleston-style home. A 60-foot

The Road Goes On Forever

Side trips, tidbits, adventures, and treasure hunts

Use the bottom-half of a styrofoam egg carton as a seed-starting container. The lid can serve as a drip tray.

veranda provides a comfortable spot to ponder the interesting collection of metal sculptures, dogwoods, tulips and azaleas. Summer romance blooms in the roses, Japanese magnolias, herbs, hydrangeas, holly, hostas, and peonies. (888)797-8211. www.secretgardennc.com
Across from the Weaverville Library.

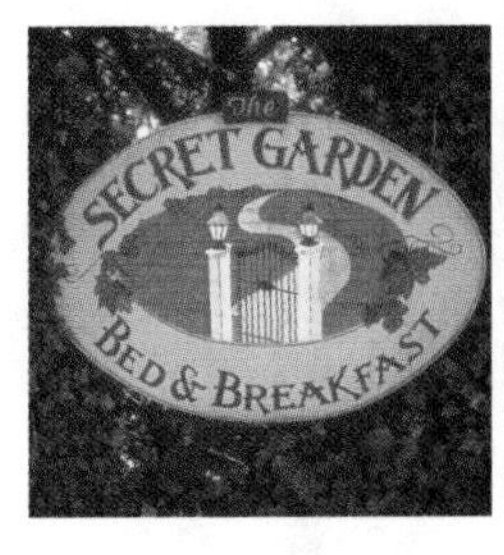

41 **Inn on Main Street** 88 S MAIN ST – A lovely garden walk bordered by herb and organic vegetable gardens await you at this romantic Victorian B&B. Old-time perennials and birdbaths provide a refuge for the world-weary heart. (877)873-6074. www.innonmain.com
Travel S down Main St just past the primary school. Inn is on L.

Ox-Ford Farm's cow Daisy is, remarkably, 28-years-old and still mooing.

42 **Ox-Ford Farm Bed and Breakfast** 75 OX CREEK RD – Dr. Edith Hapke takes pride in the working farm she started 25 years ago, and well she should. Cattle, sheep, peacocks, chickens and ducks take stock of visitors with a charming air of detachment. Walking trails criss-cross the property surrounding the four-guest room farmhouse. Open Apr–Dec. Closed Jan–Mar for lambing. (828)658-2500.
Turn L off of Main St onto Reems Creek. Travel approximately. 4.5 mi to R onto Ox Creek. Go .5 mi and look for sign on R.

Eggshell Fertilizer

Add 8 smashed eggshells to a gallon jug filled 3/4-full with water. Let mixture set for several days, then shake it up. Use it as a fertilizer for blooming perennials to give them a calcium boost.

43 **Dogwood Hills Farm** 367 OX CREEK RD – You might find your thrill on this blueberry hill, and you'll also find sweet and sour cherries, thornless blackberries, raspberries, apples, pumpkins and candyroasters. Blueberries in Aug. Cherries June 15–July 10. Blackberries July 1–Aug 10. Raspberries Aug 15–Oct 1. Apples June 30–Oct 30 (picked or pick-your-own). Pumpkins and candyroasters Oct 1–15. Bring your own containers. Mon–Sun 8am–6pm during season. (828)658-1800.
Continue on Ox-Creek Rd for 1.5 mi to R into farm.

Wildwood Herbal Flower Farm 817 REEMS CREEK RD – Alan Salmon chose the site well for his herb and perennial farm nestled in the pristine Reems Creek Valley. Garden and nursery walks amongst the display beds of culinary herbs, flowering shrubs, and perennials. The Sourwood Cottage is available for weekly rental. Tue–Sat 10am–5pm. Sun by appointment. (828)645-4342.

Follow Ox Creek Rd back to Reems Creek and turn R. Go about .5 mi to first drive on R.

For a good source of vitamin A and minerals, pick up some parsley at Wildwood.

Vance Birthplace 911 REEMS CREEK RD – The pioneer homestead of Zebulon B. Vance features a two-story cabin of hewn yellow pine and six log outbuildings. Demonstrations of pioneer living at this former North Carolina governor's home take place in the spring and fall. Apr 1–Oct. 31 Mon–Sat 9am–5pm & Sun 1pm–5pm. Nov 1–Mar 31 Tue–Sat 10am–4pm & Sun 1pm–4pm. (828)645-6706.

Continue on Reems Creek Rd for .5 mi. Historic site is on R.

BARNARDSVILLE

Cecile's Bed and Breakfast 25 PAINT FORK RD – Organic rock gardens of roses and perennials, a vegetable garden, permaculture blueberry garden, cutting garden, old barn, and spring-fed swimming pond surround the three-guest room home of this Reiki master. Permaculture and floral design workshops available. Open to public Wed–Thu 11am–7pm

Turn an old stump into a birdbath by hollowing it out and filling it with water.

The Road Goes On Forever

Side trips, tidbits, adventures, and treasure hunts

or by appointment. (828)626-3195 or (877)694-0939. www.homewithcecile.com

Take Reems Creek Rd to end and turn L on Maney Branch Rd. Travel 5.1 mi (road turns into Paint Fork Rd). Turns into dirt road for a stint. Consider the Lilies Lily Farm on L. Continue on to L just before elementary school where playground is on L. Take school exit and it turns into her driveway. (Note: In inclement weather, access Hwy 19/23 N from Weaverville Blvd and continue N to the Barnardsville exit (Hwy 197). Continue approximately 7 mi to R on Paint Fork. Cross bridge and just past the school, turn R on private driveway with sign.)

47 **The Hawk & Ivy Holistic Country Retreat Bed & Breakfast** 133 NORTH FORK RD – Over the river and through the woods you will find the lovely home of James and Eve Davis, a joyful haven from the outside world. Extensive organic kitchen gardens of fruits, vegetables and flowers surround the green farmhouse. Wander to the upper pasture where a restored, but rustic, barn serves as the setting for many a country wedding. A labyrinth is available for meditative strolls while a handful of raspberries will confirm that love is always in season here. Eve's gardening and floral design studio is a delight to visit and indicative of the "From Gourmet Garden to Gourmet Kitchen" series held with Mark Rosenstein of Asheville's "The Market Place." B&B open year-round. Grounds open Apr–Oct Wed 11am–4pm. Or, call for appointment. (828)626-3486.

Continue on Paint Fork Rd to Hwy 197 (North Fork Rd/ Barnardsville Hwy). Turn R and go approximately 1 mi and look for sign on R.

48 **Tuscan Hill B&B** 370 BARNARDSVILLE HWY – Mario and Norma Cortonesi found this valley surrounded by mountains, hemlocks and wildflowers reminiscent of their native Tuscany. They invite guests to pick a basket of fruits and vegetables from their lush gardens to take with them on their journey. A 15-minute drive from the 70-foot waterfall at Craggy Mountain Scenic area. (828)658-1877.

Travel S on Hwy 197 (Barnardsville Hwy) through Barnardsville for approximately 5.5 mi. Turn R at sign.

Call Hawk & Ivy for the schedule for the "From Gourmet Garden to Gourmet Kitchen" workshops.

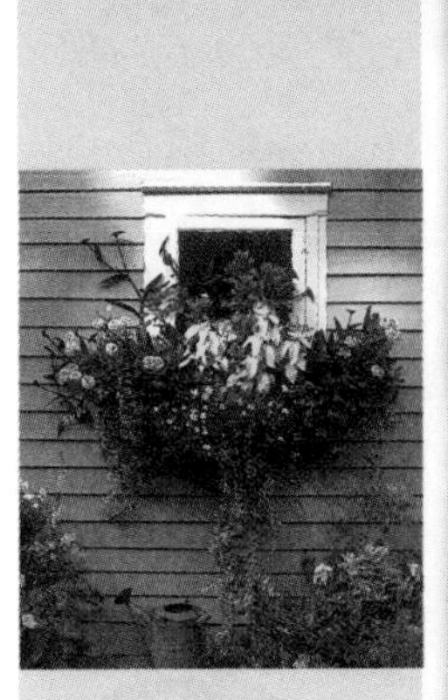

Need some low maintenance plants for your garden? Try these four:

Ajuga
Cranesbills
Creeping Jenny
Lily of the valley

The map is not the territory.
–Alfred Korzbybski

WEAVERVILLE

49 Freedom Escape Lodge 530 UPPER FLAT CREEK RD – Within the 25 acres of this old farmstead you will find log barns, a turn-of-the-century grist mill, a bass and brim catch and release, self-guided walking trails, a blacksmith, grazing cow, llamas and miniature horses (from nearby Claxton Farm) and magnificent views. Locally crafted quilts grace the inside of this lodge for individuals and groups. (828)658-0814. www.freedomescapelodge.com

Take Hwy 197 for 1.3 mi to intersection with Hwy 19/23 and turn L heading S. Travel 2.1 mi to Flat Creek Rd exit. Turn R off exit to immediate R on Murphy Hill Rd. Travel .8 mi to R on Upper Flat Creek Rd. Go 2 mi, turn L and continue on dirt road.

50 Reems Creek Valley Nursery 70 MONTICELLO RD – After 20 years in business, this nursery is known and loved by locals for its border gardens, water gardens and large selection of native plants, annuals, bedding plants, trees, hanging baskets, perennials, shrubs and organic gardening supplies. Mon–Fri 8am–5pm & Sat 9am–4pm. Closed Sun. (828)645-3937. www.reemscreek.com

Take Hwy 19/23 S towards Asheville to the 25/70 exit. Take R at light onto Monticello Rd. Nursery is .5 mi on R.

51 Dunromin Cabin 64 GREEN RIDGE RD – This antique hand-crafted log cabin makes for a great trail retreat at the end of the day. Proprietors Dee and Tom Howald generously offer their swimming pool up the hill for tired trail-worn tootsies. (800)457-2740.

Turn L on Monticello Rd and then R on Ollie Weaver Rd. Turn L at stop sign onto Clark's Chapel Rd at end of road. Proceed .1 mi, and bear L onto Green Ridge Rd. Proceed .3 mi to fifth driveway on L. Look for sign.

52 Barnwell's Orchard NEW STOCK RD – If you find yourself in the area in the fall, swing by this apple orchard for a taste of Gala, Golden Delicious, Red Delicious, Winesap and Granny Smith all in one stop. Recycle your grocery bags by filling them up with apples for the return trip home and apple pie memories of the trail

The Road Goes On Forever

Side trips, tidbits, adventures, and treasure hunts

from your own kitchen. Labor Day weekend–Oct Fri–Sun 8am–6pm. (828)692-0118.

Turn R on Monticello Rd, cross Hwy 25/70 (Weaverville Blvd) and continue on Monticello Rd approximately 2 mi. Turn L on New Stock Rd. Travel approximately .75 mi. Look for apple sign on L.

For a quiet afternoon stroll, head to the Botanical Gardens, located beside the campus of UNC-Asheville.

ASHEVILLE

53 **The Botanical Gardens at Asheville** 151 W.T. WEAVER BLVD – This 10-acre site showcases the plants, trees and shrubs native to the southern Appalachian region. The bog garden is the most recent addition. Call for schedule of plant sales, tours and workshops. See Heritage Site listing on page 118. Gardens open daily year-round dawn–dusk. Gift shop and visitors center open mid-Mar–mid-Nov 9:30am–4pm. (828)252-5190.

Continue down New Stock Rd to intersection with Hwy 19/23. Continue S on 19/23 towards Asheville to the Hwy 251/UNC-Asheville exit. Turn L and cross under 19/23. Travel about .5 mi and turn L on W.T. Weaver Blvd. Gardens immediately on L.

54 **Richmond Hill Inn** 87 RICHMOND HILL DR – Acres of well-manicured and natural gardens surround the 1889 mansion listed on the National Register of Historic Places. Lose yourself in the heathers, heaths, hollyhocks and hydrangeas to name only a few. See Heritage Site listing on page 118. (888)742-4554. www.RichmondHillInn.com

Take W.T. Weaver Blvd. back to R on Broadway to L on Hwy 251. Turn R on Pearson Bridge Rd and travel across French Broad River to R on Richmond Hill Dr. Inn is on R.

Guidebook Symbols

Kid Friendly Site

1 Farm | 1 Trail | 1 Lodging | 1 Special Attraction

1 Garden | 1 Festival | 1 Restaurant | 1 Garden Art

To prevent losing your tools in the garden, paint the handles with bright colors so they are easily seen against the earth and foliage.

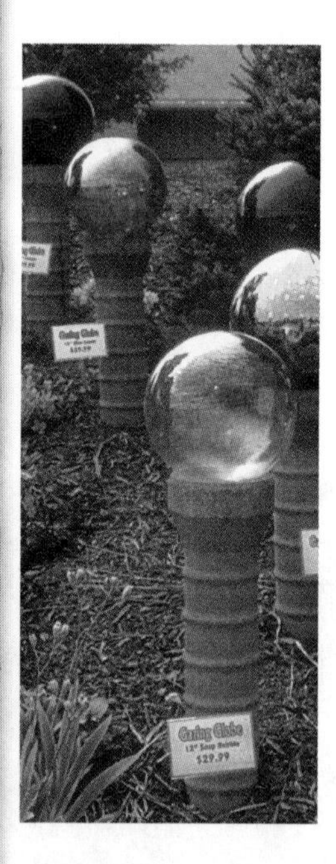

55 **WNC Farmer's Market** 570 BREVARD RD – This is the one-stop destination for an incredible cornucopia of locally grown fresh fruits and vegetables, plants, flowers, lawn and garden supplies, and mountain crafts. Open daily year-round. Winter 8am–5pm. Summer 8am–6pm. (828)253-1691.

Take 19/23 S to W on I-240. Take Brevard Rd exit. Turn L over 240. Travel approximately 1 mi Farmer's Market on L.

56 **The Moose Café** 570 BREVARD RD – The restaurant features farm-fresh produce cooked down–home mountain style and the best apple butter you'll ever eat. It has a great distant view of Biltmore House. Open daily year-round. Mon–Thu 7am–8:30pm, Fri–Sat 7am–9pm & Sun 7am–8pm. (828)255-0920.

57 **Jesse Israel & Sons Nursery & Garden Center** 570 BREVARD RD, LOT 16 – A garden of statuary provides walkways of whimsy as you enter the store for birdhouses, grass seed and garden supplies. Roses and bonsai abound, as do experts on water gardens. Mar–Dec Mon–Sat 8am–6pm & Sun 10am–6pm. Jan–Feb Mon–Sat 8am–5pm & Sun 10am–5pm. (828)254-2671.

Located at the Farmer's Market.

58 **WNC Herb Festival** 570 BREVARD RD – Count yourself lucky if you happen to be in the area the first weekend of May or the second weekend in October. Herb farmers come from the hills and beyond bringing their expansive collection of nature's finest herbs to the WNC Farmer's Market. Call for dates and times. (828)253-1691.

Located at the Farmer's Market.

59 **Appalachian Natural Soaps** 587 BREVARD RD – Victor Taylor's small soap-making business has grown into a nationally known supplier of all-natural and creative combinations of heavenly scented ingredients like lemon/poppyseed and almond/honey/

The Road Goes On Forever

Side trips, tidbits, adventures, and treasure hunts

Did you know that if you simmer a handful of lavender in boiling water it makes a great natural disinfectant and cleaning solution? It also fills the room with a heavenly aroma.

oatmeal to name a few. Mon–Fri 9am–6pm & Sat 9am–5pm. (828)251-0772.

Directly across the street from The Moose Café.

Plan to visit The NC Arboretum again and again; it's never the same place twice!

60 **The North Carolina Arboretum** 100 FREDERICK LAW OLMSTED WAY – Acres of unusual gardens greet the fortunate visitor to this facility of the University of North Carolina. Miles of hiking and biking trails weave through the grounds around the Visitor Education Center and the state-of-the-art greenhouse. Educational workshops and exhibits galore. See the Heritage Site listing on page 118. Hiking and biking trails open daily year-round 8am–9pm. Center open Mon–Sat 9am–5pm & Sun 12noon–5pm. Greenhouse open Mon–Fri 8am–4pm, but closes Wed at 2pm. (828)665-2492. www.ncarboretum.org

Continue S on Brevard Rd (Hwy 191) past Biltmore Square Mall for 2 mi. Turn R at BRP entrance.

FLETCHER

61 **Mountain Horticultural Crops Resource & Extension Center** 2016 FANNING BRIDGE RD – Tours are conducted through botanical demonstration gardens, herb gardens, and an arboretum with an assortment of Christmas trees. Open Tue 1pm–4pm & Fri 8am–12pm. Call for tour times. (828)687-0570.

Take Hwy 191 S past Long Shoals Rd and Glen Bridge Rd to L on Old Fanning Bridge Rd. Center will be on your L.

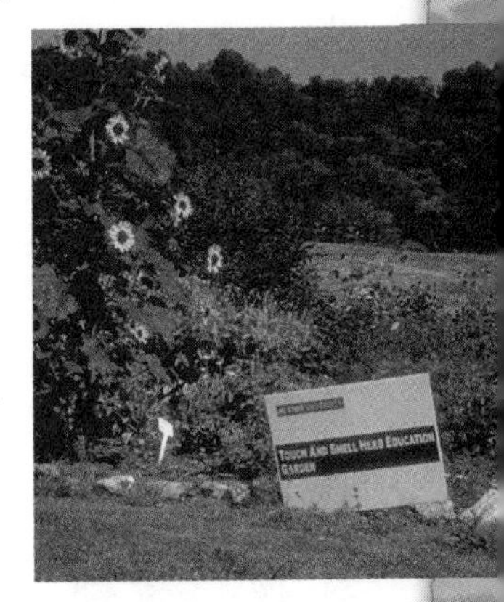

62 **WNC Agricultural Center** 1301 FANNING BRIDGE RD – This is the site for the annual "Growin' in the Mountains" Lawn & Garden Show at the end of April as well as the North Carolina Mountain State Fair in September. The center also hosts horse shows and cattle sales throughout the year. Open Mon–Thu 8am–5pm. Call for weekend show times and information on events. (828)687-1414. www.ncmountainstatefair.org

Continue on Fanning Bridge Rd. Center will be on your L.

Trail of the Tailgates

In a world of pre-packaged "virtual" food, tailgates offer a shifting panoply of seasonal produce. Early markets bring bundles of pungent ramps for orange-yolked omelets stuffed with home-dairy goat cheese. Pyramids of beet clumps rise from bins, damp soil clinging to ruby spheres. Elephant garlic bouquets meet frost-kissed organic kale. Can you resist a dozen ears of summer's Silver Queen, artfully displayed by a freckled farmer's daughter? Vendors tempt with August samples of "Moon and Stars" heirloom melon.

Like to grow your own? Transplant a homesite's hardy offshoots: rugged hostas, bright old-fashioned primroses, maroon toad lilies, blue flag iris. Take home organic starts of cold-resistant rosemary, chocolate mint or holy basil. Annuals, perennials, berries and baked goods are served up on tailgates' periodic menus. Snack on a fudgy walnut brownie or slice of buttery pound cake while you shop.

Mountain homesteads' finished goods make memorable take-home presents. Choose from gem-like jellies in stained-glass rows, pale locust and dark poplar honey, home-cured bacon. Or, gifts for other senses: rustling dried flowers, quilts simple and sumptuous, the fantastic natural sculptures of the paper wasp.

From Black Mountain to Fairview, from Swannanoa to Biltmore, tailgate markets spring up like mushrooms after soft rain. And, like stalking the wild mushroom, timing is everything. Check the list below for seasons, market hours and specialties before setting out to gather your own hand-picked harvest. Check out the list of markets on the next page, and visit them all!

HORSESHOE

63 **Plants Direct** 4076 HAYWOOD RD – Seeing this state-of-the-art greenhouse and garden center may seem a little surreal on this country road into Hendersonville. But, exploring the modern, open-roof greenhouse feels natural amongst the myriad of annuals, perennials and tropicals. There is also a gift shop with gardening tool and supplies. Mon–Sat 9am–6pm. (828)890-8333.

Turn back onto Hwy 191S. Travel 5 mi to greenhouse on R.

The Road Goes On Forever

Side trips, tidbits, adventures, and treasure hunts

Shrubs used for landscaping are also good for you. They serve as natural air purifiers by helping to remove smoke, dust and other pollutants from the air.

HENDERSONVILLE

64 The Historic Johnson Farm 3346 HAYWOOD RD – What was once a 19th-century tobacco farm is now a popular summer tourist retreat. Owned by the Henderson County Public Schools, the farm features two self-guided nature trails and 15 acres of grassy fields, forests of white pine, walnut and the rare Carolina Hemlock. A barn-loft museum features farm life artifacts from early to mid 1900's. May–Oct Tue–Sat 9am–2:30pm. Nov–Apr Tue–Fri 9am–2:30pm. Guided tours are available daily year-round at 10:30am and 1:30pm. (828)891-6585 www.johnsonfarm.org

Continue on Hwy 191 S. Travel 1.4 mi. Farm is across from Rugby Middle School. School is on L.

65 The Apple Inn 1005 WHITE PINE DR – Majestic oaks and hemlocks surround this century-old home, featuring 300 azaleas, 50 dogwoods, and an assortment of laurels, maples and numerous perennial beds. (828)693-0107. www.appleinn.com

Take Hwy 191N back about .6 mi and turn L on Rugby Rd. Travel about 4 mi to L on Brevard Rd (Hwy 64W). Take 64W towards Hendersonville for about 2.8 mi to R on White Pine Dr. Inn is on the L.

66 The Waverly Inn 783 N MAIN ST – Hendersonville's oldest inn features fourteen rooms named after local flora such as the Birdfoot Violet, Ox-eye Daisy and Closed Gentian. Walking distance to downtown. (800)537-8195. www.waverlyinn.com

Continue on 64W into Hendersonville to L onto Main St.. Inn is through light on L.

67 Mast General Store 527 N MAIN ST – Charles Kuralt said, "All general stores are satisfying to visit, but one of them, Mast General Store, is a destination." The old-timey mercantile features bird houses, goat's milk and lye soap, windchimes, hammocks, as well as rosebud and cloverine salves. Mon–Sat 10am–6pm & Sun 1pm–6pm. (828)696-1883.

TAILGATE MARKETS TO CHECK OUT

Biltmore Station Farmer's Market – Located in the parking lot of Trevi Restaurant, 2 Hendersonville Rd. Wed 5pm-7:30pm.

Biltmore Tailgate Market – Located in the parking lot of Common Ground and Screen Door, 115 Fairview Rd. Sat 8am–12noon. (828)274-0370

Fairview Farmer's Market – Located at Hwy 74 adjacent to new Fairview Library.

WNC Farmer's Market – See page 104. (828)253-1691.

Warren Wilson Produce Market – See page 88. (828)298-3325.

French Broad Food Co-op and Tailgate Market – See page 93. (828)255-7650.

North Asheville Tailgate Market – Above Asheville Pizza and Brewing. After 22 years, it's the oldest tailgate market in the area. Call Ira Mallard. (828) 683-1812.

Valley Garden Market in Black Mountain – See page 86.

Guidebook Symbols

Kid Friendly Site

1 Farm · 1 Trail · 1 Lodging · 1 Special Attraction

1 Garden · 1 Festival · 1 Restaurant · 1 Garden Art

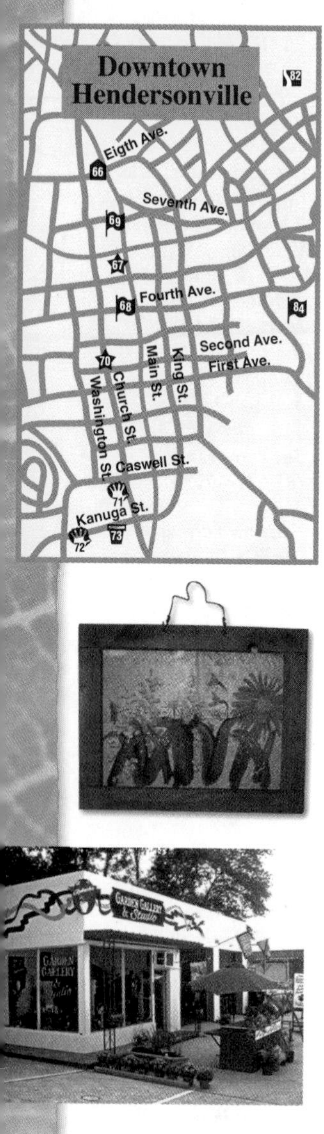

68 Garden Jubilee 401 N MAIN ST – Main Street becomes a green scene every Memorial Day weekend with garden demonstrations, workshops, and lawn and garden supplies for sale. This event is sponsored by Downtown Hendersonville Inc. (828)693-9708.

69 Hendersonville County Apple Festival MAIN ST – Johnny Appleseed would have loved this street festival featuring more apples than Carter's got liver pills. Contests, apple butter demonstrations, sidewalk sales, pancake breakfasts, live music, and apple orchard tours. Labor Day weekend. (828)697-4557.

70 Henderson County Farmer's Curb Market 221 N CHURCH ST & 2ND ST – A co-op of 100 farm families come together to sell plants, dried flowers, jams, local fresh fruits and vegetables, berries, cut flowers, annuals, perennials, wildflowers and folk crafts. Established in 1924, it's the oldest curb market in the South. Curly willow and hydrangeas will grab you at any given moment, as will the offerings of Ralph King's Lily Farm. Jan–Apr Tue & Sat 9am–1pm. May–Dec Tue, Thu & Sat 8am–2 pm. (828)692-8012.
Behind old Courthouse.

71 Rupach's Garden Gallery 402 S CHURCH ST – A renovated gas station gets a tank full of chlorophyll as an inspirational garden shop. Full of herbs, perennials, carnivorous swamp plants, vegetable plants and garden flags. Another green make-over for the downtown area. Mon–Sat 10am–6pm. (828)696-8481.
Corner of Church St and Kanuga.

72 The Classic Garden 622 KANUGA ST – Bruce and Lori Lowe have taken a small, cute house and transformed it into a hot garden architectural accent shop. It's filled with custom-ordered plants and garden items, such as statuary, birdhouses, fountains, and large architectural accents for the garden and home.

Buy some mint at Rupach's to make tea. It is said to help clear a cold and sweeten the breath.

The Road Goes On Forever
Side trips, tidbits, adventures, and treasure hunts

Blue Ridge Direct Marketing Association website: www.ncapples.com
Apple Festival website: www.ncapplefestival.org

And, there's even a lovely collection of dwarf conifers, Japanese maples, and native plants. Frequent workshops and lectures by garden experts. Tue–Fri 10am– 6pm. Sat 9am–5pm. Closed Sun & Mon. (828)698-8350.

Take S Church St to R on Kanuga. Go several blocks and shop is on L. Parking in back on Israel St.

73 **Raymond's Lawn, Home and Garden Center** 1320 KANUGA ST – Several generations of the Raymond family work together to maintain this immaculate garden center which features annuals, perennials and shrubs, most of which are grown on-site. The seven acres allow the family to grow about 90 percent of its greenery and buy the rest locally. Gingko, sweet gum, maples, magnolias, and holly mingle merrily in the fields alongside the pond and greenhouse. Mar–Nov Mon–Sat 8am–6pm. Dec–Feb Mon–Sat 8am–4pm. (828)696-8000.

Continue S on Kanuga St toward Flat Rock. Center is on L.

Teachers, take note: the Blue Ridge Apple Growers Ladies' Auxiliary has assembled an extensive educational Apple Kit for grades K-5. Songs, games, nutrition, honeybees, healthy living and...apples. Check it out at www.ces.ncsu.edu/henderson/pubs/applekit/

FLAT ROCK

74 **Carl Sandburg Home** 1928 LITTLE RIVER RD – Ravens will call to the poet in your heart as you head up the .3 mile path to the home of the Pulitzer Prize-winning author. 264 acres of beautiful grounds to walk include Connemara Farms' dairy goats, a tour of the main house, a bridge over a waterfall and ivy-covered hemlocks framing a portal into the past life of a great poet. The landscape is maintained to reflect the time in which Carl Sandburg and his family lived. Mon–Sun 9am–5pm. Closed Christmas. (828)693-4178.

From Kanuga St travel 2.6 mi to L on Little River Rd. Go about 4 mi just before intersection with Hwy 25. Turn R into entrance to home.

When Sandburg moved to Flat Rock, he brought with him more than 14,000 volumes of books and magazines.

75 **Hand in Hand Gallery** 2713 GREENVILLE HWY – David Voorhees' art impeccably imitates life as witnessed in his iris and wildlife scapes on

When mulching with newspapers, do not use the comics. The colored ink in most newsprint contains lead, which is harmful to plants.

his pottery. Partner and metalsmith Molly Sharp transforms stones from the Isle of Iona in Scotland to exquisite jewelry art. Several Muses must call this their summer home. Tue–Sat 10am–5pm. (828)697-7719.

Turn R onto Hwy 25 and gallery is immediately on R.

76 **The Wrinkled Egg** 2710 GREENVILLE HWY – Peace's Grocery (circa 1890) has been re-made into a shop of whimsy running rampant. It features folk art, metallic flower stakes, unusual statuary, as well as toys, candy, and housewares. Mon–Sat 10am–6pm & Sun 1pm–5pm. (828)696-3998.

Down the street from Hand in Hand Gallery on L.

77 **Woodfield Inn & Restaurant** 2905 GREENVILLE HWY – During the Civil War, a secret room hid the gentle ladies of Flat Rock from Union soldiers. Today the secret is out: this is the place for historically romantic events. A wedding garden, gazebo, landscaped gardens, and seven acres of nature trails provide a glimpse into another era. With 19 rooms and a restaurant serving an array of regional cuisine. (800)533-6016. www.innspiredinns.com

Continue S on Hwy 25 (Greenville Hwy) for .1 mi. Inn will be on your R.

78 **Sky Top Orchard** PINNACLE MOUNTAIN RD – At an elevation of 3000 feet, Mt. Alpine, home to this orchard, offers a glorious panoramic view of the Blue Ridge Mountains. While you are taking in the view, enjoy picking apples, a glass of cider, or a picnic. Open daily Aug–Dec 9am–6pm. (828)692-7930.

Continue S on Hwy 25 for 1 mi. Turn R onto Pinnacle Mtn Rd. Travel .75 mi to orchard at top.

79 **Highland Lake Inn** HIGHLAND LAKE RD – Whatever combination you can dream up of gardens and trails, this 180-acre haven of hospitality and homeyness already has it. With a 19-room elegant inn, a rustic lodge, family

The Road Goes On Forever

Side trips, tidbits, adventures, and treasure hunts

SPOT IT

It's somewhere on this loop. Can you find it?

A garden is the best alternative therapy.

Roaming Home and Garden Tours

Hendersonville Home and Garden Tour – The Environmental and Conservation Organization runs this tour for one day every spring or summer from 10am–5pm. The self-guided tour even visits some wildlife certified backyard habitats. $10 pp. Call (828)692–0385 for pre-registration and info.

Quality Forward Father's Day Home and Garden Tour – Quality Forward hosts this annual event at different communities throughout Buncombe County. It's a wonderful opportunity to tour inspiring gardens, while spending the afternoon with Dad or other friends and family. Call (828)254-1776 for information about tickets and locations.

Asheville Area B & B's with Garden Appeal

Abbington Green Bed & Breakfast (828)251-2454

Albermarle Inn (828)255-0027

Beaufort House (828)254-8334

Black Walnut Inn (828)254-3878

Blake House Inn (828)681-5227

Cedar Crest - A Victorian Inn (828)252-1389

Colby House (828)253-5644

Cumberland Falls Bed & Breakfast Inn (828)253-4085

The Lion and the Rose (828)255-7673

The WhiteGate Inn & Cottage (828)253-2553

Organic Grower's School

Organized by the Carolina Farm Stewardship Association, NC Cooperative Extension and Blue Ridge Community College. It's a day of workshops for beginning gardeners to advanced commercial growers. Held annually at Blue Ridge Community College in Flat Rock, it includes a trade show and seed exchange. Write or email to receive a registration form or more information: Organic Growers School, PO Box 984, Asheville, NC 28802. organicgrowersschool @main.nc.us

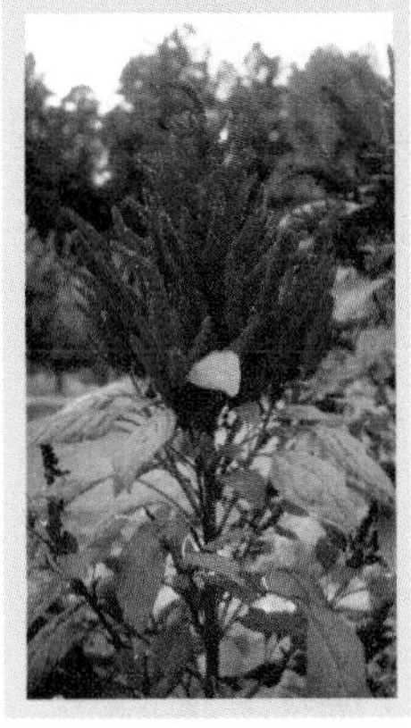

Guidebook Symbols Kid Friendly Site

Farm · Trail · Lodging · Special Attraction

Garden · Festival · Restaurant · Garden Art

cottages and cabins, it should be able to handle any accommodation needs you just might have. Not to mention the renowned restaurant featuring divine breakfast, lunch and dinner entrees straight from the vast organic gardens on-site. In amongst the periwinkle, laurel, honeysuckle, azaleas, dogwoods, and waterlilies, you will find trails for walking and mountain biking, tennis, pool, canoeing, bass and bream fishing, massage, whirlpools, and a gift shop. There are even goats to milk, peacocks parading and farm animals to nuzzle. And, you won't believe the gardens and aquaponic greenhouse. They're absolutely spectacular. (800)762-1376. www.highlandlake-inn.com

Travel N on Hwy 25. Turn R onto Highland Lake Rd. Inn will be on your R.

HENDERSONVILLE

80 **Weeping Creek Cottages**
65 SNAPDRAGON LN – For all we know, a family of hobbits could live in one of these charming fairytale cottages. As you enter a door flanked by hand-painted shutters and overrun atop with brambles of ivy, the voice of James Earl Jones may begin, "Once upon a time..." Flower gardens, creeks, woodland picnic areas in groves of white pine, and an ivy-lined pool provide lots of flights of fancy for fairies and factual folks as well. (800)988-4858. www.weepingcreek.com

Take Highland Lake Rd back to Hwy 25 and head N towards Hendersonville for .1 mi. Cottages will be on your L.

81 **Made in the Mountains** 927 GREENVILLE HWY – Feel your blood pressure drop as you enter the calm at this gallery and pottery studio featuring garden stepping stones by Cheryl Stippich, thrown pots and painted silk by owner Donna Kassab. Garden sculptures and ceramic and copper stakes abound. Tempting Serti technique silk painting, Japanese brush painting, and paper-making workshops by Donna, and E. Hollis Mentzer. Mon–Sat 10am–5pm.

One tree can remove 26 pounds of carbon dioxide from the atmosphere annually, equaling 11,000 miles of car emissions.

(828)697-0496.
Continue N on Hwy 25 for approximately 1.3 mi. Studio will be on L.

82 Mudcreek Basin Wetlands Trail E 7TH AVE – The answer to "how much wood could a woodchuck chuck" lies alongside this walking trail where woodchucks, mink and birds romp in the swamp. A 700-ft. bridge over cattails leads to an observation deck. Park in the five-car lot directly off 7th Ave. Open year-round. Recommend traveling in pairs or more.
Take Hwy 25 N into Hendersonville through Main St to R on E 6th Ave. Take L onto Grove St. Then R onto 7th Ave. Trail area is on L.

83 Piggy's Ice Cream/Harry's 217 DUNCAN HILL RD – OK so there are no gardens here. Haven't you seen enough already to take an ice cream break? Anyway, this combination of antique shop and smoked, pulled barbecue lunch stop is practically a heritage site for Hendersonville. And besides, how long has it been since you had an old-fashioned, I-think-I'm-gonna-die chocolate malt?! Open daily June–mid-Nov 11am–7pm. Mid-Nov–May Mon–Sat 11am–7pm. (828)692-1995.
Head E on 7th Ave across three bridges. Piggy's will be on your L. Look for large pig and ice cream sign (what else?).

84 Farm City Day JACKSON PARK – Held the first Saturday in October each year, this event features antique tools and engines, working draft horses, fishing, garden tractor pull, entertainment, food, and children's games. Open daily year-round 10am–4pm. (828)697-4891.
S on Duncan Hill Rd to R on Four Seasons Blvd (Hwy 64E). Travel several blocks to R on Harris St. At end, turn L onto Glover St which continues into Jackson Park.

An unusual garden idea: Install a mailbox in your garden. It's a great place to store tools and containers. Add a notebook and pen to keep track of harvesting dates and the names of your favorite plants.

Yes, it's another Don Stevenson hand sculpted replica birdhouse. See his site listing on page 176.

Quick Shade Trees:

Amur Chokecherry
Cucumber Tree
Japanese Pagoda Tree
Japanese Zelkova
River Birch

85 Bullington Horticultural Learning Center 140 ZEB CORN RD – Asian influence is strong at the former home and gardens of nurseryman Robert Bullington. Fifteen varieties of Japanese maples grow here, along with oriental dogwoods, native azaleas and false cypress. Open Aug–May Mon–Fri 12:30pm–4pm. Summer hours vary. Tours available. (828)698-6104. Donations welcome.

Take Hwy 64 E towards Chimney Rock. Cross I-26 and travel approximately .6 mi to L on Howard Gap Rd. 1 mi to R on Zeb Corn Rd. Center is .6 mi on R.

86 GrandDad's Apples N' Such US HWY 64 – This is the place to be August through November when peaches, apples, mums and pumpkins create a wheel of color, tastes and smells. After you walk the corn maze, you can pick a pumpkin, pet an alpaca, or peruse the shop with local crafts, honey, jams and jellies. Throw in a line for catfish all day at $7 pp or $5 pp for catch and release. Aug–mid-Nov Mon–Sun 9am–5pm. (828)685-1685.

Turn L back on 64 E. Travel approximately 1 mi to L at gray and red barn with John Deere tractor on top of silo.

We weren't kidding about the tractor!

The Road Goes On Forever

Side trips, tidbits, adventures, and treasure hunts

Lettuce, a member of the daisy family, first became popular table fare back in Greek and Roman times. Americans today eat about 30 lbs. of lettuce each, per year.

87 **Cloud Nine House and Gardens** 3109 CHIMNEY ROCK RD (Hwy 64) – For a romantic stroll, you can't do better than this favorite wedding spot where Victorian innocence reigns. A 36-foot gazebo is the elegant centerpiece of the gardens of roses and waterlilies, perennials and annuals on 24 acres. The heart-to-heart chapel, waterfall, and lakeside arbor all add allure. Who knows, after spending all this time together on the trail, maybe a renewing of the vows is in order. Also available for parties and conferences. Call for appointment. (828)685-8217. www.cloudnineweddinggardens.com

Turn L on 64 E and travel .8 of a mi. Look for sign on L.

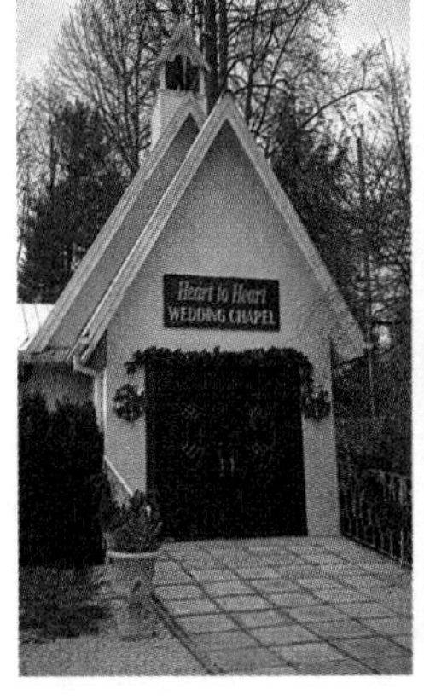

Goin' to the Chapel!

88 **The Rusty Bucket** CHIMNEY ROCK RD – When the kids get restless, stop here and appease them with the petting zoo while you wander through the aisles of handmade crafts and produce. In mid-October you can catch the Apple Harvest Festival with live local music, kids' games and a sundry of apple events. Apr–Dec Thu–Fri 10am–4pm & Sat–Sun 8:30am–5pm. Outdoor market open Sat–Sun 7am–6pm.

Turn L onto 64 (Chimney Rock Rd.) and travel 1.5 mi. Market will be on your R.

89 **Lyda's Farm** CHIMNEY ROCK RD – A paradise of produce awaits you at this farm. Apples, peaches, nectarines, tomatoes, cucumbers, cabbage, gourds, yellow and winter squash, zucchini, eggplant, Indian corn and fingers popcorn, pumpkins and candyroasters all grown on-site. Farm tours by appointment. Call for group rate. Open daily mid-Aug–mid-Nov 9am–6pm. (828)685-3459.

E on Chimney Rock Rd. approximately .25 mi on L.

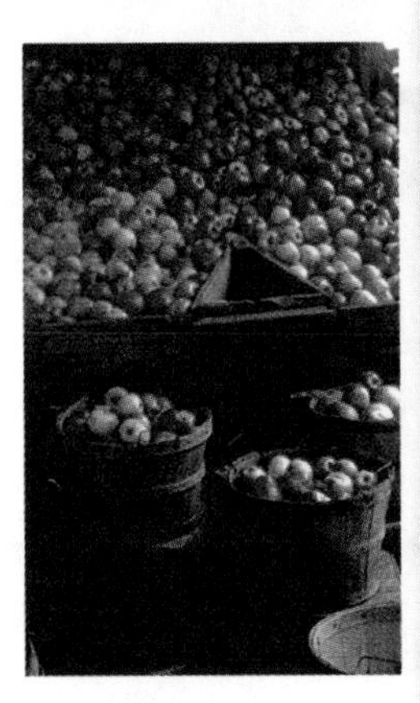

90 **Apple Blossom Trail** GILLIAM MTN RD – A nice way to end the Buncombe-Henderson trail is to take this driving tour through some of the beautiful apple orchards of Henderson County. The apple blossom trail meanders approximately 4.3 mi. through some of the many varieties of apples in their full regal Spring bloom. Mid-April

Want to spice up your yard? Why not add a crabapple tree or two or three?! Here are some varieties from which to choose your new yard additions:

'Adams' Crabapple

'Donald Wyman' Crabapple

'Prairiefire' Crabapple

'Sentinel' Crabapple

'Walters' Siberian Crabapple

through the first week of May.
At Lyda's Farm travel 1.8 mi E on Hwy 64 to R on Gilliam Mtn Rd. Turn R on Sugarloaf Rd and then L on Ledbetter Rd. Bear L on Bald Rock Rd (where there is a splendid waterfall) and then R again on Gilliam Mtn Rd.

...Side trip (on your return to Asheville)

FAIRVIEW

91 **Mountain Harvest Florist & Garden Center** 600 US 74A E – A bathtub fountain front and center tells the tale of the wide and whimsical offerings in this renovated 1920's log cabin. Local honey, chow chow and produce fill the shelves along with bunches of dried lavender and other flowers, plant fairies and cypress furniture. Outside under a gargantuan maple tree thrive geraniums, purple cone-flower, and a wide range of annuals, perennials, shrubbery and trees. Christmas trees, wreaths and garland are also available. Mon–Sat 8am–6pm & Sun 1pm–5pm. (828)298-9000.
From Asheville, travel W on the BRP to 74A E exit. Travel approximately. 2 mi on 74A to Center on L.

92 **Berry Nice Blueberry Farm** 228 MILLER RD – Regardless of your motives – jam, cobbler or muffins – a visit to this u-pick organic blueberry farm offers berries, views, and emus. With peaceful views of Arrowhead Mtn., you may have trouble convincing yourself it's time to go home and put those berries to good use. Sat 8am–7pm. (828)628-1309.
Continue W on 74A for 1 mi to L onto Old Fort Rd. Travel 1.7 mi to R onto Miller Rd. Second driveway on R. Look for the sign.

93 **Benefit Daylily Sale** – For five years, Cheryl Alderman has used her way with daylilies as a way to help children, donating the proceeds from this annual sale to WNC Child Advocacy & Prevention Services, Inc. With 400 varieties, it is a sure bet you will have trouble choosing which ones to take home. Sale happens annually the weekend before July 4th. Fri 3pm–8pm & Sat 8am–12noon. (828)254-2000.
Continue on Miller Rd to 74A. Turn L and travel 1 mi to Brush Creek Rd. Turn R and go 1 mi to Sharon Rd. Turn R. Go .5 mi to field on L.

The Road Goes On Forever
Side trips, tidbits, adventures, and treasure hunts

Apple Orchards of Henderson County

Dressed for a mid-April dance in clouds of white blossom, apple trees precisely pruned glide across mountain slopes. Produce purveyors offer first fruits in late summer- Granny Smith, Golden Delicious, Gala. Come Labor Day, a four-day Apple Festival features apple country bus tours, a music-filled street fair, an Apple Ball at Highland Inn. Rich scents from ripe apples invite a crunch. Try Rome's old standard, spicy Gingergold or popular new Honeycrisp, a sell-out sensation. Mid-October's early frost incites a riot of autumnal leaf color as the harvest keeps rolling in: golden jellies, jaunty cider and fat round pumpkins.

Home orchardists, don't miss the Apple Variety Block. This two-acre outdoor laboratory, cultivated by Henderson pomologists, is open for self-guided tours. You'll find over a hundred apple varieties demonstrating innovative pruning methods and support systems. Block plots available at the site. Call NC Agriculture Extension for directions. (828)697-4891.

Apple Orchards of Henderson County

Apple House
(828)685-9917

Apple Mill
(828)749-9136

Billy Laughter Orchards
(828)685-3241

Brown's Honey, Fruit & Vegetable Farm
(828)693-3093

Coston Farm & Apple House
(828)685-8352

GrandDad's Apple's N' Such
(828)685-1685

Henry Barnwell Orchards
(828)685-7371

Jimmy Nix and Sons
(828)685-7222

Lively Orchard Outlet
(828)692-6605

Lyda Farms
(828)685-3549

MacJackson Orchard
(828)685-3882

Ottanola Farms
(828)685-7508

Piney Mountain Orchards
(828)685-3235

Riverview Orchard
(828)687-1936

Stepp's Hillcrest Orchard
(828)685-9083

Tall Pine Apple Orchard
(828)685-7422

U-Pick/We-Pick Apples Sky Top
(828)692-7930

The Big Botanicals

To stand on the South Terrace of the Biltmore Estate—to take in the rolling parklands enfolded in the wild embrace of the French Broad River, the vast sylvan stretches of the middle distance, the hazy rim of faraway mountains, and the limitless over-crowning heavens—is to walk into a 19th century canvas painted by a member of the Hudson River School. Below you, widely spaced oaks, their gracefully spreading limbs a blur of silvery green, cast soft shadows on the vibrant grass. The satiny pewter sheen of the river's surface is almost lost amid the green hues. The view before you is so vast and breathtaking that it makes the storybook French chateau to your left—so large when you first faced it, after that three-mile sinuous drive that never hinted at what was to come—suddenly adjust its scale. You see what architect Richard Morris Hunt and his patron George Vanderbilt must have grasped. For a landscape this magnificent, a house like that is only a fitting complement.

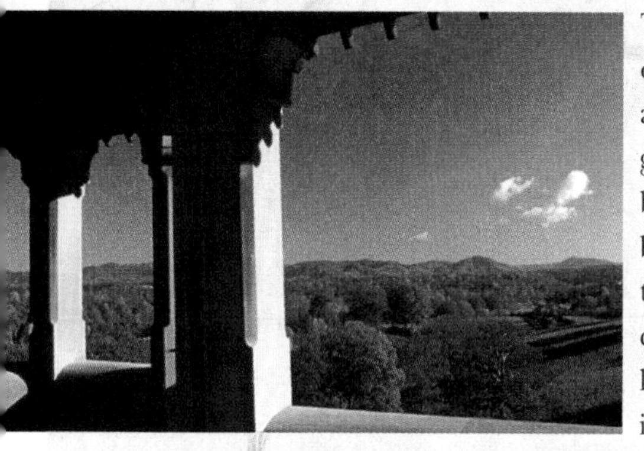

Tucked into an undulating rock wall in Asheville's Botanical Gardens, ephemeral spring beauties offer delicate pink-striped faces to the sun. They're as lovely in their way as the pastel palette of perennials splashed across Richmond Hill Inn's parterre garden. As the extraordinary beds of miner's lettuce, arugula and nasturtiums flourishing in Highland Lake Inn's greenhouses, or the NC Arboretum's flowery Quilt Garden, its beautifully articulated bonsai. Together they make up the "big botanicals" of Buncombe

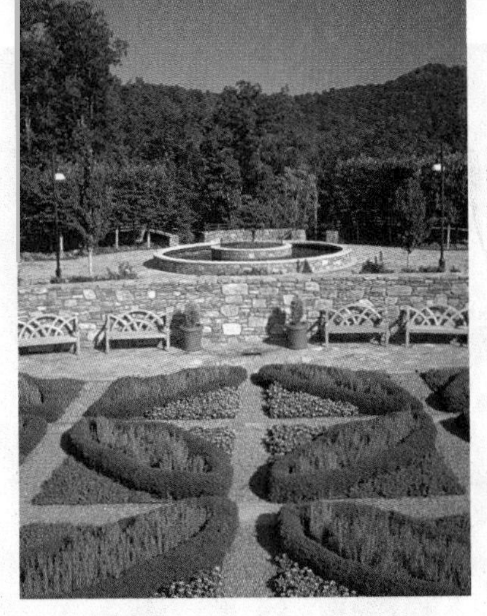

and Henderson Counties. Marriages made in heaven that flower from informed collaborations between man and nature. Their glory is that they work on every scale, from the monumental to the minute.

For sheer inspiration, none of these places will steer you wrong. Will a backdrop of somber blue-black conifers tame a riot of feverishly blooming azaleas? Frederick Law Olmsted's ramble through Biltmore's gardens says it can. Heard of indigo, madder, wormwood and woad, but never seen them growing? Put a face to a name in the Arboretum's heritage craft gardens. Looking for a way to temper traffic sounds? Find solutions in the falling waters at Richmond Hill, the Botanical Garden's woodland screen. Interested in an organic garden buzzing with beneficial insects, bolstered by blooming buckwheat cover crops? Hasten to Highland Lake Inn for a garden stroll, then sample its restaurant's "Salade Maison," an eclectic blend of top-notch greens and their seasonal accompaniments.

In the Botanical Gardens varied habitats, discover the subtle harmonies of natural plant communities reunited by a landscape architect imitating the wild. Consider planting vines for every hour, then try the effect under the arbor at Richmond Hill. Morning glories open to rising river mist; purple clusters of hyacinth beans beguile bees at noon; moonvine's huge white blooms surrender to swooping hawkmoths as evening settles in. And, should the hothouse flowers of Biltmore's Conservatory threaten to overwhelm, return to the South Terrace for a final promenade. Watch a bluebird nesting in a box on the swale below you take to the air. Catch that flash of unearthly blue. It's hard to imagine, in that instant, that a bird at home in an 8,000-acre paradise could feel any happier than you.

The Ribbon Garden

Daniel Webster defines a garden as "a public recreation area or park usually ornamented by plants and trees" and as "a rich well-cultivated region." The nation's first rural national parkway, the Blue Ridge Parkway, is indeed a 470-mile ribbon of garden, delighting millions of annual visitors and serving as a reminder of the value of retaining glimpses into our rural heritage.

Originally the landscape architect, Stanley W. Abbott, emphasized that the basic reason for the existence of the Parkway was "to please (visitors) by revealing the charm and interest of the native American countryside." This was not an easy accomplishment in dealing with a chosen route featuring cultivated farm land, heavy commercial development, problematic erosion and mountainous terrain. But in 1933, with a $4,000,000 appropriation fund for the Public Works proposal, Abbott began the tedious and meticulous project that would provide a link between the Shenandoah and Great Smoky Mountain National Parks, while creating labor for large numbers of unemployed mountain folks during the depths of the Great Depression. Abbott, a modern–day Renaissance man of great vision, sought to explore how Americans of that era were reevaluating their relationship to the natural environment.

From Rockfish Gap in Virginia to the Oconaluftee River Bridge this is one spectacularly long garden!

A 470 Mile Garden?

Under the admonishment of the first park roads developer, General Hiram M. Chittenden, that "all park roads must lie lightly upon the land," Abbott strove to dovetail beauty and utility of the Parkway by "following a mountain stream for awhile, then climbing upon the slope of a hill pasture, then dipping down into the open bottom lands and back into the woodlands."

Today, the panoramic views from the Parkway can be attributed to Abbott's dedication to 1) manipulate the route beyond ridge tops to other prime locations; 2) salvage and preserve architectural favorites such as Mabry Mill and Brinegar Cabin; 3) use Scenic Easements that made conservationists out of the farmers tilling the adjacent lands by agreeing to perpetual restrictions upon how these lands could be used; 4) emulate the local mountaineers' use of native stone and specify that stone used on walls, tunnels or bridges, as at Linville River, come from within a certain distance of that site; and 5) employ slope reduction as a means of reducing road hazard and future maintenance while also sodding, seeding and planting these areas with native materials. Further enhancement of the Parkway came from "the beads on a string – the rare gems in a necklace" that were added in the form of recreational parks.

Gardens tend to be full of flowers, and the Blue Ridge Parkway is no exception.

Its many wild and and endangered varieties include trillium, fire pink, crested dwarf iris, mountain laurel, day flower, pink lady's slipper, Indian paintbrush, trout lily, Heller's Blazing Star, the Blue Ridge goldenrod and three types of rhododendron. But flowers and native plants are not the beginning and end of this "ribbon garden" that Abbott and his successors, through great attention to detail, framed with walls, tunnels and bridges that mimic and mirror the natural environment.

From the stone arches laid so carefully by Italian and Spanish immigrant stone masons, to the post-and-rail fences put up by local mountain men, to the many trees and tons of top soil moved for landscaping by the Civilian Conservation Corps, the Blue Ridge Parkway is truly a garden that was handmade in America.

Reference: *Painting with a Comet's Tail* by Harley Jolley, p. 16, 6, 16, 17.

Whistlestop Tour

A catbird salutes dawn's early light with snatches of stolen melody. Thunder and lightning rock the cradle of the ancient Cherokee. All around this looping track, domestic tranquility and wild nature contend, combine and complement. ✠ Begin at Balsam Mountain Inn, an airy hillside presence, then steam on down to Waynesville. Redbrick sidewalks lead to cafés, galleries, shops and ice cream parlors. At a street-corner mini-park, follow "Chicken Thief's" foxy nose to his creator's lair in a fanciful sculpture garden. ✠ Fringe-tree and silverbell canopy clumps of glossy-leaved ginger along Junaluska's nature trail. In student-tended plots, parsley, marigolds, broccoli–and tidy scarecrows–practice the gentle art of companion planting. ✠ Rail-straight rows of squash, tomatoes, peppers and corn file across fertile river valleys. A paradise of rosy mountain laurel, flaming azalea, penstemon and fire pink rims Parkway curves. Embraced in a haze of blue mountains, find forestry's cradle. Where crosscut saw and axe laid waste to virgin growth, a German visionary sowed experimental plots. ✠ Frolic with squealing children in a waterfall's splash pool. Wildlife gardens, talking signs and unlimited trout inform a visit to Pisgah's wildlife education center. Once you know rainbow from brookie, conduct yourself to Brevard. Orchestral and olfactory symphonies float on every breeze. ✠ Station yourself near Rosman, where marine blue larkspur shores up a boardwalk edged with foxgloves and waves of warm-hued daylilies.

Nature's own version of fast food isn't just for the birds.

Stop and smell the sunflowers

Cashiers is just the ticket for a dabble in aquatic gardening. Or, heap a grapevine basket with take-home treasures. Reflect on Lake Thorpe's placid waters, then plunge down a forested chute to Tuckasegee Valley. ✂ Jackson County's courthouse sits bright as buttermilk at the foot of Sylva's Main Street. This hillside-clinging community invites a stroll. Window shop, then sip a very berry smoothie with nasturtiums at your elbow. Edible orchids accent the eatery's well-dressed spinach salads. ✂ Sidetrack to an English cottage garden. Pale pink primroses, cool blue Stokes' asters and Queen Anne's lace are a sculptor's antidote to stone's intensity. Tread a thyme carpet through falls of climbing roses toward a rustic barn studio. ✂ Train your eye on Dillsboro. Ribbons of rail connect its craft-filled shops to Swain's county seat. A pre-school engineer, in red bandana and railroad cap, eyes his hero at steam engine's throttle. On a depot platform, cloggers in plaid sundresses stage a hoedown to a country trio's "Honey, You Can't Love Two." A massive bark-shingled lodge shares a knoll above Bryson City with a gable-roofed country inn. ✂ Outdoor commissaries at the Smokies' backdoor entrance serve up innertubes, snacks and horses by the hour. In Cherokee, blowguns and baskets blend natural and native resources. Dip into the Oconaluftee. Study Sequoyah's syllabary. Explore an Indian village. At day's end, it's all aboard the high road for a bird's eye view of Qualla Boundary. Then toot back to Balsam and make tracks for home. ✂

Whistlestop Tour

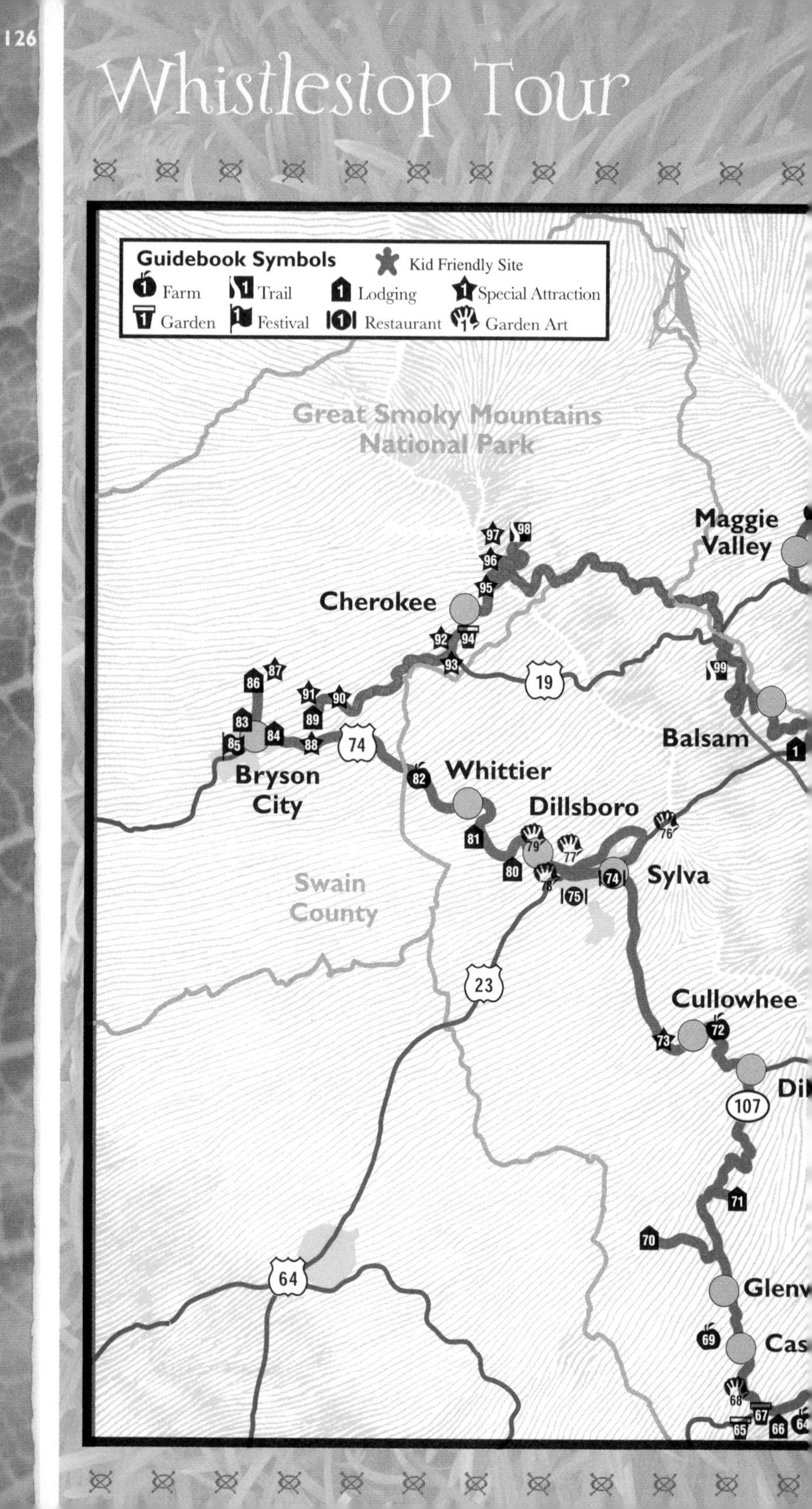

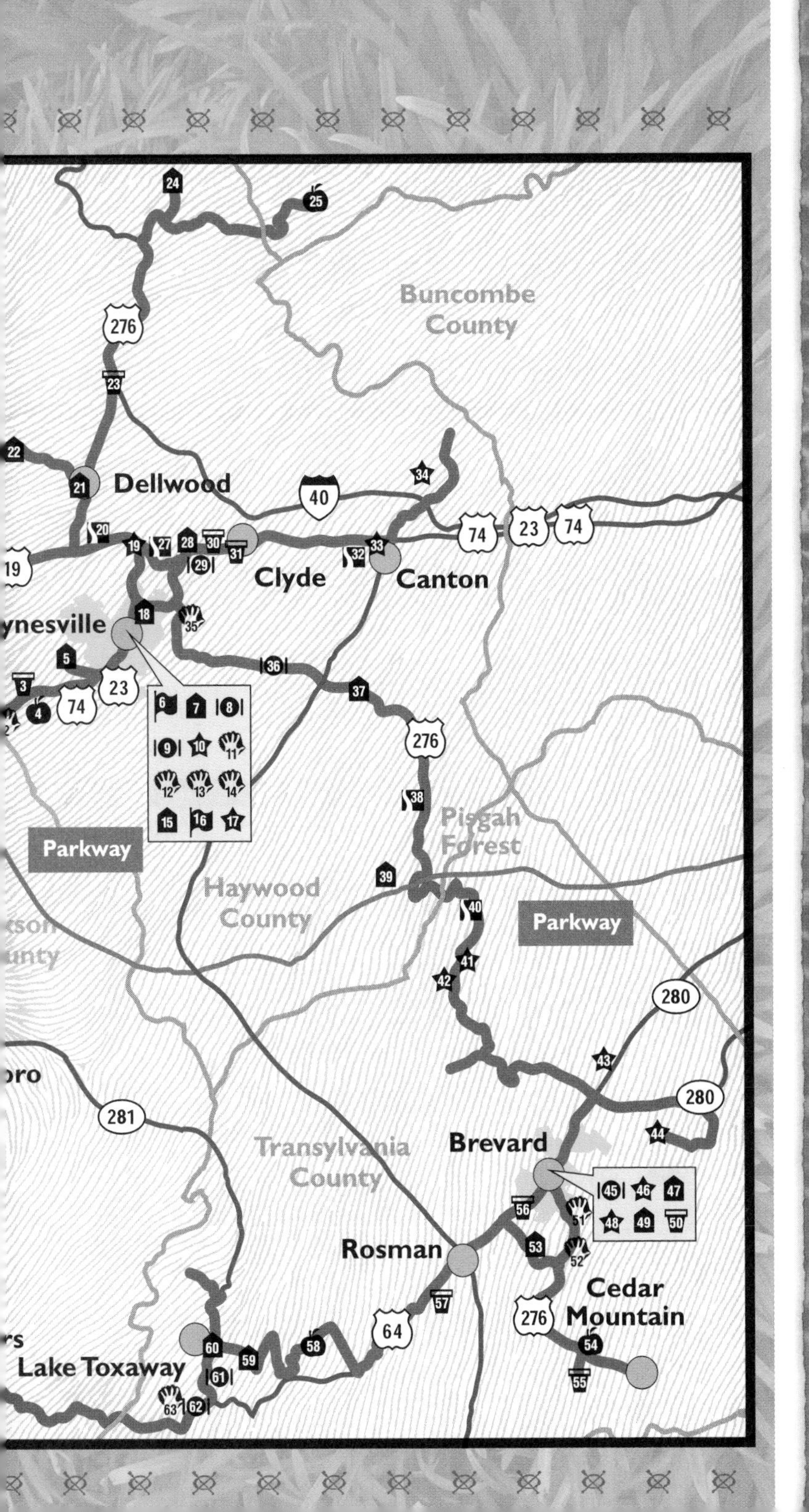

Buncombe County
Dellwood
Clyde
Canton
Haywood County
Pisgah Forest
Parkway
Parkway
Transylvania County
Brevard
Rosman
Cedar Mountain
Lake Toxaway

Hallway of the Balsam Mountain Inn. Spend some time admiring local crafts and meandering through the Inn's gardens.

BALSAM

1 Balsam Mountain Inn 68 SEVEN SPRINGS DR – For those seeking solace in higher elevations, this retreat situated at 3500 feet offers peace, quiet and a lovely country inn among showy orchids, trillium, trout lilies, dolls eyes, jack in the pulpit, red oaks and the two biggest buckeyes in North Carolina. Walking trails abound with the NC Mountains to the Sea Trail just .25 mile away. (800)224-9498. www.balsaminn.com

Exit at Mile Post 443 off the BRP at intersection with 74/23 and turn S toward Sylva. Turn L off 74/23 about .25 mi S of the BRP overpass at green sign of village of Balsam. Make immediate R up hill on Carin Flats Rd, cross railroad, travel .3 mi. Inn is on L.

2 Mud Dabbers Studio HWY 23/74 – Mud dabbers work as a team, as do the eight family members and five friends who work together to create a space full of planters, bird baths, feeders and wind chimes among their famous dinnerware sets. Mon–Sat 10am–6pm & Sun 1pm–5pm. (828)456-1916.

Turn R onto Hwy 23/74 towards Waynesville. Studio will be on your R just before the Rest Area.

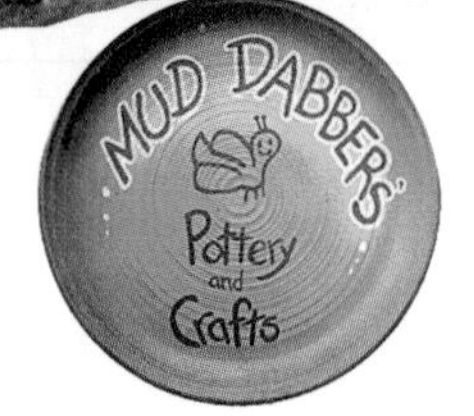

WAYNESVILLE

3 Rainbow Garden Center 2930 OLD BALSAM RD – Rainbows are possible with the size of the waterfall garden displayed at this garden retail business. St. Francis watches over impish gnomes and other statuary while visitors roam through butterfly bushes and display gardens of perennials, trees, shrubs, roses and herbs. Large cactus house is a draw. Apr–Nov 1 Mon–Sat 8am–6pm & Sun 1pm–6pm. Call for hours in the off-season. (828)456-4621.

From Mud Dabbers, travel E on 74/23 heading towards Waynesville about 1.4 mi and turn R at Old Balsam Rd.

From apples and corn to home-cooked goods, Barber's Orchard is a must stop for your tummy.

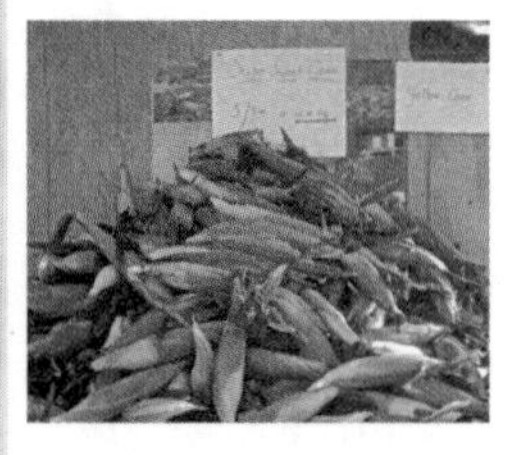

4 Barber's Orchards Fruit Stand OLD BALSAM RD – Keep the doctor away with one of 15 varieties of locally grown apples. And, you can have your cake and eat it too with the on-site

bakery shop full of apple cakes, turnovers and tarts. First opened in 1932, this landmark of the community is now owned by Benny and Jane Arrington. Aug 1–Dec 31 Mon–Sat 9am–6pm & Sun 11am–6pm. (828)456-3598.

Located across from Rainbow Garden Center.

5 The Yellow House 89 OAKVIEW DR – If you're like Emerson and love to wander, these are the grounds you've been looking for. Bleeding hearts, butterfly bushes, bachelor buttons, columbine, clematis, peonies, daylilies, yarrow, and rhododendron join together in a riot of color and pattern to make your walk worthwhile. The lovely B&B and cottage offer two perennial gardens, a bird garden, herb garden, tranquil pond, and a lovely Asian pear tree. Very mellow yellow. (828)452-0991. www.theyellowhouse.com

Back on 73/24 travel approximately 4.5 mi. Take Hazelwood exit - #100. Turn L and travel 1.1 mi to R on Oakview.

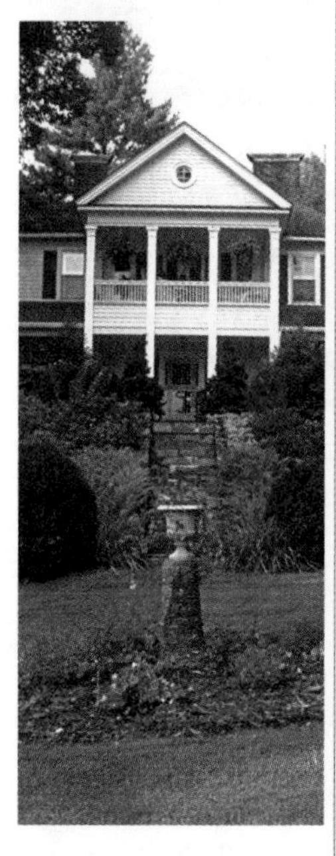

At the Yellow House, you'll find a beautiful mix of the formal and informal.

6 Ramp Festival WELCH ST – Every May the locals tastefully celebrate the glory of this rambunctious vegetable at the Waynesville American Legion Post with arts, crafts and food. Call Waynesville Chamber of Commerce for exact dates and times. (828)456-8691.

Take Plott Creek Rd back under Hwy 23 to become Hazelwood Rd. Travel .9 mi to intersection with Main St. Turn L onto Main St. At intersection with Pigeon St on R.

7 Herren House 94 EAST ST – Only a block from downtown, this 19th century Victorian

Rosemary, sage, oregano, thyme, and marjoram all belong to the mint family.

Guidebook Symbols

Kid Friendly Site · Farm · Trail · Lodging · Special Attraction · Garden · Festival · Restaurant · Garden Art

We found these morning glories winding their way through the arbor at the Herren House. What struck us wasn't just their brilliant color, it was their blooms. They were almost five inches in diameter!

B&B features a two-tiered English cottage garden full of annuals, perennials, and native azaleas. Herbs from the garden show up in the morning in fresh baked eggs and homemade chicken sausage. Wrap-around porches and latticed garden shelters offer shady respite. (828)452-7837. www.herrenhouse.com

Several blocks to R on East St.

8 Lomo's Grill, Bakery and Café 44 CHURCH ST – The Argentinian Fernandez family have got a good thing going for Waynesville folks and anyone else fortunate enough to wander into this smorgasbord for the senses. Local farmer's market vegetables and garden-grown herbs grace the entrees of the fine dinner dining, casual lunch, and Lomo-to-go and bakery items. Lomo bakery and Lomo-to-go Mon–Sat 10am–5pm. Lunch available 11am–3pm & dinner available 5:30pm–10pm. (828)452-5222.

Cross over Main St. East St changes to Church St.

9 Whitman's Bakery 18 N MAIN ST – These folks start rolling in the dough at 3am every day to produce over 50 varieties of bread and rolls, making some using wheat seeds that they sprout themselves. Trust the locals who have known since 1945 where to get a great sandwich for lunch. Good luck looking at all these cakes, pies and donuts without having to take along a sampling for the road. May the Force be with you. Tue–Sat 6am–5:30pm. Closed Sun & Mon. (828)456-8271.

Oh, the art we found for the garden at Twigs and Leaves Gallery!!!

10 Mast General Store 63 MAIN ST – The Mast tradition continues. You'll find just what you need for gardens and trails, including clothing and footwear to outdoor gear and gardening supplies. Mon–Sat 10am–6pm & Sun 1pm–6pm. (828)452-2101. www.mastgeneralstore.com

11 Twigs and Leaves Gallery 98 N MAIN ST – Enchantment exists in this gallery of exquisite nature gifts such as pine needle baskets, Kaaren

The Road Goes On Forever

Side trips, tidbits, adventures, and treasure hunts

Peppers can contain up to six times as much vitamin C as oranges! The highest levels are found when the peppers are in their "green" stage.

Stoner pottery and Journal Thomas oak burl bowls. Unusual fountains gurgle streams of inspiration. Jan–Mar Tue–Sat 10am–5:30pm. Apr–Dec Mon–Sat 10am–5:30pm. (828)456-1940. www.twigsandleaves.com

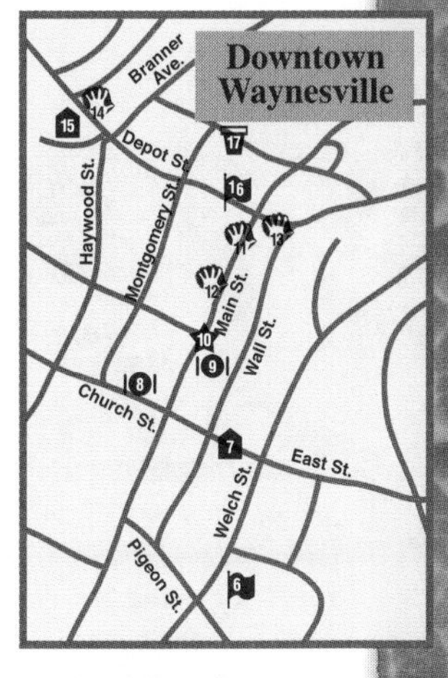

12 **Hardwood Gallery** 102 N MAIN ST – A new way to appreciate a hardwood forest. Dennis Ruane and Jean Alvarez use their working studio to transform walnut, cherry ash, maple, birch, apple and oak into functional and artistic items of mountain and contemporary themes. A hard act to follow. Mon–Sat 10am–5:30pm. Closed Sun. (828)456-3500.

13 **Burr Studio & Gallery** 136 N MAIN ST – Patio art gets special attention by Dane and Mary Etta Burr with wall suns and rock fountains. The lush garden at the studio entrance will cool you off. Mar–Dec Mon–Sat 10am—5pm & Sun 12noon–5pm. Closed Jan & Feb. (828)456-7400.

14 **Grace Cathey Sculpture Garden** 136 DEPOT ST – Metallic butterflies prepare for flight while an iron turtle forever creeps out of a stone-lined pond. Grace has got it together in this steel garden of trellises and animals adjacent to her husband's service station. Mon–Fri 8am–5:30pm. (828)456-8843.

Turn L off Main St onto Depot St. The garden is immediately on R at Phillips 66 gas station.

15 **Suyeta Park Inn** 31 SUYETA PARK DR – An 1890 grand hotel sitting on a bluff in the heart of Waynesville pulses with life in the innovative raised beds of vegetables and herbs that Scott and Lisa Fleanore created behind the inn. A brick-lined walk-through herb garden will capture your heart. (828)456-5266. www.suyetapark.com

Across street from the sculpture garden.

Guidebook Symbols

Kid Friendly Site

1 Farm 1 Trail 1 Lodging 1 Special Attraction

1 Garden 1 Festival 1 Restaurant 1 Garden Art

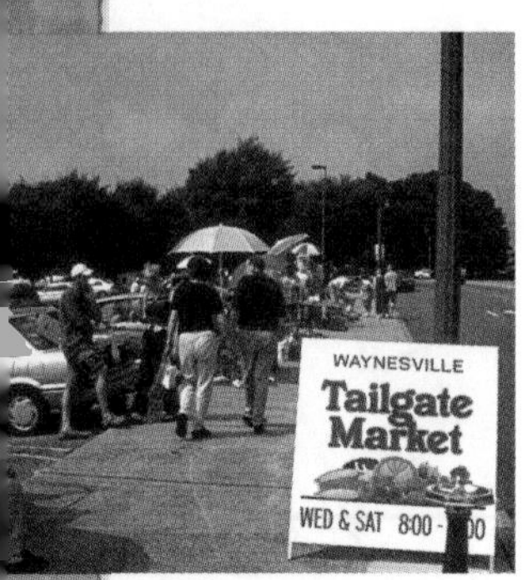

Just another one of the many tailgate markets you'll find along the way. This one happens to be conveniently located within walking distance of downtown Waynesville.

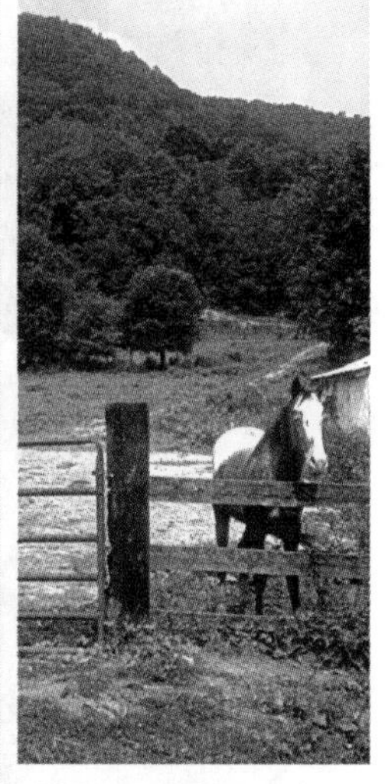

At Queen's Farm Riding Stables the horses are "chompin' at the bit" to get saddled up and show you the valley from atop the mountain.

16 **Haywood County Apple Festival** MAIN ST NEAR COURTHOUSE – Apple delicacies, mountain music and crafts await visitors the third week of October every year. (828)456-3517

Off Main St at intersection with Depot St at courthouse.

17 **Waynesville Tailgate Market** MAIN ST – Gardens live a fleeting but fragrant existence in the back of pickup trucks for several hours every Saturday and Wednesday morning beginning in early-June. 8am–12noon. (828)456-3517.

Off Main St at intersection with Depot St at courthouse.

18 **Old Stone Inn** 109 DOLAN RD – Wooded hills and mossy brook banks beckon at this peaceful mountain retreat where innkeepers Robert and Cindy Zinser's pet bunnies scamper about in the herb garden and gazebo. An expansive and impressive array of European dishes awaits guests in front of a massive stone fireplace in the timbered dining room. Eighteen guest rooms and four cottages offer lots of comfortable options. (828)456-3333. www.oldstoneinn.com

Continue on Depot St for .2 mi and turn L on Love Ln. Go .1 mi and turn L on Dolan Rd. Go .1 mi to entrance to Inn on L.

19 **The Red Barn** 1850 DELLWOOD RD – Karen Collis created a legacy to be proud of: a mountain museum with wheat cradles, treadle grindstones, and other farm artifacts and family heirlooms from three generations of Blue Ridge roots. Otherwise rooted at this garden center are perennials, bulbs, herbs, tropical foliage, ferns and annuals – 80 percent of which are grown on site. Mon–Sat 10am–5:30pm & Sun 1pm–5pm. (828)926-1901.

Backtrack to Depot St, now named Dellwood Rd. Turn L and go .4 mi to light at intersection of Russ Ave. Turn L and go 1.8 mi to intersection of US 19 and turn L. The Red Barn is .5 mi on R.

20 **Queen's Farm Riding Stables** 2180 DELLWOOD RD – Since 1947, wildflowers and wildlife greet riders headed up the private Ad Tate Knob on Utah Mountain for one-to two-

The Road Goes On Forever

Side trips, tidbits, adventures, and treasure hunts

hour rides. After bringing Lidge, Joker or one of the other horses back to the barn, enjoy the breeze on a tire swing, a game of horseshoes or a picnic near the Japanese chestnut and apple trees. Open year-round Mon–Sun dawn–dusk. Call ahead in winter. (828)926-0718.

Continue another .3 mi. On R.

Side trip to Jonathan Creek/Fines Creek...

21 **Boyd Mountain Log Cabins** 445 BOYD FARM RD – Six authentic hand-hewn restored log cabins offer resplendent reprieve from the real world amidst the Christmas tree farm, two stocked fishing ponds and beautiful mountains at Dan and Betsy Boyd's 130-acre family farm. (828)926-1575. www.boydmountain.com

From Queen's Stables, travel 1.5 mi to intersection of US 19 and Hwy 276. Turn N (R) onto Hwy 276 and go 2.3 mi to L on Hemphill Rd. Cross bridge, go .02 mi and turn L immediately onto Boyd Farm Rd.

22 **The Swag** 2300 SWAG RD – Wandering in the gentle wilderness at this exclusive family retreat offers 50-mile views regardless which one-hour or all-day trail you choose. Enjoy a day of wildflower discoveries, waterfall explorations and bird song symphonies before returning for a sumptuous four-course dinner at the renowned country inn. Open May–Oct. Call about special birding, wildflower and hiking events. (828)926-0430. www.theswag.com

Return to Hemphill Rd and turn L. Travel 3.8 mi to L at The Swag gate. Drive 2.5 mi up the private driveway.

23 **The Lily Patch** CLAY HOLLOW RD – How many daylilies can you get in eight beds? About 30,000 at Joe Cathey and Lou Adcock's farm. 250 varieties ranging from the Spider Miracle daylily at 45 inches tall with an eight-inch bloom to the Eenie Weenie at 10 inches tall with a two-to three-inch bloom. May–Aug 9am–5pm. (828)926-3076.

Backtrack to Hwy 276 and turn L continuing N another 2.7 mi. Turn L onto Bob Boyd Rd. and go 1/2 mi to L on Farmland Rd. Travel .03 mi to R onto Clay Hollow Rd, the entrance to the farm. .02 mi to parking area.

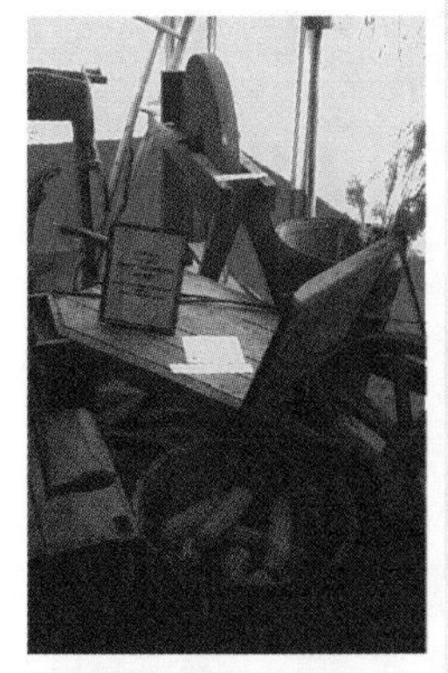

Lots of stuff to look at in The Red Barn.

Christmas Tree Facts:

Over 35 million live Christmas trees are sold in North America every year.

For every live Christmas tree harvested, two to three seedlings are planted in its place the following spring.

Over 250 varieties at The Lily Patch.

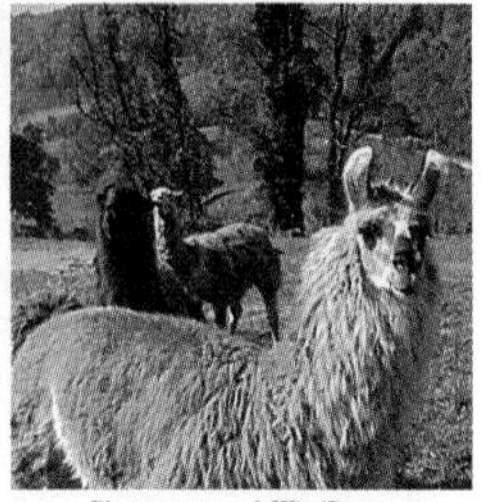

Photo courtesy of WindDancers Lodging and Llama Treks.

Vegetable Garden Pest Repellent

1/4 cup chopped garlic
1/4 cup chopped hot pepper
1/4 cup chopped onion
1 1/2 cups water
1/2 cup wood ash
1/4 cup hydrated lime

Puree garlic, pepper & onion in blender. Add 1/4 cup of water and blend to mush. Strain through a cheesecloth into a glass jar. Add wood ash and lime to the mixture. Stir well. Add the rest of the water. Store in a cool, dry place for up to one month. Use it to spray the upper and lower surface's of the plant's foliage and the roots.

24 WindDancers Lodging and Llama Treks
1966 MARTINS CREEK RD – While 21 llamas loom large on the landscape, the name of this retreat is owed to the healthy population of yellow finches that seem to waltz on the wind. Of the 270-acre property, 230 acres are in a conservancy easement. There are three contemporary log lodges with nine guest accommodations, numerous trails for hiking or llama trekking, overnight camping facilities for llama trekkers, and crystal views from your rocking chair nine mountains deep. Don't miss a gourmet lunch at the "trek deck" with the head waters of Martins Creek flowing directly under your feet. (828)627-6986. www.winddancersnc.com

Backtrack to Hwy 276 and turn L continuing N. Go 1 mi to the entrance ramp to Interstate 40. Continue W on I-40 for 5 mi to Exit 15. Turn R onto Fines Creek Rd and travel 1.5 mi to L on Martins Creek Rd. Go 2 mi up gravel road to ranch on L.

25 Jehovah-Rah Farm 170 JOE MOONEY RD – Fiber-producing animals such as Shetland sheep, llamas, alpacas, Angora goats, and Angora rabbits keep Julie Wilson busy spinning wool, teaching and conducting educational tours of her 20-acre farm. Other incentives to make the trip out here include a hemlock forest, circa-1875 log cabin, barns and corn crib, a rushing creek and a non-rushing view of Hebo Mountain and the serene Pisgah National Forest. Fee per group per hour. (828)665-2242 or (828)627-3362.

Turn L on Martins Creek Rd and travel approximately. 4.2 mi to R on Max Patch Rd. Go approximately. 1.2 mi to L on Betsey's Gap Rd (Hwy 209). Travel approximately. 3.4 mi to L on Joe Mooney Rd and continue to end of road.

Side Trip...

MAGGIE VALLEY

26 Cataloochee Ranch VIE TOP RD – "Steak-out" a claim for a day or two at this open meadow and woodland sprawl ranch. Aside from the steak barbecues and horseback riding, all other activities of hiking, trout fishing, and

The Road Goes On Forever

Side trips, tidbits, adventures, and treasure hunts

swimming, are at your own pace. With the scent of wood smoke and crisp air comes the anticipated ski season at the nearby slopes. Romantic cabins and a superb restaurant. (800)868-1401. www.cataloochee-ranch.com

Return to intersection of Hwys 276 and 19 at Dellwood. Turn R and head W on Hwy 19 for approximately. 5 mi to Ghost Town on R. Turn R at Ghost Town on Vie Top Rd. Continue up road for 3 mi and ranch is at top of the mountain.

...Meanwhile, back on the trail

27 Corneille Bryan Nature Center STUART CIRCLE – The Tuscola Garden Club works diligently all year to maintain this verdant uphill trail through 500 species of wildflowers and native flora. There are specimens of every mountain wildflower in western North Carolina. Black walnut, oak and locust nurture an understory of silverbell, hawthorne, fringe tree, and sourwood amidst several small springs and a waterfall. Pausing to ponder the beauty of growing things is free. www.lakejunaluska.com.

Turn around on Dellwood and head back E on Hwy 19. From intersection of Russ Ave travel .3 mi to entrance to Lake Junaluska. Turn L onto Lakeshore Dr. Go .5 mi to Stuart Circle. Turn L and go .1 mi to trail entrance.

28 The Sunset Inn 979 N LAKESHORE DR – Enjoy a tasty lunch from the porch overlooking beautiful Lake Junaluska. Lunch is open to the public and offers a variety of unusual vegetarian items such as mushroom and wild leek soup. Full accommodations and child-friendly. (800)221-8499. www.innspirit.com

From Stuart Circle, circle back to Lakeshore Dr and turn L. (There is a lovely rose walk here if you need to stop and smell the roses.) Continue on Lakeshore Dr and go .6 mi to Inn on L.

Trees That Need No Cleanup:

Bald Cypress
Gingko
Sweet Bay Magnolia
White Fringe Tree
'Winter King' Green Hawthorn

An easy way to dry roses for potpourri is to wrap rose petals in a paper towel and put in the microwave on medium heat for two minutes or until dry.

Guidebook Symbols

Kid Friendly Site
Farm · Trail · Lodging · Special Attraction
Garden · Festival · Restaurant · Garden Art

Basil, rose petals, mint, rosemary, nasturtium flowers or pods and other edible flowers are great as a garnish for your fine dining and are a pleasant alternative to parsley.

CLYDE

29 **Carolina Gourmet** 100 SPICEWOOD DR – For a picnic with pizazz, you can't do better than a quick stop at this to-go catering cabin. Local produce finds starring roles in specialty sandwiches such as the toasty walnut hummus wrap and Waldorf chicken salad. Mon–Fri 8:30am–2:30pm. (828)452-3004.

Continue on Lakeshore Dr across the dam for .3 mi to L at stone gate and .1 mi to intersection. Turn R on Crabtree Rd, go .5 mi and turn L on Hospital Dr. Turn R onto Spicewood Dr. On R.

30 **Mountain View Nursery** 1456 HOSPITAL DR – Flame azaleas, hemlocks, herbs, and other native alpine plants can be enjoyed from the vantage point of a bench in the demo garden. This is a good spot to sit and gaze at the goldfish while mulling over which homegrown native tree or shrub to take home with you. Mon–Fri 8:30am–5pm & Sat 8:30am– 1:30pm. (828)627-9015.

Go back to Hospital Rd and go .8 mi on R.

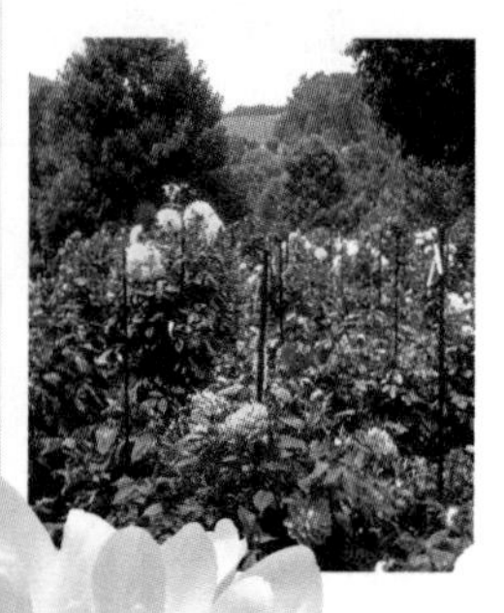

31 **Haywood Community College** 185 FREEDLANDER DR – This is a one-stop spot for touring an arboretum, grist mill, nature walk, and dye garden. The greenhouses are full of cacti and other succulent plants, begonias and geraniums, staghorn and asparagus ferns, and tropicals such as ficus and fantail palms. Call for guided tours. Mon–Fri 7am–11pm & Sat 7am–4pm. Closed Sun. (828)627-4640.

Continue .2 mi to Dead End and turn R. Go .1 mi on L. Turn L and go .02 mi uphill to Sawmill Dr. Turn R and immediately turn R onto Mill House Dr.

Side trip...

CANTON

32 **Pigeon River Scenic Walking Trail** 36 PARK ST – Between the memory trees planted along the 1.5-mile trail and the pristine surface of the river, there's a lot to reflect on at this park. Playground and picnic facilities are also available. Open dawn–dusk. (828)648-7925.

From Haywood Community College, take Exit 106 from Hwy

The fastest snail is the ordinary garden snail.

23/74 which changes to 19/23 N. Come through Clyde and continue to Canton. At 4th red light in Canton, turn R on 215 S. At yield sign, bear R on Penland St. Park will be .25 mi on L.

Canton Farmer's Market ACADEMY ST – Green beans, potatoes, tomatoes, cucumbers, squash, apples, blueberries, blackberries, pumpkins, gourds, honey, and flowers turn a parking lot into a farm paradise. Mid-June–Oct Tue & Thu 8am–12noon. (828)648-7925.

Turn R out of parking lot onto Penland St. Go to first light and turn R onto Main St. Travel to second light at bank and turn L onto Academy St. At next block, turn L into the municipal parking lot across from Town Hall.

Old Pressley Sapphire Mine 240 PRESSLEY MINE RD – With the largest sapphire ever discovered having come from this mine, be on the lookout for Indiana Jones. Weather permitting Mon–Sun 9am–6pm. (828)648-6320. www.oldpressleysapphiremine.com

Travel to the light at Town Hall and turn R. Go to stop sign and turn L on Depot St. Go to stop sign and turn L onto Main St. Cross railroad tracks to red light. Stay straight through two lights and cross the overpass. Go to North Hominy Rd and turn L. Turn L onto Willis Cove Rd and then L on Pressley Mine Rd to end.

...Meanwhile, back on the trail

The Wood'n Craft Shop 4061 PIGEON RD – Woody Woodpecker would be a good mascot for this art shop full of wood carved birds and other wildlife of artisan Ron Mayhew. Ceramic feeders and birdbaths provide creature comforts for any of the realistic carvings that might take wing. Apr–Dec Mon–Sat 10am–5pm. (828)648-2820.

Take Hospital Rd W back to L on Asheville Rd (Business Hwy 23). Go 2 mi and turn L on Ratcliff Cove Rd. Go .04 mi and turn R on Raccoon Rd. Travel 1.2 mi to L on Pigeon Rd (Hwy 276). Go 2.2 mi and shop is on L.

The art of the Tea Way consists simply of boiling water, preparing tea and drinking it.
– Rikyu

If you plan on doing any canning, use vinegar to clean and deodorize the old jars you want to reuse. You can also use the vinegar to remove fruit stains from your hands.

Guidebook Symbols

Kid Friendly Site

Farm | Trail | Lodging | Special Attraction

Garden | Festival | Restaurant | Garden Art

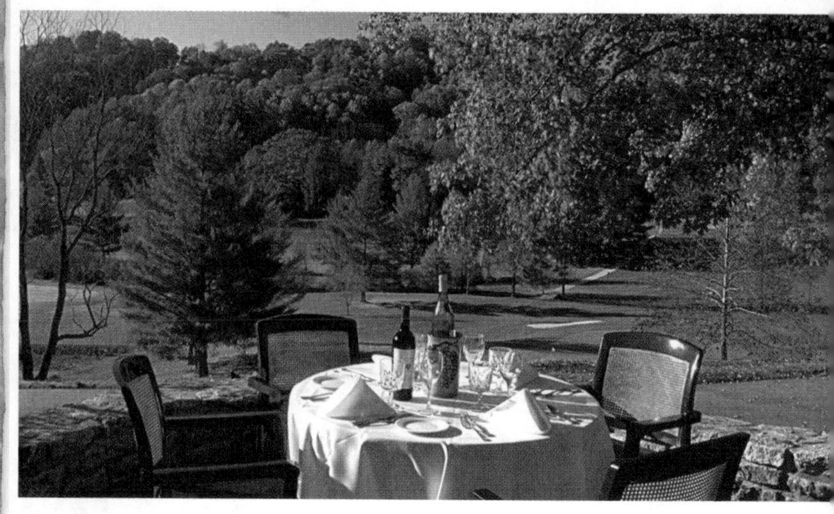

SLIDING ROCK
Each year, thousands of children, and adults, slide down sixty-feet of pitched granite, propelled by 11,000 gallons of water per minute. It's a quick trip down the rock to a cold dunking into a chilly pool. Asked why they do it, most respond with steely resolve, "Because it's there."

As we have said before, "Find a trail and go for a walk".

36 Sourwood Grille US 276 S – Where else could you find a cozy old log cabin slap dab in the middle of an elite country club? At Springdale Country Club's Sourwood Grille, . Chef Donny Paleno grills local salmon-trout cakes on a wood-burning fire enticing both those in the sand trap and those on the trail. Apr 20–Oct 31. Lunch daily 11:30am–3pm. Dinner Wed-Sun 6pm–9:30pm. (828)235-9105.

Continue 7.1 mi. further on Hwy 276 to entrance of Springdale Country Club on L.

37 Heritage Cove Cabins US 276 S – OK, so the guy that runs this is in a Bahamas state of mind. It works here at an elevation of 3500-feet with five cabins on 58 acres of creeks, cool breezes and charismatic scenery. So what if you have to bring your own bananas and coconuts, mon? (800)646-4020. www.heritagecove.com

Continue 4.4 mi through the Cruso community to R at the sign, just before Camp Hope.

Big East Fork
TRAILHEAD
PISGAH
National Forest

38 Big East Trailhead US 276 S – This trailhead provides a beautiful entrance to Pisgah National Forest with two rarities for this section of the mountains: a mostly level trail

All Aboard for "Cradle of Forestry"

Chug down the Blue Ridge Parkway to the Forest Discovery Center for a first-hand encounter with America's conservation history. In 1889, George Vanderbilt (Biltmore Estate) engaged Frederick Law Olmsted (creator of NYC's Central Park) to manage his gardens and grounds. Traipsing the vast property, Olmsted confronted evidence of poor forestry practices: abused and depleted land. He recommended Gifford Pinchot to begin the reforestation.

"The object of the plan was to return a profit to the owner while improving the forest," said German forester Dr. Carl A. Schenck, Pinchot's successor. For fourteen years, this born teacher and his forestry school transformed the woodlands known today as Pisgah National Forest. Schenk describes "improvement cutting" as, "removing the fellows which were 'no good' and giving the promising boys more air to breathe and more light to enjoy." His students, "promising boys" who followed him everywhere, matured into our first forest rangers.

Open spring through mid-fall, the 6,500 acre "Cradle" offers two one-mile paved trails. Guided tours cover basic forestry concepts: habitat, decomposition and species succession. Special lay-overs include "Bugs, Bogs and Beavers" and "Terrific Tree Day". Visit the 1915 Climax logging locomotive - designed for heavy loads, sharp curves and crude track - before you steam along the trail.

and plenty of parking. Popular among fishermen, the trail follows along the banks of the East Fork of the Pigeon River offering an abundance of pristine primitive camp areas as well as access to the Shining Rock Wilderness Area trail system for adventurous explorers. (828)877-3265.

Continue on 276 for 1.7 mi and park on R.

39 **The Pisgah Inn** BLUE RIDGE PARKWAY BETWEEN MILE POST 408 & 409 – The name "Pisgah" means "Promised Land" and this inn, true to its name, delivers. Whether it's panoramic views, fine dining or pleasurable accommodations you're after, you're sure to find it here. A land of milk-and-honey with a craft and gift shop to boot. Open daily Apr–Oct 7:30am–10:30am, 11:30am–4pm & 5pm–9pm. Hours shorten slightly in Apr & May. (828)235-8228. www.pisgahinn.com

2.7 mi from Big East Trailhead turn L on BRP.

Monotony is the law of nature.
Look at the monotonous manner in which the sun rises.
The monotony of necessary occupations is exhilarating and life-giving.
– Gandhi

Guidebook Symbols

Kid Friendly Site
1 Farm · 1 Trail · 1 Lodging · 1 Special Attraction
1 Garden · 1 Festival · 1 Restaurant · 1 Garden Art

The Pink Beds offer a blast of color as the rhododendrons bloom

Pink Beds Trail US 276 S – Rhododendron, mountain laurel and azaleas combine to create a five-mile pink heaven to walk through during the spring and early summer. Numerous picnic tables provide a divine dining area. (828)877-3265

3.5 mi from the BRP.

Cradle of Forestry 1001 PISGAH HWY – In the span of one mile, you can talk to spinners, weavers, quilters, woodsmen and blacksmiths about early 20th century life in the Appalachian mountains. The Biltmore Campus Trail takes you through the homesteads of George Vanderbilt, Gifford Pinchot and Dr. Carl Schenck, pioneers in forestry conservation. Children love the scavenger hunts in the Forest Fun exhibit in the Visitor Center. Admission: Adults $5 & Children ages 4-17 $2.50. Open daily mid-Apr–Oct 9am–5pm. (828)877-3130. www.cradleofforestry.com.

.5 mi on L from the BRP on Hwy 276 S (Pisgah Hwy).

Pisgah Center for Wildlife Education 475 FISH HATCHERY RD – A one-quarter-mile interpretative trail meanders through a wildlife garden with 75 percent all native plants, and all the plants support wildlife. Observe butterflies, birds and bunnies at their daily buffet. Open year-round. Mon–Sun 8am–5pm. Closed Christmas, Thanksgiving & Easter. (828)877-4423. www.ncwildlife.com.

5.7 mi to R turn on Fish Hatchery Rd. Follow signs.

BREVARD

Allison-Deaver House NC HWY 280 – The oldest house (1815) in Transylvania County and west of the Blue Ridge boasts a nature trail that borders a pasture, rambles behind an 1827 barn and is interspersed with native plants. Admission $2pp or $5 per family. Open Fri and Sun 1pm–4pm & Sat 10am–4pm. (828) 884-5137

L off of 276 onto Hwy 280 just .1 mi on L.

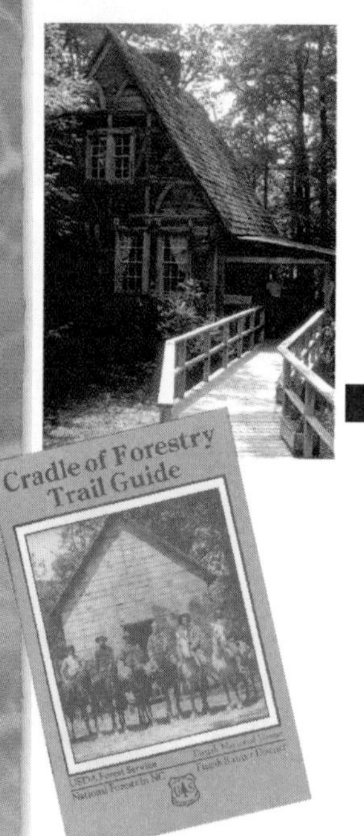

The Road Goes On Forever

Side trips, tidbits, adventures, and treasure hunts

If you want to attract Robins to your bird feeder and your yard, use raisins as the tempting treat in the feed or just scattered on your lawn.

44 Blue Ridge Corn Maze 570 EVERETT RD – If you're going to get lost on the trail, this is the place to do it. Taylor Mackey's corn maze provides real adventure in late summer and early fall and is a howling hangout at Halloween. Aug 1–Oct 31 Mon–Fri 5pm–9pm & Sat–Sun 1pm–9pm. (828)884-4415. www.cornfieldmaze.com

Turn S on Hwy 280 to immediate intersection with Hwy 64 and go E for 3.7 mi to Penrose. Turn R on Crab Creek Rd for 1.5 mi to Everett Rd. Turn R on Everett and continue 1.5 mi to maze on R.

An "amazingly" fun thing to do!!

45 Bracken Mountain Bakery 34 S BROAD ST – Organic stop for apple spice bread, croissants, European style bread—sunflower oat and honey cracked wheat bread, to name a few. Your nose will know the way. Open May–Oct Mon–Fri 8am–5pm & Sat 8:30am–5pm. Nov–Apr Tue–Fri 8am–5pm & Sat 8:30am–5pm. (828)883-4034.

Take Old Hendersonville Hwy L to L on Hwy 64 W into Brevard. Downtown on R before First Union Bank.

46 DD Bullwinkel's 38 S. BROAD ST – This general store is full of notable North Carolina merchandise such as twig furniture, pottery and handcrafted jewelry. After close scrutiny you will discover a gardening corner and a nice selection of herbal soaps. Conveniently located next to an old-fashioned lunch counter and soda fountain. Mon-Sat 10am–5:30pm & Sun 11:30am–5pm. Summer hours are Mon-Sat 10am–7:30pm & Sun 11:30am–5pm. (828)862-4700. www.ddbullwinkel.com

Just past the bakery on R.

The Land of Sky Music and Arts Festival is held annually at Blue Ridge Corn Maze on the third weekend in September. Admission: Adults $6, Children ages 6-12 $4 & Children under 6 free. (828)884-4415. www.slideguitar.com

47 The Red House Inn 412 PROBART ST – Since 1851, this house has served as a trading post, railroad station, post office, private school and the predecessor to Brevard College. Now surrounded by a hedge of hemlocks, you can admire the bluebells from the greenhouse

Guidebook Symbols

Kid Friendly Site
1 Farm · 1 Trail · 1 Lodging · 1 Special Attraction
1 Garden · 1 Festival · 1 Restaurant · 1 Garden Art

Looking out one of the antique stained glass windows at the Red House Inn.

sitting room where stagecoach tickets were once sold. (828)884-9349.

Turn L on Main St, to R on Caldwell St to L on Probart St. B&B is on R.

48 Transylvania County Tailgate Market
299 S BROAD ST – The South Broad Park with its fragrant lilac bushes and dogwoods is the perfect backdrop for the July–October tailgate market in Brevard. Tue, Thu & Sat 7am–1pm. (828)884-3109.

Take Probart St E back to S Broad St and turn R. Travel three blocks and park will be on your L across from the Cardinal Drive-in.

Trout

Trout - they're upstream and down; in ponds, rivers and creeks, in hatcheries and wild waters. Native brooks, with greenish backs and worm-like markings, keep company with Pacific Northwest rainbow and European brown, both introduced in the late 1800's. Brook demand water that's clear, cold and moving. Rainbow and brown are tolerant of warmer, stiller water. All are beautiful, and abundant, on this trail.

Many fly fishermen, each toting specialized lures like Royal Wuff or Bead Head Hare's Ear and rods springy as whips, enjoy the challenge of seeking trout in unstocked waters or the sport of catch and release. They head for Wild Trout Waters, high quality waters sustaining trout populations by natural reproduction where special fishing restrictions apply. For more prosaic angling, try Hatchery Supported Waters - 1100 miles of them in NC. They're stocked periodically with trout (40% rainbow, 40% brook and 20% brown) to sustain fishing. There's no size limit or bait restriction, and the creel limit is seven trout per day.

If catch, keep and eat is clearly your game, stop by a local trout farm to be certain of your supper. Land your own (gear and bait provided) or have them netted and cleaned for a per fish or pound fee. A well-stocked, and friendly, commercial trout pond provides a great family outing. (Tip: the colder and more oxygenated the water, the tastier the trout. More delicious if the fish snag occasional bugs or tiny shrimp.) Take home your cleaned catch to grill, bake, broil or smoke. Better yet, try it mountain style: coat with cornmeal inside and out and pan-fry the whole fish. Don't look for leftovers!

The Road Goes On Forever
Side trips, tidbits, adventures, and treasure hunts

The nearby Davidson River is a favorite among fly fishing enthusiast.

The Inn at Brevard 410 E MAIN ST – Where have all the flowers gone? A number of them spring up here on the ground where Stonewall Jackson planned battle strategies with his troops. No doubt he ate trout and stoneground grits similar to the offerings of Howard and Faye Yager at this old Civil War home. Dinner should begin and end with a stroll through the European garden behind this elegant inn. Restaurant open June–Aug Sun 5pm–9pm. (828)884-2105. www.innatbrevard.8m.com

Take Broad St N three blocks and turn R on Main St towards Hwy 276. Inn will be on your L just past the shops.

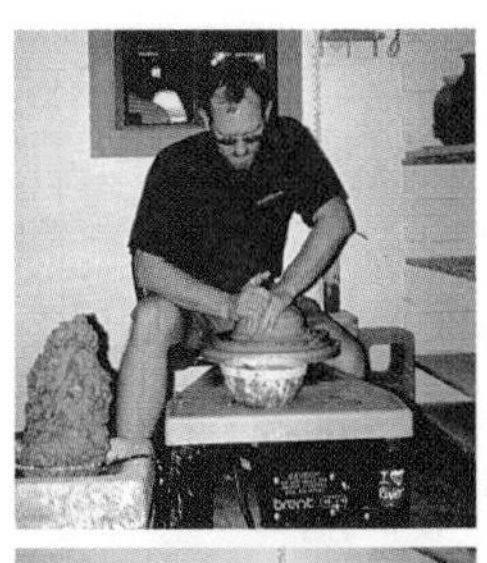

Silvermont Park E MAIN ST – A 1917 Old Colonial home on the Historic Register of Deeds provides an anchor in a sea of green. On the stone path through the grounds, you can enjoy the cool cover of hemlocks over dogwoods with daffodils at your feet. Rick Frye, the city horticulturist, designed a beautifully-laid out herb garden behind the house. Picnic tables available.

Across and down the street from The Inn at Brevard on the R.

Mountain Forest Studio 2991 GREENVILLE HWY – An English country garden and a contemporary sculpture entitled, "Alabama Resurrection" by Daniel Millspaugh greet guests at the pottery studio of Mary Murray's century-old farmhouse. Open Mar–Dec Mon–Sat 10am–5pm & Sun 1pm–5pm. Closed Jan–Feb. (828)885-2149.

Continue on Main St which turns into Hwy 276. Travel 2.5 mi. Studio is on L.

Mud Dabbers Pottery GREENVILLE HWY OR HWY 276 – The mud dabbers have built another nest like the one in Balsam. The historic Powell's Store is the site not only for these talented potters but also for the Connestee people of 500 A.D. Ancestors of the present day Cherokee also knew a thing or two about creating durable clay pottery from this same spot on Earth. Mon–Sat 10am–6pm & Sun 1pm–6pm. (828)884-5131.

Travel 1 mi past Mtn Forest Studio on L.

Mud Dabber's Magic!

Guidebook Symbols

Kid Friendly Site
Farm · Trail · Lodging · Special Attraction
Garden · Festival · Restaurant · Garden Art

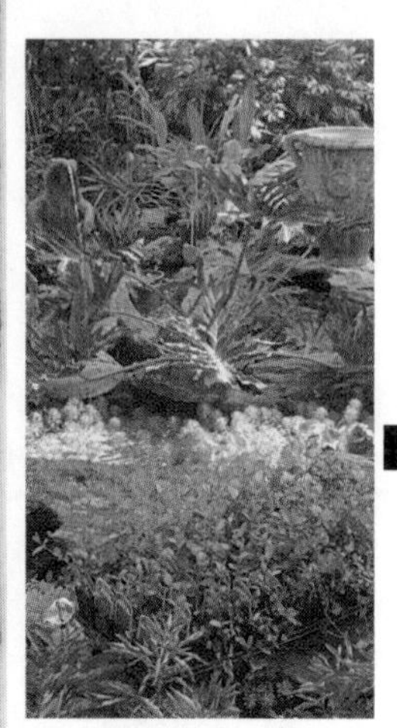

Cooking with herbs? Remember that finely chopped fresh herbs will produce a stronger flavor than dried herbs.

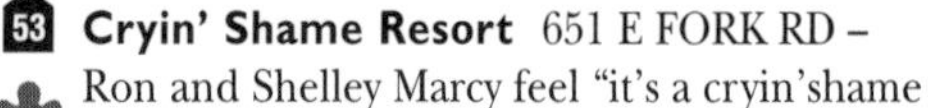

53 Cryin' Shame Resort 651 E FORK RD – Ron and Shelley Marcy feel "it's a cryin'shame you can't stay longer" at one of their four mountain cottages what with all the waterfalls, rafting and hiking trails available. (828)885-7216. www.carolina-cabins.com

Go 4 mi past Mud Dabbers down Hwy 276, turn R on East Fork Rd. Travel .75 mi and turn L into resort.

CEDAR MOUNTAIN

54 Whistle Stop Produce 125 ANDERS RD – It's no surprise that the special offering of this produce stand is tomatoes – green, red and yellow. Hanging baskets of ferns and perennials keep watch over an assortment of produce, homemade bread, and Mason jars of homemade soup. But the secret's in the sauce. Just ask the hanging rattlesnake skin by the door. Apr 1–Oct 30 Mon–Sun 8am–6pm. (828)877-5081.

1 mi past E Fork Rd intersection on L.

55 The Extended Garden HWY 276 – The Green Giant of canned vegetable fame comes out every morning to preside over this herb farm and nursery extraordinaire. Clair and Eric Stephenson celebrate life with the healthy propagation of 250 varieties of scented geraniums as well as green zebra tomatoes, gota kola, Asian cucumbers, watermelon radishes, rosemary, and assorted herbs. In the valley of the giant, ho ho ho, feng shui giant, live good people with green thumbs and a great sense of placement. Worth the drive. Open Apr 1–Oct 31 Mon–Sat 9:30am–5pm & Sun 12noon–4pm or by appointment. (828)883-5656.

1 mi past Whistle Stop on R.

56 Whitewater Gardens 259 ROSMAN HWY – John and Linda Sarpy will help you plan your own garden while you listen to classical music in a beautiful space of topiary, ornamental garden art, and English and French country antiques. Hard-to-find annuals, vines and bulbs in and around the greenhouses with display

There are more than 1,000 varieties of tomatoes currently being grown in the U.S. It's hard to "ketchup" with them all!

water gardens. Mon–Fri 9am–4pm & Sat 9am–2pm. Closed Sun. (828)884-2656.

Travel about 5.2 mi back up Hwy 276 towards Brevard and turn L on Camp Illahee Rd. Go about 2 mi to intersection with Hwy 64. Turn R. Gardens are on R.

57 **Henderson's Greenhouses** 3940 OLD ROSMAN HWY – If rabbits ruled, they would undoubtedly choose the realm of Henderson's Greenhouses. Twenty-seven acres with 12 greenhouses full of vegetables, ferns, shrubs, perennials, annuals, and impatiens. Mon–Sat 8:30am–5pm. Closed Sun. (828)883-3003.

Turn L onto Hwy 64W and travel 4.25 mi to L onto Old Rosman Hwy. Travel 2 mi to greenhouses on L.

LAKE TOXAWAY

58 **Salmonid's Trout Farm** TWIN PONDS RD – Yes, it's a beautiful lake full of brook and rainbow trout. There's also an apple and cherry orchard, wild raspberries and blueberries, a shady picnic area, Christmas trees and a 1.5 mile hiking trail to explore. A soul-soothing stop. A fishing fee is charged. Thu–Sun 10am–6pm or by reservation. (828)966-4604.

Turn L on Old Rosman Hwy and travel .7 mi to intersection with Hwy 178. Turn R and take 178N back to intersection with 64 W and turn L. Travel about 3.75 mi and turn R on Silversteen Rd at the gas station. Go .7 mi and turn L on Golden Rd. Continue for 2.8 mi to intersection with Twin Ponds Rd. Turn L and farm will be on your R.

59 **Twin Streams Bed & Breakfast** TWIN PONDS LN – If you're tired of the vicarious lifestyle of reading torrid romance novels, put the book down and lead your love to this 11-acre charming hideaway. Walking trails abound along with a duck and stocked trout pond and views of a cascading mountain stream from your room. And if your spouse wants to fish and you don't, take a break from each other to finish the last chapter of happily ever after. This is a good place to outdo the book. (828)883-3007.

From Salmonid's, turn L on Twin Ponds Ln and pass the turn-off for Golden Rd. Continue on Twin Ponds Ln about 1.2 mi. Turn L into the B&B.

Looking to keep pests out of your flower garden?
Try this non-toxic Flower Garden Pest Repellent

1/4 cup chopped garlic
2 cups water
2 teaspoons mineral oil
1 oz oil-based soap

Puree garlic in a blender. Add 1/4 cup of water and blend to mush. Strain through a cheesecloth into a glass jar. Add oil and soap to the mixture. Stir well, then add the rest of the water. Store in a cool, dry place for up to one month. Use it to spray the upper and lower surface's of the plant's foliage and the roots.

Guidebook Symbols Kid Friendly Site
Farm · Trail · Lodging · Special Attraction
Garden · Festival · Restaurant · Garden Art

Want to spice up your honey? Add some herbs! Add two teaspoons of your favorite fresh herb to a quart of honey. Warm over low heat. Place in a canning jar and store for two or three weeks to get the full flavor. We suggest you try sage and rosemary. Yummy Honey!

60 **The Cabins at Seven Foxes** HWY 281 S – There's no room for the mundane at this new mountain retreat with cabins such as The Bear Cave, The Squirrel Nest or The Fox Hole. The barnyard meadow in view of the cabins is full of miniature horses and goats for the young and young-at-heart. (828)877-6333.

Turn L on Twin Ponds Ln to intersection with Hwy 281. Go approximately ,5 mi and turn R on Slick Fisher Rd. Travel 2.5 mi to the retreat across from Indian Lake Estates. Check-in, however, is at the Brown Trout Mountain Grille.

61 **Brown Trout Mountain Grille** 35 HWY 281 – The trout didn't have to jump far to land on the dining table at this fine restaurant just across from Lake Toxaway. Aside from fresh fish, there's also fresh, live entertainment. Tue–Sun 5:30pm–10pm. Bar open until 2am Tue–Sun. (828)877-3474.

Return to Hwy 281 and turn R heading S. The restaurant is .25 mi on your L.

62 **October's End Restaurant** 115 HWY 64 W – When the entrée ingredients are Morgan Mills trout, fresh rosemary, basil, and Highlands tomatoes, if it were any fresher, you'd slap it. Fire-grilled roasted peppers taste even better when eaten from the balcony overlooking Toxaway Falls. Herbs are grown on the deck of this scenic and tasteful stop. Mon–Sun 11:30am–3pm & 5:30pm–9:30pm from Apr 1 through (you guessed it) Oct 31. (828)966-9226.

Take Hwy 281 S to 64 W. Turn R and travel .6 mi. Restaurant will be on your L just past the bridge over Toxaway Falls.

63 **Maxine's** HWY 64 W – Birdhouses of stone and moss beckon winged creatures next to bramble wreaths and rustic furniture at this garden shop. Bedding plants, herbs and garden flowers provide a riot of color and great hiding places for fairy and angel statuary. Mon–Sun 10am–6pm. (828)966-4847.

Just beside October's End.

The Road Goes On Forever

Side trips, tidbits, adventures, and treasure hunts

Babe Ruth wore a cabbage leaf under his cap to keep cool. He changed it every two innings.

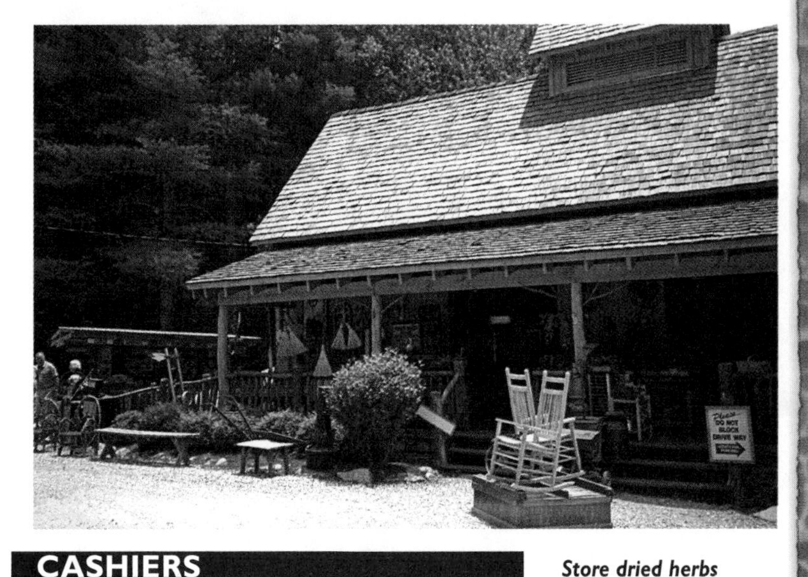

CASHIERS

64 Cashiers Farmer's Market US 64 & NC 107 – An old farm wagon in front of the store should be a clue that this is the place to load up on fresh produce. But this is also a good stop for twig baskets, local jellies and honey. They even sell music that will put you in a mountain state of mind. Easter–Thanksgiving Mon–Sat 10am–6pm & Sun 10am–4pm. (828) 743-4334.
Continue on Hwy 64 to intersection with NC 107 as you turn S on 107, market will be on your L.

Store dried herbs in glass bottles, preferably dark bottles. Store out of direct sunlight, which bleaches and deteriorates the herbs.

65 Chattooga Gardens HWY 107 S – The greenhouses with fountains, hanging baskets, perennials, annuals and herbs all complement an antique cabin that's full of gardening books. There's even a walk-through garden of stone birdhouses and arbors abounding everywhere. Mar–Dec Mon–Sat 9am–5pm during the high season. Closed Jan–Feb. (828) 743-1062.
.3 mi on R past Farmer's Market on Hwy 107 S.

66 High Hampton Inn HWY 107 S – The majestic Rock Mountain mirrored in Hampton Lake provides the frame for this picture-perfect inn and its manicured grounds. Worth noting are the Halsted Dahlia Gardens and the

Guidebook Symbols
Kid Friendly Site
1 Farm | 1 Trail | 1 Lodging | 1 Special Attraction
1 Garden | 1 Festival | 1 Restaurant | 1 Garden Art

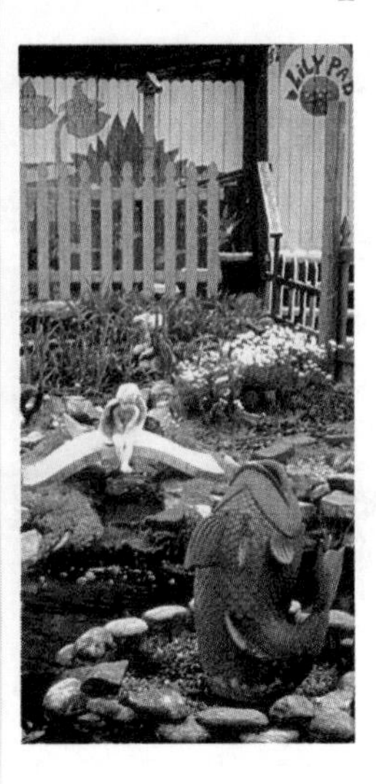

Honeymoon/Anniversary Cottage on Jewel Lake which was originally a grist mill. Half-day guided walks are scheduled weekly with picnic lunches provided by the Inn. One of the eight estate trails goes to the peak of Chimney Top Mountain at 4618 feet. June 1–Labor Day there are even kids' activities such as hayrides, donkey cart rides and nature walks. (800)334-2551. www.highhamptoninn.com

1.5 mi S on Hwy 107 from the intersection of Hwys 64 and 107 in Cashiers.

67 **Lily Pad Aquatic Nursery** 41 PILLAR DR – If the Beatles had seen this place, it would have become immortalized as an album cover. Lotus flowers, water lilies, goldfish, koi, brightly painted picket fences and ponds aplenty create a magical mystery tour of funky yet classical proportions. Water garden seminars available. Apr–Nov Mon–Sat 11am–5pm. Closed Dec–Mar. (828)743-5783.

Across the street from Village Walk and behind Tommy's Restaurant on Pillar Dr parallel to Hwy 107.

68 **The Bird Barn'n Garden** HWY 107 S – North Carolina-made birdhouses and hummingbird feeders, orchids, wind chimes, garden statues, and locally made planters fill this shop to the brim. You can spill out into the garden in front of the shop where butterfly bushes, lady's mantle and blackberry lilies thrive. Mon–Sat 10am–5pm. (828)743-3797.

Traveling back to Cashiers, just before intersection with Hwy 64, store will be on L in the Village Walk Shopping Center.

Fun Christmas Tree Facts:

Evergreens were first decorated with apples and called "the paradise tree," symbolic of the story of Adam and Eve.

It can take as many as 15 years to grow a Christmas tree of average retail sale height of six feet.

There are about 15,000 Christmas tree growers in North America, and over 100,000 people are employed full- or part-time by the growers.

GLENVILLE

69 **Tom Sawyer Tree Farm** LAKESIDE CIRCLE DR & CHIMNEY POND RD – Tom and his buddy Huck Finn didn't have any reindeer adventures, but you'll find them at a real Tom Sawyer's tree farm. A serene mountain pond welcomes you to this choose and cut Christmas tree farm located alongside Glenville Lake, one the highest lakes east of the Mississippi. Reindeer

The Road Goes On Forever

Side trips, tidbits, adventures, and treasure hunts

SPOT IT

It's somewhere on this loop. Can you find it?

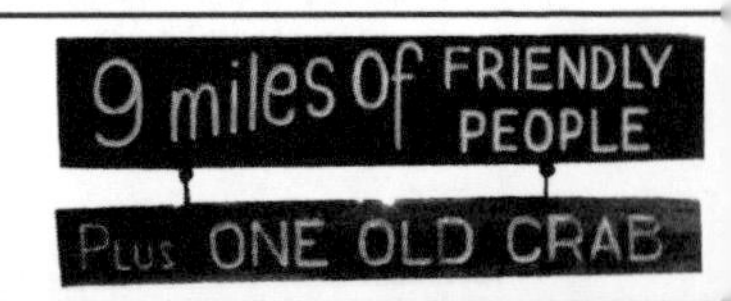

abound along with spiced cider, wreaths, garland, and Santa on weekends. Open daily Thanksgiving–Christmas 9am–5pm. (828)743-5456. www.tomsawyertrees.com

Continue on Hwy 107 N approximately 7 mi from intersection of 64 in Cashiers. Just at Happ's Restaurant on R, turn L on Lakeside Circle Dr and go .5 mi to farm.

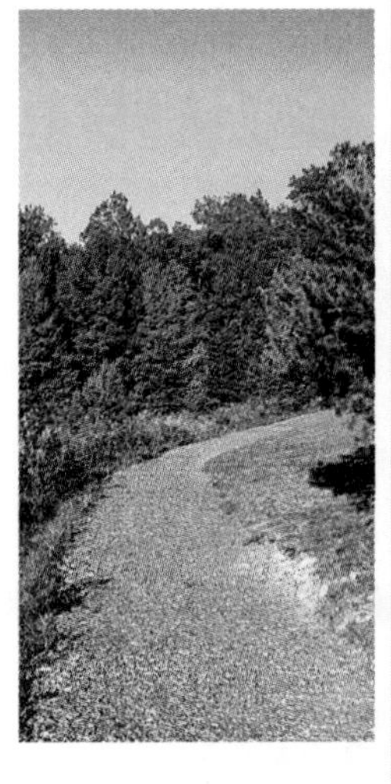

70 **Arrowmont Stables and Cabins** 276 ARROWMONT TRAIL – View the mountain tops from a higher perch at this English and Western wilderness riding adventure ranch. Enjoy trail riding on Flame Azalea, Fern Forest, or Scenic Valley Trail, or practice in the ring. Open year-round Mon–Sat. (800)682-1092. www.arrowmont.com

Turn L back onto Hwy 107 N and travel approximately. .4 mi to Citgo on R. Turn L onto Pine Creek Rd (SR 1163) for 3.1 mi traveling around Lake Glenville, over one of the largest earth dams of its kind and in view of the lake's islands. Turn R onto Cullowhee Mtn Rd (S.R. 1157) and go 1 mi. Turn R on Arrowmont Trail to stables on your R. If gate is shut, just open and come on in. (Can't let the horses out!)

TUCKASEGEE

71 **Singing Waters Camping Resort** 1006 TROUT CREEK RD – Birch bark blows in the breeze like so many Tibetan prayer flags as you enter a pristine sanctuary of cascading waterfalls with embankments of bloodroot and maidenhair fern. Two playgrounds, a stocked trout pond, and a swimming pond ensure fun for all ages. Rustic and full–amenity cabins and tent sites. Closed Jan–Feb. (828)293-5872. www.singingwaterscampingresort.com

Back on 107 N, travel approximately 3 mi and turn R on Trout Creek Rd. 1 mi to resort.

CULLOWHEE

72 **Thomas Berry Farm** 78 MEDALLION DR – Researchers at Tufts University in Boston and the USDA have found blueberries to have the highest content of antioxidants. Therefore, the folks at the farm here say that if you eat a half cup of blueberries daily for 1200 months you

Blueberry Liquer

3 cups fresh blueberries
1 clove
1/2 cup sugar syrup
2 cups of vodka
Peel of 1 scraped lemon wedge

Rinse berries and lightly crush. Add vodka, lemon peel and clove. Pour into dark bottle. Store for 3-4 months. Strain through cheesecloth. Squeeze out all juice. Add sugar syrup to taste. Store for 4 weeks. Liquer will be slightly watery. To thicken, add glycerin. Great for baking.

While on the campus of Western Carolina University in Cullowhee, don't miss the Cherokee Garden. The folks at the Mountain Heritage Center can help give you directions. It's between the Stillwell Building, Natural Science Building and Campus Library. Also, ask for help to find the on-campus Rhododendron Garden. It's near the infirmary.

will live to see your 100th birthday. Do the math and steer clear of transfer trucks. That aside, the Thomas family can keep your picked berries for you in a walk-in cooler up to three weeks as you're traveling until you're ready to head home. Open early July–late Aug Mon, Wed & Fri 8am–6pm. (828)293-5132.

Turn R back onto Hwy 107 N for 10.1 mi to just before a bridge. Turn R on Old Cullowhee Rd (SR 1002). Stay on this road until you cross the river twice. After second bridge, turn R on Wayehutta Rd. Travel .5 mi to the farm.

73 **Mountain Heritage Center** WESTERN CAROLINA UNIVERSITY – You can walk the path of Western North Carolina's Scottish and Irish ancestors at this educational stop on the WCU campus in the H.F. Robinson Administration Building. Open year-round Mon–Fri 8am–5pm & June–Oct Sun 2pm–5pm. (828)227-7129.

Go back to Old Cullowhee Rd and turn L to cross the river. Turn R at blinking light and follow to Wachovia Bank. Turn R and follow the road to the Center.

SYLVA

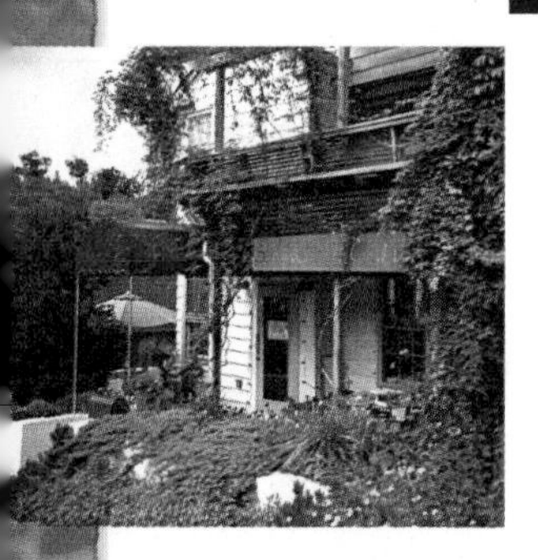

74 **Spring Street Café** 3 E JACKSON ST – For fresh and healthy, eclectic and homestyle food, you'll do well to dine at this upbeat downtown café. From Jamaican Jerk BBQ to Babaganouj (roasted eggplant salad) to buttermilk biscuits, local produce takes on wildly different personas, all of them tasty. Don't miss the homemade herbed goat cheese. Tue–Sat 11:30am–3pm & 5:30pm–10pm. Sun 10am–3pm. Closed Mon. (828)586-1800.

From WCU, turn R onto 107 N and travel approximately 6 mi to Sylva. Follow Hwy 23 Business (Mill St) one way to L on Spring St. Cross Main St and go one block. Restaurant is on L with blue awning.

75 **Alan's on Main Street** 553 W MAIN ST – OK, trail hoppers. How about a salad bouquet of mixed baby field greens arranged in a vine ripened tomato vase with hearts of palm, cucumbers and a champagne vinagrette? Chef Alan Gould creates works of heart-smart art directly from the garden to the kitchen

The Road Goes On Forever

Side trips, tidbits, adventures, and treasure hunts

The Daisy got its name because the yellow center resembled the sun. It was commonly known as the "day's eye" and, over time, was eventually called daisy.

with his greenhouse behind this renovated 1904 house-turned-fine dining restaurant. There is also a lovely sitting area with flowers and shrubs adjacent to the greenhouse. A good place to contemplate the glory of green, growing things. Tue–Sat 11am–2pm & 5pm–9pm. Closed Sun & Mon. (828) 631-4545

Turn R back onto Main St. Alan's is on the R.

76 **Karcher Stonecarving Studio & Rose Gardens** 260 N BETA RD – A little bit of heaven is here on earth at this working studio and gallery located in a century-old barn. Collene Karcher brings marble, alabaster and limestone to life as human torsos, Medusa and angel reliefs. Were you made of stone, you'd still be moved. An antique rose garden with herb and perennial beds alongside a stream provides the perfect setting for her garden art which also includes works in wood and casts in bronze. The Karchers can and sell homemade raspberry jam. They also offer some pick-your-own days during mid-August depending on the yield. Apr 1–Oct 31 Sat 10am–5pm. By appointment during the rest of the year. (828)586-4813. www.collenekarcher.com

Take Hwy 23/74 E towards Asheville to Steeple Rd on L by Amoco Station. Follow Steeple Rd to L at stoplight. Take R on N Beta Rd. Fifth drive on R.

DILLSBORO

77 **The Nature Connection** 150 FRONT ST – Garden books and garden art prevail with a nice selection of local handmade crafts and nature paintings. May–Dec Mon–Sun 11am–5pm. Jan–Apr Thu–Sun 11am–5pm. (828)586-0686.

Turn R on Hwy 23/74 W back towards Sylva to Exit 81. Turn L on Haywood Rd and then the second R on Church St. Take the first R onto Front St. Halfway down the block on the R.

Honeybees have shown a preference for yellow and blue flowers.

Looking for a new toothpaste? Why not try an old-timey one instead?

Rosemary Toothpowder

Rosemary has great antibacterial effects. Just burn the stems of rosemary and grind the coals into a powder. Brush your teeth with the powder.

To freshen your breath after a meal, try eating some parsley. It neutralizes mouth odor.

Guidebook Symbols

Kid Friendly Site
Farm · Trail · Lodging · Special Attraction
Garden · Festival · Restaurant · Garden Art

Pickles and relishes are closely related. For pickles, vegetables are left whole, or cut to size for the recipe. For relishes, vegetables and/or fruits are chopped before you put them in a vinegar mixture. Pick up a sample of each at Dogwood Crafters.

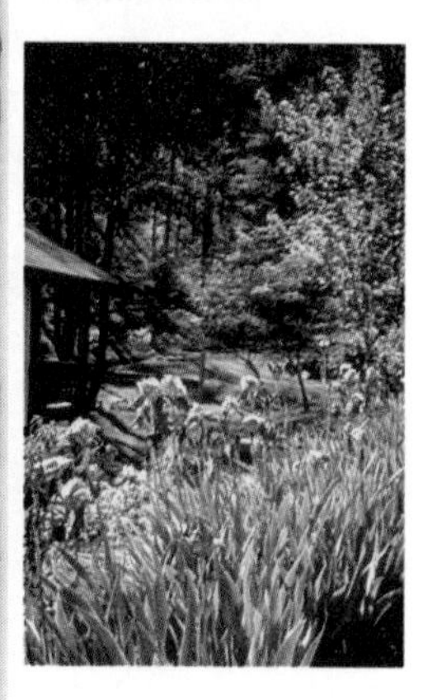

78 **Dogwood Crafters** 90 WEBSTER ST – This cooperative features a local group of artisans and crafters who give demonstrations once a month on a variety of topics including growing herbs. Situated in a renovated log cabin, these folks seek to preserve the unique craft skills of the people of Southern Appalachia. Corn shuck flowers, wreaths of native nuts and pine cones, homemade jams, jellies, pickles, relishes and preserves are just a few of the offerings at this homey shop. Open daily 9am–5pm. During the high season 9am–9pm. Closed Jan–Feb. (828)586-2248.

Continue down Front St to R on Webster St. First store on R.

79 **Oaks Gallery** 29 CRAFT CIRCLE - There could be no other name for this gallery since a 300-year-old oak tree (the second oldest in the state) graces the spot with a daylily garden and gazebo to keep it company. The gallery includes a variety of garden art and wood carvings. Mon–Sat 10am–5pm. Closed Sun. (828)586-6542.

Travel to Haywood Rd and turn L. Go to the light and turn L on US 441. Turn L onto River Road and then first L onto Craft Circle.

80 **Squire Watkins Inn** 657 HAYWOOD RD – Built in the late 1880's, the gardens were designed by Doan Ogden who designed the UNCA, Cherokee and Warren Wilson botanical gardens. The two-acre property extends to the river and has a walking trail connecting to downtown Dillsboro. Other features of this beautiful inn include a small pond, waterfall, herb garden and rock garden. (800)586-5244.

Backtrack to R on Hwy 441 to light and turn L. Inn is on the L.

81 **The Chalet Inn** 285 LONE OAK DR – For all you know, you could suddenly have been transported to the Black Forest region of Germany at George and Hanneke Ware's idyllic inn. Twenty-two acres of mountain forests, naturalized gardens, brook, and stocked pond, and hiking trails full of wildflowers and

The Road Goes On Forever

Side trips, tidbits, adventures, and treasure hunts

There are 250,000 known species of flowering plants on our planet.

birds. The family Volksmarsch offers children an opportunity to find checkpoints on a trail map and receive a zeichen (souvenir token). From your flower-bedecked balcony in the Alpine "Gasthaus", you can almost hear yodeling from a distant ridge. Gardens and hiking trails open to public (Children 12 & older) Apr–Sep 11am–3 pm. Inn hosts guests from third Friday in March through New Year's Day. (800)789-8024. www.chaletinn.com

From Exit 81 head N on 441/74 for 3 mi to L on Barkers Creek Rd across from the Shell Station. Travel .02 mi to R on Thomas Valley Rd. After 1.1 mi turn L on Nations Creek Rd and travel .03 mi to R on Lone Oak Dr.

American Indians were cultivating strawberries as early as 1643. They crushed the strawberries in a mortar, mixing them with meal to make a strawberry bread.

82 **Shelton Farms** 500 THOMAS VALLEY RD – A greenhouse full of hydroponic lettuce makes a refreshing stop. And, why not pick up a few fresh tomatoes and strawberries too? (828)497-5323.

Turn L back onto Thomas Valley Rd and travel 4.1 mi (stay R) to farm on R.

BRYSON CITY

83 **Randolph House** FRYEMONT RD – This 1895 12-gabled mansion fills up regularly with folks who then fill up themselves with homemade breads, vegetables harvested from the nearby gardens and mountain trout from local waters. Closed Nov–Mar. (828)488-3472.

Take Thomas Valley Rd to Whittier continue under Hwy 74. Take R at Post Office and access Hwy 74 W. Travel 3.7 mi on 74 W to 19 N (Exit 67) towards Bryson City. Continue .3 mi to Fryemont. On L.

84 **Historic Calhoun Country Inn** 135 EVERETT ST – Fifteen rooms featuring handmade quilts, antique and period furniture. Family style meals served Friday and Saturday to guests. Breakfast from 7am–9am and dinners 6pm–8 pm. Teas, fresh breads, homemade jams and cobblers, sourwood honey and biscuits. Maybe Calhoun descendants move to the front of the line. Check your family tree to be sure. (828)488-1234. www.calhouncountryinn.com.

Continue on 19N. Turn R onto Main St. Take L onto Everett St. Inn is .5 mi block on L.

Strawberry and Tarragon Jam

4 cups of granulated sugar
5 cups crushed strawberries
1/2 cup chopped tarragon leaves

Combine sugar and strawberries in saucepan. Bring to a boil. Add tarragon leaves. Let simmer and stir often until thick. Skim off foam.

Recipe makes 3 one-pint jars.

85 Heritage Festival RIVERFRONT PARK – Every Memorial Day Weekend this event hits the town with log sawing contests, spinning, woodworking, pottery and basket making, inner tube races, community heritage displays, food, crafts and games. Fri 6pm–10pm & Sat 10am–6pm. (800)867-9246.

Continue N on Everett St to stoplight and turn L onto Mitchell St. Halfway down block is County Administration Building on L. Festival is held on grounds at Riverfront Park.

86 Folkestone Inn 101 FOLKESTONE RD – This is a great country B&B with walking trails that include gardens set back in the woods and the ambling Deep Creek to keep you company. Maps provided of trails but not hobbit holes. (888)812-3385. www.folkstone.com

Backtrack to Everett and turn L. Railroad depot on R. Cross tracks onto Depot St. Take Depot St E to L on West Deep Creek Rd. 2 mi near Deep Creek entrance to Great Smoky Mountains National Park. Inn is on L.

Plant strawberries as soon as it's warm enough for the soil to be worked. Pinch the flowers off the plants until July.

87 Great Smoky Mountains National Park DEEP CREEK RD – Bryson City is a charming entrance to the quieter side of the National Park. Picnic, camp, try tubing in Deep Creek or stroll to three spectacular waterfalls. Enjoy the changing seasons – accessible year-round. (865)436-1200. www.nps.gov/grsm.

Entrance just past Folkestone Inn. *See Main Entrance on page 163.*

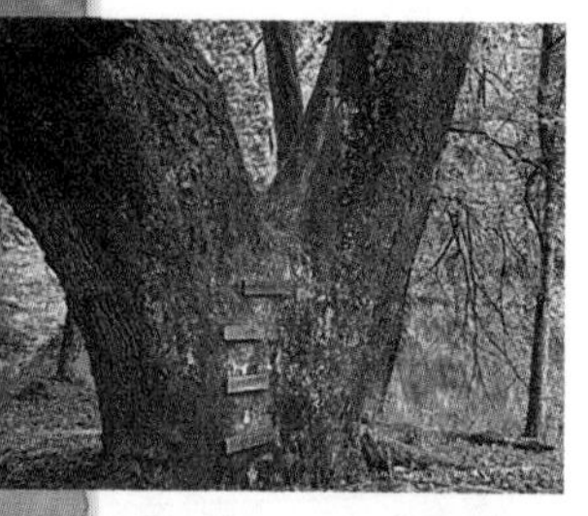

Check out the Wedding Tree at Darnell Farms. Ask for the complete story when you visit.

88 Darnell Farms/Corn Maze HYATT CREEK RD – Strawberries, green beans, tomatoes, okra, peppers, cucumbers, and squash are grown at the farm on Thomas Valley Road in Whittier and also here in the fertile valley at Governor's Island. The Strawberry Jam is a bluegrass and berry festival held on a weekend in May every year. Admission: Adults $5 & Children ages 6–11 $3. Farm open May–Nov 15 Mon–Sat 8am–6pm. Corn maze open Sep–Oct Tue–Thu 4pm–10pm, Fri 4pm–11pm & Sat 10am–11pm. Closed Sun & Mon. (828)497-2376.

Take East Deep Creek Rd back to US 19 and turn L. Travel about 1 mi and turn L on Galbraith Creek Rd. Turn L onto Old River

---

The Road Goes On Forever

Side trips, tidbits, adventures, and treasure hunts

The Great Smoky Mountains National Park straddles the North Carolina/Tennessee border. Roughly 250,000 acres are in North Carolina. The park is the largest undisturbed high-elevation forest in the Southern Appalachains.

Rd (scenic dirt road by river). Turn R onto Hyatt Creek Rd. Farm is on R across bridge at Governor's Island.

89 **Hemlock Inn** GALBRAITH CREEK RD – What was once a mountain farm is now an unpretentious country inn overlooking three valleys to the big mountains across the way. A favorite stop for vacationing Adirondack chairs. (828)488-2885.
Turn R onto 19. Travel .5 mi to L on Galbraith Creek Rd. Inn is on L.

The science of apple growing is called POMOLOGY.

90 **Valley Produce** HWY 19 E – This roadside stand, the oldest one in the Smokies, carries almost every fruit and vegetable in the alphabet. In the spring there is also a nice selection of hydrangeas, hanging baskets, statuary and perennials. Open daily Apr–Dec 9am–7pm. (828)488-8426.
Turn L on 19 toward Cherokee. Stand is on L.

The coarse trailing vine of pumpkins can overtake a smaller garden quite easily. Make sure you give them plenty of space.

91 **Kituhwa Corn Maze** HWY 19 E – Walk the Tribal Seal of the Eastern Band of the Cherokee in this maze situated on the grounds of Kituhwa, the Mother Town of Cherokee. The original Council House Mound adjoining the maze deserves at least a moment of reflection and respect. In the middle of the maze is a seven-sided tower honoring the seven clans of the Cherokee. Indian corn, gourds and pumpkins add festive color and mood as you bounce along on the hayride. But can you find your way out of the maze through educational clues about Cherokee heritage? Admission: Adults $5 & Children under 12 $3. Aug–Oct Fri–Sun 12noon–10pm. (828)497-7605.
Directly across Hwy 19 from Valley Produce.

CHEROKEE

92 **Oconaluftee Island Park** INTERSECTION US 19 & US 441 N – Where river cane was once cut for baskets stand nine talking trees speaking in both Cherokee and English. The trees will tell

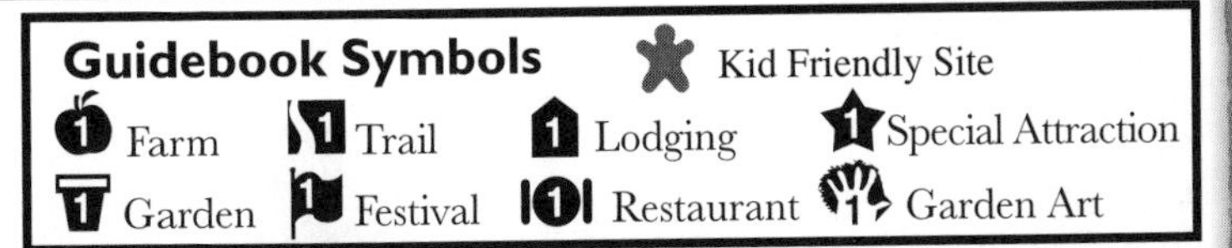

Shrubs are a wonderful addition to any garden. We've come up with a couple of lists of ideas we hope will help you when making your shrub choices.

Groundcover shrubs:

American Elderberry
Fragrant Sumac
Japanese Kerria
Red-Osier Dogwood
Rugosa Rose
St. John's-Wort
Summersweet
Sweet Fern
Ural False Spirea
Winter Jasmine

Fast-growing shrubs for quick screening:

Amur Maple
Border Privet
Bottlebrush Buckeye
Flowering Quince
Heavenly Bamboo
Jetbead
Pineapple Guava
Redleaf Rose
Spreading Cotoneaster
Winter Honeysuckle
Yaupon

you of the legends and medicinal uses of the various trees and plants growing in this sanctuary of solitude and river stones. Muse over the mystical presence of ancient elders as you walk around the island on the beautiful river trail. Picnic shelters, tables and grills on the grounds. Open year-round sunrise to sunset. Call for more information about the park and other general Cherokee information. (828)497-9115.

93 **Museum of the Cherokee Indians** HWY 441 N & DRAMA RD – Journey back in time to prehistoric North America, through the Revolutionary War, the legacy of Sequoyah, the Chamber of Discord, Tsali's cave and along the Trail of Tears. You won't come out without stirred emotions. On a whimsical note, where else can you play a centuries-old butter-bean game? An interpretive facility for the Trail of Tears National Historic Trail, administered by the National Park Service. Admission: Adults $8 & Children ages 6 and older $5. Open daily except Thanksgiving, Christmas and New Year's Day 9am–5pm. (828)497-3481.

On L.

94 **Oconaluftee Indian Village, Herb Garden and Nature Trail** HWY 441 N – Black birch and yellow poplar were once used to make dug-out canoes while red spruce, sycamore and

The Road Goes On Forever
Side trips, tidbits, adventures, and treasure hunts

SPOT IT
It's somewhere on this loop. Can you find it?

For some old-fashioned, sweets and treats to make using your finds from the gardens along the trails, try these recipes.

Sweet Potato Pie

2 cups sweet potatoes, diced and cooked
2/3 cup molasses
1/2 teaspoon ginger
1/2 stick butter
1/2 cup sweet milk
pinch of salt
biscuit dough
other spices if desired

Mix together all the ingredients except the dough and bring to a boil. Cut rolled dough into cubes and drop into boiling mixture. Put thin slices of dough on top. Put pan in oven and bake until crust is brown.

Blackberry Cobbler

blackberries, enough for one pie
sugar to taste
butter, small amount
biscuit dough, enough for several biscuits

Cook the blackberries until they come to a boil, add as much or little sugar as you want, and then add some butter. Cook until thick. Roll out the dough, cut as for biscuits, and drop into the blackberries. Then roll some dough thin, cut into strips, and place on top of the blackberries. Set the pan in the oven until the crust on top is brown.

Recipes are from The Foxfire Book, edited by Eliot Wiggington, Anchor Books, 1972.

No, you didn't miss this building along the trail. It's one of folk artist Don Stevenson's hand sculpted replica bird-houses. Stop at his studio in Morganton. (Page 176 Site 20.)

To learn more about the flora and fauna of the Great Smoky Mountains National Park, pick up any of the guidebooks published by the Great Smoky Mountains Natural History Association. For more information, call (865)-436-0120. Or, check out the website. www.smokiesstore.og

Eastern hornbeam were used for a tea to remedy toothache pain. Walking through the garden, you will learn about the ingenious ways that the Cherokee used nature to heal themselves and improve their living conditions. Dog hobble, jelly berry, mockernut hickory and the tree of heaven line the walking trail along with hundreds of flowers, shrubs and ferns. See Heritage Site on page 161 for detailed description. In the Indian Village, guides will lead you through the history of the Cherokee through hands-on demonstrations of such timeworn crafts as weaving, pottery, beadwork, and chipping flint into arrowheads. Indian Village Admission: Adults $12 & Children ages 6-13 $5. Discounts for groups of 15 or more. No charge for enjoying the Nature Trail. Open daily May 15–Oct 25 9am–5pm. (828)497-2315. www.oconalufteevillage.com

Turn R onto Drama Rd. Follow to top of the hill.

95 Great Smoky Mountains National Park HWY 441 N – Relax and refresh your spirit deep in a forest, alongside a mountain stream or from the edge of a ridgetop with miles of view. Explore the half million-acre International Biosphere Reserve featuring diverse plants and animals. Travel the scenic Newfound Gap Road and enjoy hiking, camping, fishing, picnicking and horseback riding. At the Great Smoky entrance sign, you will find one end of the 1.5 mile river trail running to the Mountain Farm Museum. (865)436-1200. www.nps.gov/grsm

Approximately. .5 mi N of Cherokee on 441.

96 Oconaluftee Visitor Center and Mountain Farm Museum HWY 441 N – Stop at the historic Oconaluftee Visitor Center in season to see native plants and wildflowers nestled alongside the building and to ask where you can explore wild growing species. At the Museum, explore the early 1900's farming lifestyle through self-guiding exhibits and a collection of historic log farm buildings moved to the site in the 1950's. Spring through fall see

The Road Goes On Forever

Side trips, tidbits, adventures, and treasure hunts

Pick up a copy of "Our Southern Highlanders" by Horace Kephart for an historical perspective on life in the Smoky Mountains. Kephart was one of the early proponents of the National Park

representative fields and gardens with a variety of heirloom crops such as broomcorn, turnips and berries. Open daily except Christmas from sunrise to sunset. (828)497-1904.

At the entrance to the Park just past the BRP exit and 1.5 mi N of Cherokee on Hwy 441.

Mingus Mill HWY 441 N – This 1886 gristmill ground corn into cornmeal and wheat into flour for local residents for 50 years. Unique, even for its day, the Mingus Mill is powered by a water-driven turbine instead of a traditional waterwheel. Open Apr–Oct 9am–5pm.

Located .5 mi N of Oconaluftee Visitor Center on Hwy 441.

98 **Mingo Falls** BIG COVE RD – A 200-foot high waterfall sparkles from the vantage point of the foot-trail bridge and provides refreshing inspiration.

Backtrack to Cherokee to L onto Acquoni Rd. Take 1st L onto Big Cove Rd. Continue 5 mi to Mingo Falls Campground area on R and walk the trail (about a five minute hike).

99 **Waterrock Knob** BLUE RIDGE PARKWAY MILE POST 451 – This is the place for a 360-degree panoramic view of the Smokies. While the overlook is a spectacular spot to watch sunrise or sunset, the vista from the trail will have you whistling in admiration at the end of your Whistlestop Tour.

Enter the BRP at its southern beginning at the entrance of the Great Smoky Mtn National Park. 18.2 mi on L past Mile Post 451.

Ever tried to fry corn? Take 6 ears of corn and shave the kernels off the cob. Heat a lump of butter the size of a small egg.

When the butter is hot, put the corn in and fry it. Add salt and pepper. Break 3 eggs and scramble with the corn. Voilà - you've got fried corn!

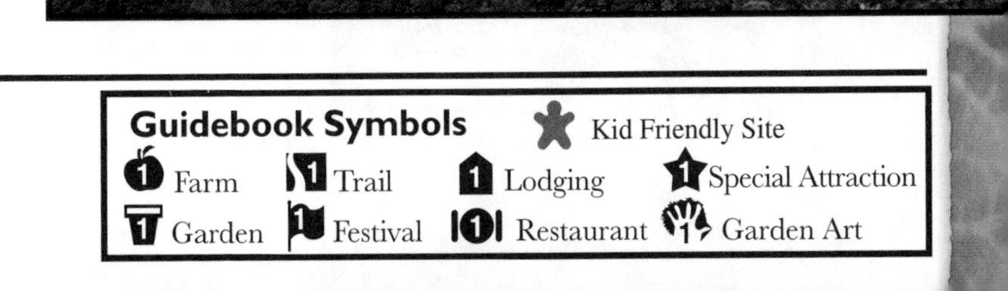

Guidebook Symbols Kid Friendly Site

Farm · Trail · Lodging · Special Attraction

Garden · Festival · Restaurant · Garden Art

Oconaluftee Indian Village

They occupied a kind of Eden, the Principal People, as they called themselves. In the heart of the Southern Appalachians, the area botanists salute as the seed cradle of the continent, the Ani'-Yun'wiya tended soil enriched by the rise and fall of flood waters. Amid mountains of vast beauty and natural wealth—75 percent of medicinal plants known to grow in the United States grow here—they recognized and revered the forest and its trees.

Harmony rather than hierarchy, balance rather than dominion. These were values the Principal People embraced, values neither esteemed nor understood by the white conquistadors, traders and settlers who overwhelmed a people we call Cherokee. Even the name had "no meaning in their own language," wrote ethnologist James Mooney, who spent four years among them (1887-90).

The Principal People's culture was inclusive. Men, women and children attended councils. A matrilineal society whose members belonged to seven clans—among them the Deer, Wolf and Bird. A man moved in with his wife's family after marriage. Men's business was hunting and war; women's tending home, hearth and crops. Foremost among the latter were the "Three Sisters": corn, beans and squash.

In the Principal People's gardens, climbing beans twined round cornstalks and squash, gourd and pumpkin vines ran riot. Most revered of crops was corn, or "selu," around which the Green Corn Ceremony—the tribe's most solemn annual function—revolved. Part propitiation and expiation for past sins, part amnesty for

criminals, part prayer for coming year's happiness and prosperity, the ceremony preceded the first taste of the season's new crop. Care was taken not to blow on the piping hot feast for fear of causing a wind that would flatten the stalks in the field.

Ritual observances attended every aspect of corn's raising. Seven seeds, the sacred number, went into every hill. Shamans entered fields, after the final hoeing to sing songs of invocation to corn's spirit. If properly performed, stalks showed a blessing of ears. A clean trail from field to house encouraged corn to stay at home, to refrain from wandering.

Their "old country is a region of luxuriant flora, with tall trees and tangled undergrowth on the slopes and ridges, and myriad bright-tinted blossoms and sweet wild fruits along the running streams," Mooney wrote. Living in a sylvan paradise, they regarded plants as man's ally, "constantly at [the shamans'] willing service... to counteract the jealous hostility of the animals."

Fragrant cedar, with its evergreen needles and richly hued, fine-grained, warp- and decay-resistant wood, they held in highest esteem. The Principal People learned that pounded chips of walnut bark, cast on a stream's ribbed surface, would stupefy the fish they came to gather in baskets woven of river cane. In root, bark, flower and fruit, they found powerful cures and abundant succor.

Foothill Forays

A cornucopia of treats tucked into rolling hills is template for this trail. Man-made lakes lure wild life. A haze of blue mountains unscrolls as backdrop all along this foothills foray. Now hit the trail in Valdese, where the industrious immigrants transplanted old world values to a new and fertile land. These alpine families fashioned flax into linens, fermented grapes into wine and baked the Word into the staff of life. In nearby Morganton, find history well-preserved in Quaker Meadows. Enjoy a judicious plate of saucy barbecue at an eatery amid swaying willows. Wander an orchard's green aisles with perfect clusters of ripening fruit. Sink your teeth into Blushing Arlet's crisp flesh or drain a glass of fresh-pressed cider. Skirt the South Mountains to Rutherford, through an undulating landscape of field and forest. A frilly pair of Victorian B&Bs share an old English garden. In Sandy Plains, ancient cedars, lily ponds and statuary-studded lawns set off a stately plantation. Guineas forage beside an old general store turned pottery. At Columbus, a restored courthouse presides over Polk County. Take a park bench break to absorb its graceful lines. It's only a hop, skip and jump to Tryon. Horse around this equestrian epicenter, whose mascot Morris, recalls a local toy manufacturer's signature product. Inns, massive 19th century residences

...Pumpkins. From the foothills back into the high country, you'll even find pies that will delight the eyes.

Plantations, Pottery and ...

and even a former sanitorium enjoy sumptuous second bloom. Twist through rock-walled chasms past the cardinal flower and goldenrod along a scenic byway that parallels the nation's steepest railroad grade. Pause at picturesque Pearson's Falls. A town blossomed where a railroad halted at Saluda. On Main Street find a general store unchanged in a century. Forging this community together are cafes, garden shops, galleries and a bakery named Wildflour. The road to Lake Lure hints at Low Country landscapes. Produce stands proclaim okra and fresh figs. Swans reflect in a farm's peaceful pond. Trace the lake's fingers, then wind up Rocky Broad to Chimney Rock for lunch in a rustic inn. The mountain gateway town of Old Fort sports an arrowhead, three museums and a man-made geyser. On to Marion, thistles bristle and scarlet trumpet vine runs rampant. Rambling Carson House tells well-heeled tales of a family's political past. Enjoy iced tea on the veranda of a Greek Revival mansion, then press on to a state park where Lake James invites a dip. Fields of corn and candyroasters ripen in North Cove, at the hem of rugged Linville Mountain. Rise through the trees maintaining toeholds in blocky brown sandstone, past cool limestone caverns carved by water's slow seep. Before you kick off your shoes at trail's end, hike up to Linville Falls. You've crept into High Country.

Foothill Forays

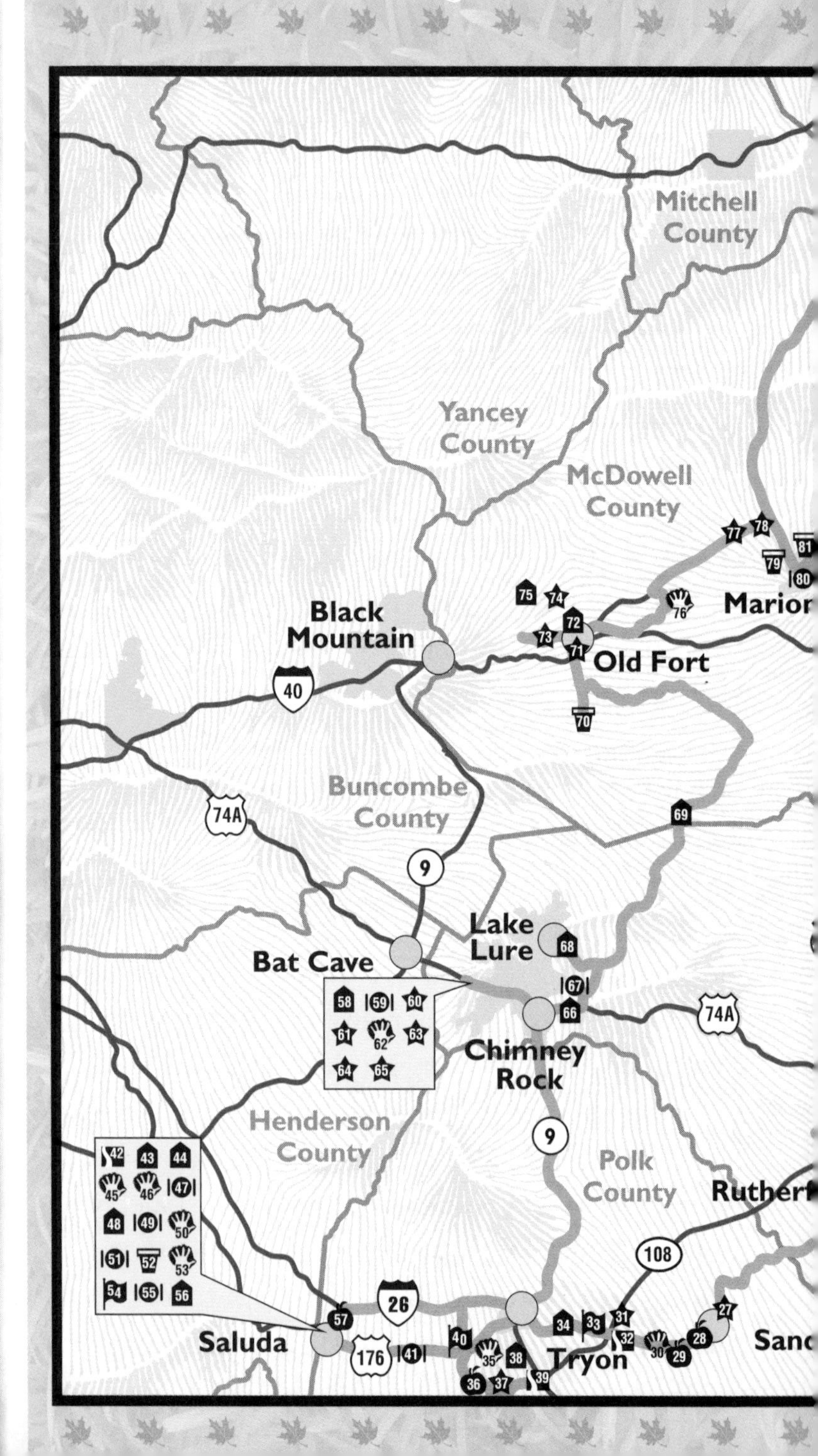

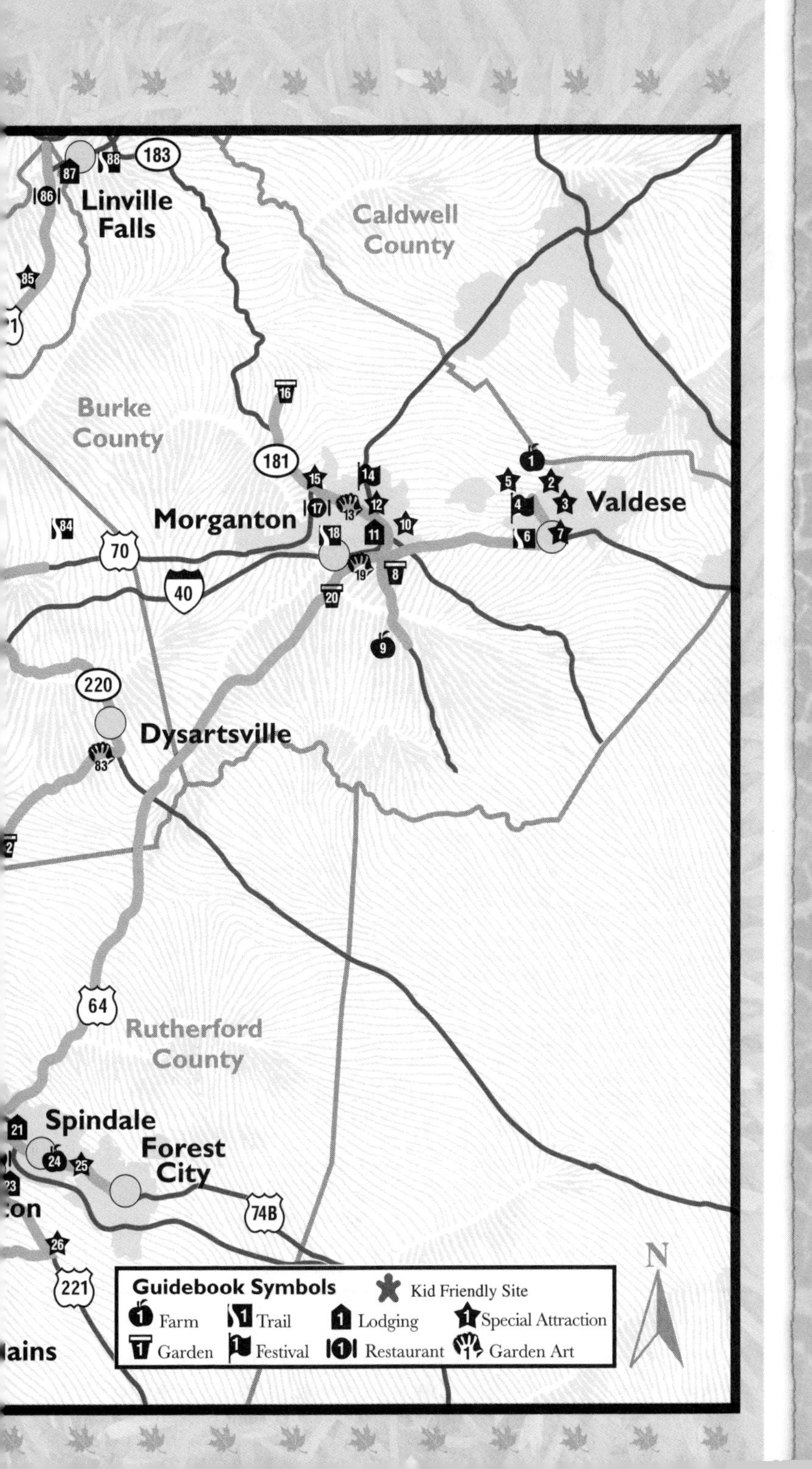

Linville Falls
Caldwell County
Burke County
Morganton
Valdese
Dysartsville
Rutherford County
Spindale
Forest City
183
181
70
40
220
64
74B
221
Guidebook Symbols
Kid Friendly Site
Farm
Trail
Lodging
Special Attraction
Garden
Festival
Restaurant
Garden Art
N

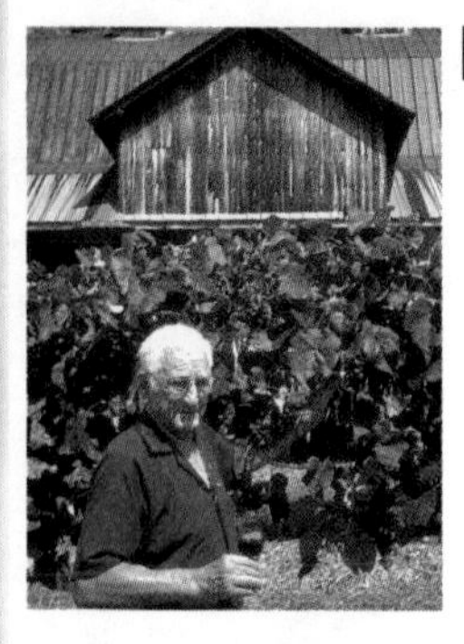

Join Joel Dalmas for a taste of wines made in the hills of WNC.

Don't forget to pack a picnic to enjoy with your Waldensian Wines. Might we suggest you include some of the following items in your basket:

Brie and Gouda Cheeses
Prosciutto and Salami
Sliced Apples and Pears
Grapes
A crusty loaf of fresh-baked bread!

VALDESE

1 Villar Vintners of Valdese 4959 VILLAR LANE NE – "Life is too short to drink bad wine," says Joel Dalmas, a descendant of one of the original Waldensian families of the Cottian Alps that settled in this area. Concord and Niagara grapes are crushed, fermented, filtered, blended, bottled and labeled to evolve into eight different dry, semi-sweet and sweet wines. Conducted tours are followed by free wine tasting whenever the winery is open. Groups of 10 or more by appointment only. Fri, Sat & Sun 1pm–6pm. (828)879-3202. www.ncwine.org

Take Exit 112 off Hwy 40 at Valdese. Go .9 mi on Eldred Rd through Main St. Continue straight on Eldred (it will become Laurel St) for 1.3 mi and turn L on Villar Ln. Go .1 mi and turn L into Waldensian Heritage Wines. Winery is on R.

2 Waldensian Presbyterian Church 109 E MAIN ST – You can't miss the beautiful stone church on Main Street with the adjacent well-manicured grounds of Centennial Park: Featuring a large fountain, picnic tables, bocce court and room to romp on the expanse of grass.

Return to Main St and turn R. Go .4 mi to church on L at intersection with Rodoret St.

3 Waldensian Heritage Museum RODORET ST – Learn the story of the Waldensians, religious immigrants who have kept their heritage and traditions alive since founding the town of Valdese in 1893. Admission is free. Open year-round by appointment. Apr–Oct 3pm–4:30pm. Mid-July–mid-Aug 5pm– 8pm. (828)874-2531.

Turn L on Rodoret St and go .1 mi. Museum will be on R.

4 Waldensian Festival MAIN ST – On the second Saturday in August folks travel to Valdese to enjoy this annual festival known as "The Celebration of the Glorious Return." For over 300 years, Waldenses around the world celebrate the return of their exiled ancestors from Switzerland to the valleys of the Cottian

---

The Road Goes On Forever
Side trips, tidbits, adventures, and treasure hunts

To prevent birdseed from sprouting since birds can be messy eaters, put it in the microwave for a short time to sterilize it.

Alps of Italy in 1689. The town honors the heritage and present day contributions of the Waldensians with music, crafts, food and foot races. 9am–4pm.
(828)879-2116. www.valdese.com/festival

Trail of Faith 307 CHURCH ST NW – A committed group of Waldensian descendants led by Jimmy Jacumin, used their ingenuity, perseverance, and a bulldozer to move umpteen tons of dirt to construct miniature Alps and fifteen buildings and monuments replicating and honoring those of the Waldensian homeland. Tour lasts approximately one to two hours. Admission: Adults $5 & Students $3. Open year-round Mon–Fri by appointment. May–Oct Sat–Sun 2pm–5pm. (828)874-1893. www.waldensians.com.

Turn R on St Germain and go .2 mi. Turn R on Waldo St and then L on Main St. Go 2 blocks and turn R on Church St. Travel .3 mi to Trail of Faith and amphitheater on R.

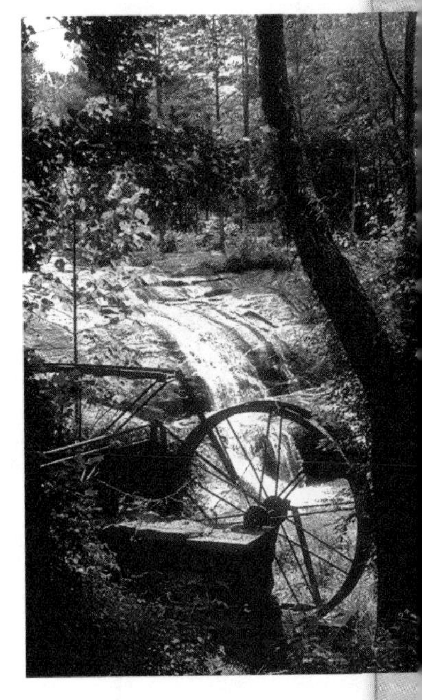

McGalliard Falls/Meytre's Grist Mill CHURCH ST – The Valdese Recreation Department maintains this beautiful park featuring Meytre Mill, a replica of an early gristmill. Other highlights include a 45-foot waterfall, nature trails, picnic facilities and a children's play area. Shelter can be reserved for a fee. 8am–dark. (828)879-2132.

Continue 1 mi up Church St to park on R.

Burke County Farmer's Market MAIN ST – About the time the dew dries, farmers pull into the parking lot across from City Hall to form a colorful strand of glistening, fresh Burke County vegetables. Turnips, green beans, sweet corn, tomatoes, okra and cabbage beckon in the mid-morning sun. Open late-May–Oct. Wed & Sat 10am–12noon. Fri 4pm–7pm. (828)439-4460.

Return to Main St and turn L. Travel one block to the parking lot on R across from City Hall and Myra's Restaurant.

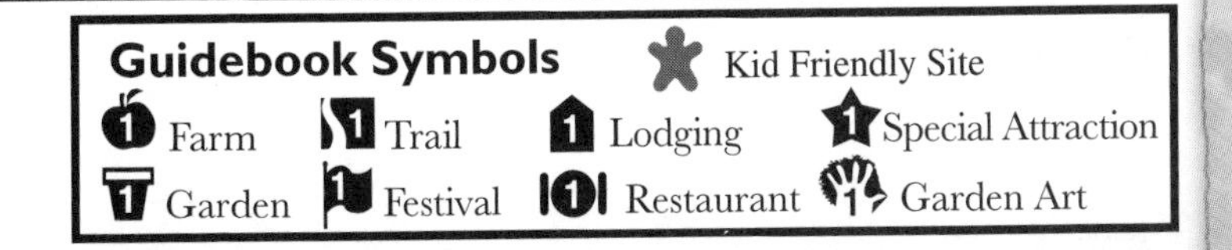

If you are in need of some flowers to grow successfully under trees in your yard, try these:

Astilbes

Epimediums

Hostas

Lenten Rose

Lily-of-the-valley

Plumbago or Leadwort

Serbian Bellflower

MORGANTON

8 **Western Carolina Center** 300 ENOLA RD – The herb garden, vegetable garden, corn field, and flower garden all show evidence of the loving care bequeathed to them by Don Chapman and his greenhouse students at this center for the disabled. With wheelchair access into the greenhouse, students may learn to grow cabbage, kale, pansies, mums and other plants as well as create their own propagation pots. Stevie Wonder once said, "Just because a man lacks the use of his eyes doesn't mean he lacks vision." Indeed. Mon–Fri 9am–3 pm. (828)433-2665. The South Mountain Craft Village at 104 ENOLA RD, features handcrafted items made by WCC residents as well as a Farmer's Market on Thu 8:30am–12noonish. (828)433-2607.

In Valdese, return to Hwy 40 W and continue to Morganton. Take Exit 104 and go L on Enola Rd for .2 mi to Craft Village on R. Then continue on Enola Rd for .4 mi to wooden picket fence on L. Turn into lot in front of greenhouse.

9 **Apple Hill Orchard & Cider Mill** 5205 APPLETREE LN – For over 70 years, locals have honored teachers and kept doctors at bay with either a Gala, Red Delicious, Golden, Jonagold, Stayman, Winesap, Red Rome, Red Fuji, Braeburn or Granny Smith apple. The farmer's market here is stocked with jams, jellies, and cider that the Prewitt family presses each year. School tours available for fee. Late-Aug–Dec Mon–Sat 9am–sundown. (828)437-1224.

Continue S on Enola Rd 3.4 mi to R on Pleasant Hill Ave just beside Pleasant Hill Baptist Church. Go .1 mi and turn R at Apple Hill Orchard sign.

10 **The Penny Patch Produce and Garden Center** FLEMING RD – Produce, pickled beets and pigs' feet make way for the delectable confections of Two Harts Bakery, such as blackberry wine cake, whole wheat sourdough bread and peach almond cake. Mon–Fri 9am–6pm & Sat 8:30am–4pm. Closed Aug.

The Road Goes On Forever

Side trips, tidbits, adventures, and treasure hunts

(828)433-0791.
Go 4.8 mi back up Enola to L on Sterling for .8 mi to R on Fleming. Travel .9 mi to produce stand on L.

 **The College Street Inn** 204 S COLLEGE ST – For proximity to the historic downtown district with its vibrant shops, boutiques and restaurants, you can't get any closer to the action than the College Street Inn. Spacious rooms, customized gourmet meals and small but intensive landscaping. (828)430-8911. www.thecollegestreeetinn.com.
Return R on Fleming for .9 mi to across Sterling to first R on College St. Go .5 mi to inn on L.

12 Burke County Farmer's Market COLLEGE ST – Not long after the rooster crows and early birds sing, you'll find local green and growing things on tempting exhibit in an otherwise ordinary parking lot. Late May–Oct Wed & Sat 6:30am–8:30am. (828)439-4460.
Turn L on College St and go .1 mi to lot on the R. Look for the Bradford pear trees in front of the lot and just past a school.

Since tomatoes are the most widely grown plant in vegetable gardens, you'll definitely find plenty to choose from at the Burke County Farmer's Market.

13 Purple Penguin and Petals and Pots 106 W UNION ST – Teresa Fitzpatrick and the McBain sisters continually unearth and reveal beyond the ordinary treasures such as dried flowers, stained glass stepping stones, live plant topiaries, wreaths, painted pots and birdhouses. Great gift shop for a fun and funky dig. Tue–Fri 10am–5pm & Sat 10am–4pm. (828)439-9030.
Take Business 70 downtown (Meeting St) to L on Hwy 18 (Green St) to L on Business 70 (W Union St). Shop is on R on second block.

14 Historic Morganton Festival DOWNTOWN – Join locals the weekend after Labor Day to pay tribute to the town named after Revolutionary War leader Daniel Morgan and where Senator Sam Ervin, Jr. once practiced law at the 1837

Lily Growing Tips

Lilies grow best in groups of three or more. Plant lilies in late October when bulbs are "resting". Leave at least 12-18 inches between bulbs since they will multiply and use the extra space. Cover tightly with soil to prevent air pockets that could dry out the roots.

Mulch lilies with grass clippings or compost. Mulching helps to conserve moisture, keep soil cool, and prevent the weeds from germinating. Keeping mulch on bulbs in winter helps to moderate the soil temperature. In spring, it can help to prevent the early emergence of lilies, hopefully preventing frost-damage.

Fall housekeeping for lilies includes removing the dead foliage. It will help to prevent disease problems and allow for good drainage and air circulation for the bulbs.

Burke County Courthouse. Over 400 craft vendors and musicians create a cacophony of colors, smells and sounds through the city's greenway district. Fri 11am–10pm. Sat 9am–10pm. Sun 11am–5pm. (828)438-5252.

15 **Quaker Meadows House** ST MARY'S CHURCH RD – Zinnias and bee balm sway in the breeze where once stood the "Council Oak," the site of patriot soldiers meeting to plan the defeat of loyalists at the Battle of Kings Mountain, the turning point of the Revolutionary War in the South. Now in peaceful times, the garden provides pause for reflection in among the cucumbers, sweet potatoes, chamomile, basil and echinacea. The 1812 Federal–style house is on the National Register of Historic Places and a certified site on the Overmountain Victory National Historic Trail. Admission: Adults $3, Student $1 & Children under 12 Free. House tours Apr–Oct Sun 2pm–5pm. Grounds open year-round sunrise to sunset. (828)437-4104.

Take Union St on back to College St and turn R. Go .6 mi to L on Green St (Hwy 181). Go 1.2 mi to R on St Mary's Church Rd. House is on L at .1 mi.

16 **Millstone Meadows** 2595 HENDERSON MILL RD – Welcome to Lily Land! Charles Henson's 1400 varieties of daylilies express themselves in several gardens including the Tasty Treat bed (lilies representing ice cream flavors), the Guitar bed (lilies to take musical note of) and the Heart bed. Lined up in the sun in colorful rows, the lilies swoon with the sound of their own names such as Passion Portals, Dressed to Kill, Rainbow Eyes and Muscadine Pie. A '46 Ford pick up parks permanently with a bed of purple petunias in tow. This American Hemerocallis Society display garden is open mid-June–mid-July Tue–Sat 9am–6pm. Closed Sun & Mon. (828)437-7277.

Double back on St Mary's Church Rd and turn R on Hwy 181. Travel 4.2 mi to R on Goodman Lake Rd. Continue to Henderson Mill Rd and turn R. Go .4 mi to R into Millstone Gardens for .1 mi.

The Road Goes On Forever
Side trips, tidbits, adventures, and treasure hunts

SPOT IT
It's somewhere on this loop. Can you find it?

Judge's Riverside Restaurant GREENLEE FORD RD – It's the law to enjoy smokehouse barbecue on the outdoor dining deck beside the graceful Catawba River. For a light sentence, try the Balsamic chicken salad but best to begin with a preliminary hearing such as fresh Brunswick stew and finish in the witness box with homemade chocolate fudge pie. Case closed. Open daily 11am–10pm. (828)433-5798.

Return by Goodman Lake Rd to L on Hwy 181 to Morganton. Go 4.9 mi to R on Sanford Dr (Hwy 64 bypass). Go 1.1 mi to R on Hwy 70. Travel .4 mi to R on Greenlee Ford Rd. Go .2 mi to L to restaurant.

Sit back, relax and take time to enjoy the sounds of the river while you enjoy your meal at Judge's.

Catawba River Greenway GREENLEE FORD – The over 6 miles of paved hiking, biking, running and walking trails along the Catawba River and adjacent to Judge's is a good place to walk off the pounds of evidence you acquired at the restaurant. Nature observation areas, fishing piers, shops and picnic areas. Open sunrise to sunset. (828)438-5270.

Fourth Creek Folk Art Studio 308 FOREST HILL RD – These birdhouses are not just for the birds. Don Stevenson's miniature historic replicas of old barns, general stores and mills offer sanctuary for feathered friends and delight for trail hoppers looking for evidence of the restoration of our vanishing rural scene. Tue–Thu 9am–12 noon & 1pm–5pm. (828)433-6118.

Return on Hwy 70 (W Union St) towards Morganton for 1.4 mi to R on Hwy 64 (Burkemont Ave). Go .3 mi to R on Patton and then .1 mi to L on Forest Hill St. Travel .2 mi to studio on R.

You can find more of Don Stevenson's birdhouses, like the one pictured below, at Fourth Creek Folk Art Studio.

Western Piedmont Community College 1001 BURKEMONT AVE – A curly willow tree beckons you to the campus greenhouses with exotic orchids and ferns. Down the hill on the far side of the campus parking lot, a nature trail leads to an amphitheater by a reed-lined lake. The

arboretum focuses on native trees such as serviceberry, contorted white pines, and Carolina hemlock. It serves as a seed source or, in collegiate terminology, The Return of the Native, for anyone wanting to perpetuate these species. Horticultural classes and workshops available. Greenhouse tours by appointment. Open Mon–Fri 8am–10pm. Closed Sat & Sun. (828)438-6075. www.wp.cc.nc.us

From Forest Hill Rd, turn L on Greenbriar Ln and go .1 mi to R on Burkemont (Hwy 64). Travel .6 mi to the campus on your L and then .6 mi to greenhouse. (Also at Exit 103 off of Hwy 40).

A mulch is a layer of material spread on the surface of the soil to retain moisture and retard weed growth. Free, or minimal cost, organic mulch materials include leaves, pine needles, sawdust, seaweed, wood chips and shavings, spoiled hay, straw, rotten wood, hulls or shells, and corn cobs or stalks.

RUTHERFORDTON

21 **Carrier Houses Bed & Breakfast** 249 & 255 N MAIN ST – The vivid fuchsia of crepe myrtle blossoms provides the frame around the extensive water garden between the two Victorian homes listed on the National Register of Historic Places. The romance of a by gone era is captured somewhere between the large shade trees, hanging baskets, trellises, and flowering plants. Coneflowers and koi, fountains and fairies await. (800)835-7071. www.carrierhouses.com

Travel 17 mi on Hwy 64 to L on Cane Creek Rd for 1.5 mi. Turn L back onto Hwy 64 for approximately 10 mi to city limits of Rutherfordton at intersection. Continue through stoplight to Hwy 221 intersection. Turn L (S) and go .8 mi. B&B is on R next to the Rutherford County Courthouse.

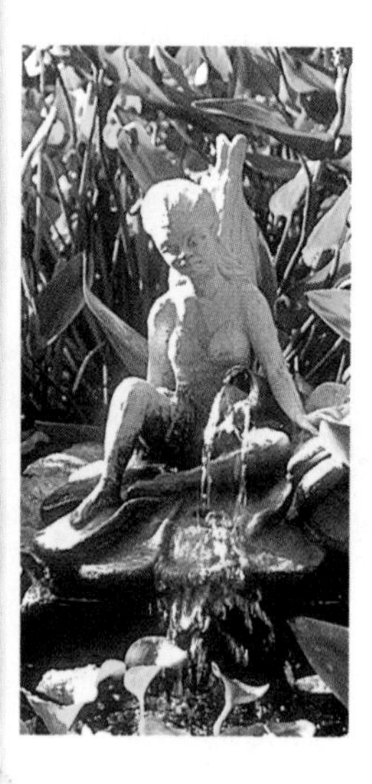

22 **The Vineyard Family Restaurant** 211 MAIN ST – Salmon–stuffed fresh tomatoes, Chicken a la Vodka, homemade crab cakes, lasagna and bruschetta with homemade marinara sauce are just a few of the entrée choices to agonize over at this café with a small water garden. Live classical and jazz music for your entertainment Thu & Fri. Koi to be coy over. Mon–Thu 11am–9pm & Fri–Sat 11am–10 pm. (828)288-0240.

Hop, skip and a jump from the B&B on the R.

23 **Pinebrae Manor** 1286 NC 108 HWY – This charming and spotless B&B was once the administration building for the early-1900

The Road Goes On Forever

Side trips, tidbits, adventures, and treasure hunts

For a refreshing drink, add one tablespoon of raspberry vinegar to a cup of iced water.

Rutherford County home for the indigent and elderly, many of whom farmed and canned produce on-site. Now the grounds of the manor on "The Hill of Pine" are home to visiting families of ground hogs, deer and fox. Your family will want to visit the .8-mile nature trail where you can nibble blackberries and raspberries as you walk. Hydrangeas, irises and gladiola grace the front lawn of the Georgian style manor. Don't miss the belt-busting breakfast. Open Mar 15–Nov 30. (828)286-1543. www.pinebrae.blueridge.net

From Hwy 221 (Main St) continue S about .2 mi to R on Hwy 108. Follow 108 signs through residential area for 2.5 mi to R into B&B.

Raspberry Vinegar
3 lbs. fresh raspberries
4 cups white wine vinegar
Sugar as needed
Wash raspberries and place in a large jar. Cover with vinegar. Allow to stand, covered, for 8 days. Stir gently every day.

Side trip to Spindale, Forest City and Lone Weak

24 Rutherford County Farmer's Market – Here's a barnful of big, beautiful fruits and vegetables to load up on as you trailblaze. May–Nov. Fri 7am–12noon in spring and early summer. Tue & Thu 7am–12noon in mid- to late-summer. (828)287-6010.

Turn R on Hwy 74 Business E and go 2.9 mi through Spindale and turn R on Fairgrounds Rd and go .3 mi. Turn R at big open-air barn.

25 Rutherford County Farm Museum 240 DEPOT ST – Have you ever seen a left-handed plow, a livermush paddle or a gas iron? Wilbur Burgin wants to show you these as well as hundreds of other artifacts dating back to the 19th century. Two large murals depict the cycle of growing cotton and the early textile mills of the county. Admission: Adults $2 & Children free. Wed–Sat 10am–4pm. (828)248-1248.

Continue E on Hwy 74 Business for 1.7 mi. Turn R on Depot St and go .2 mi and then L on S. Powell St for .1 mi. Turn R on E. Main St to museum on R.

Baked Peaches

1 dozen peaches
1 cup granulated sugar

Prick peaches all over with a fork and set them close together in a baking dish. Sprinkle with sugar, and add just enough water to cover the bottom of the dish. Bake until soft. Serve with ice cream.

Meanwhile back on the trail....

26 **Sunnyside Orchard** 1581 HWY 221 S – Pick a peck of yellow and white peaches at Larry Crowe's third generation family roadside orchard. Also a good source for watermelons, cantaloupes, corn, okra, tomatoes and locust honey. Mid-June–mid-Sep 7am–7pm. (828)287-4012.

Return to the intersection of Hwys 108 and 221 in Rutherfordton. Turn R onto Hwy 221S and travel approximately 4.3 mi to orchard on L.

27 **Green River Plantation** COXE RD – Fiddle dee dee. Scarlett O'Hara trounced out of the wrong house. It should have been this 1804 one where Union soldiers' horse hoof prints are indelibly imprinted on the heart-of-pine floor and where genteel belles tested the integrity of their diamonds by scratching them on a now 200 year-old glass pane in the front lobby. The Cantrell family's hospitality and originality is apparent in their tours, weddings, receptions, dinners and lunches, gift shop and B&B service. The 366-acre plantation features idyllic water and boxwood gardens, contented Chinese geese, ostriches, ducks and emus. Oil from the emus is gathered and sent to Pennsylvania to produce a line of emu beauty and health products that are sold in the on-site gift shop. Lots of old carriage trails to explore. Tour admission: Adults $10 & Seniors $9. (828)286-1461. www.green-river.net

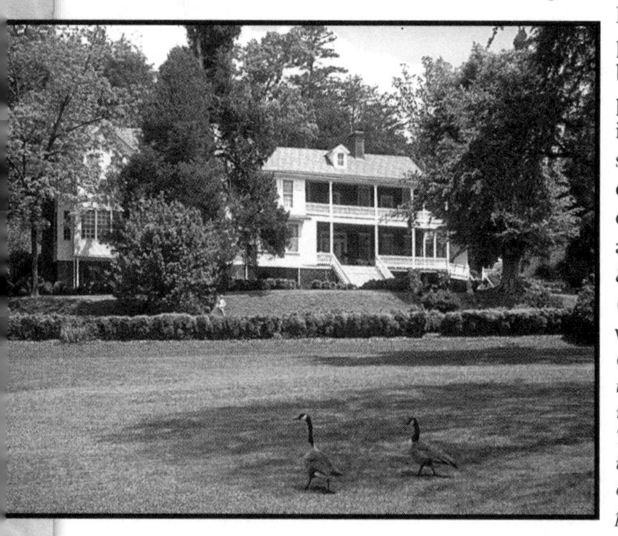

Continue on 221 S for .5 mi to R on Hwy 74 W. Go 4.5 mi to Exit 173 at Union Rd. Turn R and go .3 mi to intersection with Coxe Rd and turn R. Travel .8 mi to plantation on your R.

The Road Goes On Forever

Side trips, tidbits, adventures, and treasure hunts

Windy Hill Farm If you've never seen an "Easter Egg" chicken, check out the Araucana/Americana chickens at Windy Hill Farm where they incubate the festive multi-colored eggs. There's an heirloom garden to explore as well. Apr–Oct. Call Kay Russell exact hours. (828)272-9058

From plantation, turn R on Coxe Rd and go 1.1 mi to merge with Sandy Plains Rd. From Sandy Plains Road, turn R onto Moore Road and travel approximately 1 mi. to R onto Windy Hill Lane. Farm is at 111 Windy Hill Lane.

Egg Trivia:

About 240 million laying hens produce approximately 5.5 billion dozen eggs per year in the United States.

A hen requires 24 to 26 hours to produce an egg.

SANDY PLAINS

Rockhouse Vineyards and Winery 1525 TURNER RD – The first vines at Lee Griffin and Marsha Cassedy's 200-acre farm were planted in 1991. Since then, the Chardonnay and Chambourcin wines have won medals in various national wine competitions. they also feature the Viognier and Cabernet Franc grapes. The interesting rock building with rocks from 35 states and an assortment of oddities such as light bulbs and car parts built into the walls, some having been contributed by Mrs. Carl Sandburg. Open for tours and wine tasting Mar–Dec Thu–Sun 1pm–5pm. Closed Jan & Feb. (828)863-2784.

Backtrack to Sandy Plains Rd and turn R to intersection with Hwy 9. Turn R and go .9 mi to R on Turner Rd. Drive 1.5 mi to vineyard entrance.

Try these fast-growing flowering vines for your garden:

Clematis
Dutchman's-pipe Vine
Five-leaf Akebia
Scarlet Runner Bean
Trumpet Honeysuckle

Little Mountain Pottery 6372 PENIEL RD – Having been around the world and back again working with folk potters, Claude and Elaine Graves have tried to "capture North Carolina in clay and glaze." You can watch them at work on the potters wheel, glazing and decorating and firing and unloading kilns in a centuries-old process. Stoneware and salt-fired pieces, clay sculpture and whimsical works such as

Guidebook Symbols Kid Friendly Site
Farm, Trail, Lodging, Special Attraction
Garden, Festival, Restaurant, Garden Art

unusual birdbaths and feeders. Open Mon–Sat 10am–4pm or by appointment. (828)894-8091.

Return to Hwy 9 S and go .1 mi to R on Peniel Rd. Travel 1.3 mi to L into studio.

COLUMBUS

31 **Polk County Courthouse** 1 COURTHOUSE ST – The 142-year-old antebellum Greek Revival courthouse is the oldest active one in Western North Carolina. Open Mon–Fri 8:30am–5pm. (828)894-3301.

Turn L onto Peniel Rd and continue 5.9 mi. Turn L on Walker St and then R onto Hwy 108 (Mills St). Courthouse is on R.

32 **Stearn's Park** MILLS ST – Across the street from the courthouse is a great place to stretch your legs. Gazebo, benches, picnic tables and a gravel walking path around Stearn's School provide escape from the planet of the car seat. Sunrise to sunset. (828)863-4384.

33 **Fabulous Fourth** MILLS ST – If you are a master at impeccable timing and can time your trip so, you would do well to find yourself here on the 4th of July when food, crafts as well as Big Band, jazz, rock, beach, dance and country music invade the nooks and crannies of this American town. 8am–5pm. (828)894-8236.

Check out Rogers Park next door to Town Hall in Tryon. You'll find a beautiful amphitheater with rock walls, native plants, a small creek and short trails through which to meander. (828)859-6655.

TRYON

34 **Stone Hedge Inn** 222 STONE HEDGE LANE – Vivaldi's Four Seasons unfold beautifully in the rich hues and scents emanating from the old and new gardens surrounding the fieldstone inn. Springtime brings pink azaleas, dogwoods and royal purple iris, while summer boasts the heady magnolias and riotous perennial borders. The golden hues of autumn are enhanced with the vast camellia gardens that bravely unfold through the winter months. Access the terraced beds by the network of paths or take a short hike up the road behind the Inn to

The Road Goes On Forever

Side trips, tidbits, adventures, and treasure hunts

the locally famous Pearson's Falls. Gourmet offerings from breakfast to dinner to Sunday brunch include, for example, smoked salmon, grilled portobella mushrooms, NC mountain trout and eggplant parmesan. Dinner Wed–Sat 6pm–9pm. Sunday brunch 12noon–2:30pm. (828)859-9114. www.stone-hedge-inn.com

Continue W on Hwy 108 approximately 3 mi. Turn R on Howard Gap Rd and travel 1.3 mi. Turn R on Stone Hedge Ln and follow to top.

35 Kathleen Carson Hand Painted Tiles

66 OLAMAE WAY – If your garden or grounds are needing an extra "oomph", you may want to check out Kathleen's decorative tile signs or sculptural planters. If nothing else, absorb the beauty of her craft at her studio as she forms clay and paints tiles. You'll find more of her pieces for sale at her husband's place - Saluda Forge. Mon–Fri 9am–5pm. (828)859-8316. www.tileandiron.com

Return to Hwy 108 W into merger with Hwy 176 into Tryon. Just across from Palmer St turn R onto Olamae Way. Studio is immediately on R.

For garden flowers that return year after year with spectacular results, try these 10 annuals. They don't need replanting.

Chinese Forget-Me-Not
Cornflower
Cosmos
Garden Balsam
Love-In-A-Mist
Mignonette
Poppies
Pot Marigold
Rocket Larkspur
Sunflowers

36 Posey Hollow Farms

105 MAPLE ST – When you see the wall mural of a woman picking yellow eggplant in a field of various vegetables, you'll know you've found the entrance to a produce-packing paradise. Jeff Tempest's manufacturing facility for jams, jellies, pickles, relish, chutneys, honey and hot sauce will have you debating which of your whiney kids to leave in Tryon to get another few pickle jars in the car. OK, go easy on the kids, but wedge in a box of garden herb bread mix. Thu–Fri 10am–5pm & Sat 10am–2pm. (828)859-0110.

Turn back onto N Trade St (Hwy 176) and go R. Just past Palmer St, turn L on Maple St and park on the hill. Store is on the L.

Guidebook Symbols

Kid Friendly Site
Farm · Trail · Lodging · Special Attraction
Garden · Festival · Restaurant · Garden Art

We don't have the corn liquor recipe, but we do have one for Corncob Molasses.

Take a dozen sweet corn cobs and boil about 3/4 hour in 3 pints of water. Take out cobs and strain. Add a pound of brown sugar to the juice. Boil down to a syrup. Use it as a substitute for maple molasses.

37 **Polk County Historical Museum** 22 DEPOT ST – If old Uncle Bill had a still on the hill, it very well could have been in these here parts. In the early part of the last century, some local farmers supplemented their income with the production of corn liquor. The still is still here at this quaint little museum in the old Depot building where you'll also find a spinning wheel, quilts and dresses, oxen yokes, farming hand tools and a recipe for the illegal brew. No admission charged, but all donations are appreciated. Tue & Thu 10am–12noon. Closed July–Aug. (828)894-2505.

Turn L back onto Hwy 176 (Trade St) and then R onto Pacolet St. Take immediate R on Depot and museum will be on R.

38 **Pine Crest Inn** 85 PINE CREST LN – What once served as a tuberculosis center is now an elegant inn with an outer circle of charming cottages and extensive perennial and rose gardens. Tastes of the region are captured in such dishes as Forest Mushroom Bisque, Cornmeal Crusted Trout, and raspberry and strawberry crepes. (800)633-3001. www.pinecrestinn.com

Continue S down Trade St alongside the railroad tracks, past the historic Morris the Horse on R. Turn L onto New Market St for .2 mi to L on Pine Crest Ln.

39 **Foothills Equestrian Nature Center (FENCE)** 3381 HUNTING COUNTRY RD – Year-round nature and equestrian programs are provided by this non-profit, such as Bonsai and Oriental Gardening, birding, landscape design, and Saturday hikes. While hikes usually occur on the seven miles of trail on the property, they vary from photo hikes to wildflower hikes to children's hikes including nature adventures. Trails open Mon–Sun dawn–dusk. Nature Center open Mon–Fri 9am–12noon & 1pm–4pm. There are no hikes in July, Aug & Jan. Call for more information. (828)859-9021. www.FENCE.org

Turn L on New Market St and continue 1.5 mi to L on Hunting Country Rd. Travel approximately 2 mi to L to FENCE entrance.

The Road Goes On Forever

Side trips, tidbits, adventures, and treasure hunts

Blue Ridge Barbecue Festival HARMON FIELD – This NC Governor-sanctioned State Barbecue Championship is the real deal. Whether it's the Down East vinegar-based variety or the tomato-based Western North Carolina version, be ready to pig out the second Friday and Saturday in June each year. 10am–11pm. (828)859-7427. www.blueridgebbqfestival.com

Return on Hwy 176 (Trade St) back through Tryon past the intersection with Hwy 108. Bear L on Hwy 176 towards Saluda. Turn R on Harmon Field Rd and Harmon Field (site of the festival) will be on your immediate L.

Folks in Eastern NC serve pork with a vinegar sauce, while folks in Western NC add tomato to their sauce. Either way - Yum Yum!

Caro Mi Restaurant 3231 US HWY 176 N – Carolina country ham, cooked apples, fresh chicken livers and Rainbow Mountain trout filleted at your table. This well-known and locally favored restaurant is perched in front of the Pacolet River, accessible by an old covered bridge. Wed–Thu 5pm–8pm & Fri–Sat 5pm–8:30pm. Reservations encouraged. (828)859-5200.

At merge of Hwys 176 and 108 in Tryon, continue on Hwy 176 for 2.7 mi towards Saluda. Restaurant will be on L.

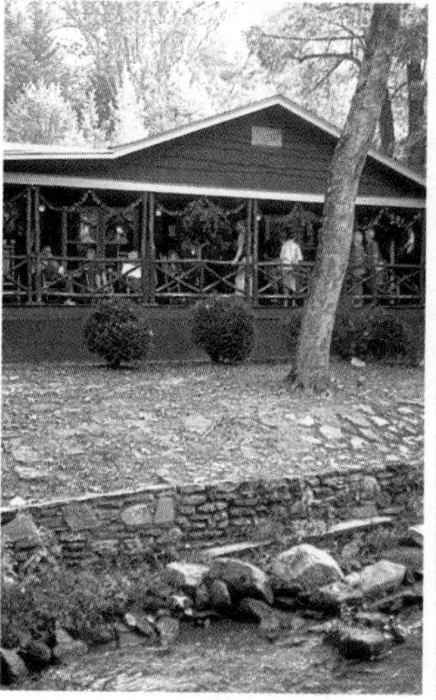

Pearson's Falls OFF HWY 176 N – In 1931, the Tryon Garden Club came to the rescue to save this wildlife preserve from a timber company. It is now an N.C. Natural Heritage Area. Ever since, these dedicated folks have kept a diligent watch over the pristine falls, the one-quarter-mile trail and the over 200 varieties of ferns, wildflowers, algae and mosses found in the glen. Picnicking permitted. Admission: Adults $2, Children over age 6 .50 & Children under 6 free. Mar 1–Oct 31 10am–6pm & Nov 1–Feb 28 10am–5pm. Closed Mon & Tue during Nov–Feb. Closed Mon year-round except holidays. (828)859-2022.

Continue on Hwy 176 towards Saluda for 1.8 mi. Turn L at sign and travel .8 mi to Falls entrance on L.

Need some moss growing around your rock garden? Pour a mixture of blended moss, water and buttermilk wherever you want moss to grow. Proportions of the items don't really matter, but add more water if it is too thick to pour.

Keep your boots in the garden where you need them. Upend your rubber boots on stakes when you're through gardening for the day. They will stay dry inside and be ready to slip on when your garden's wet.

SALUDA

43 Orchard Inn HWY 176 – On the uphill trip from Saluda, you'll want to turn off at this inn where you can take a real bite of life. Originally built for the Southern Railway folks around 1900, the inn sits on a 12-acre crest of the Warrior Range atop the Blue Ridge, offering an incredible panoramic view from the sun porch dining room. Couple that with the gourmet renderings of Chef Monte Weber such as Fresh Spinach with Roasted Red Peppers and a Champagne Vinaigrette, Zuchini and Onion Stuffed Quail with Jasmine Rice and a Marsala Sauce. Ratchet it up another notch by eating your Mountain Berry Cobbler under the grapevine arbor and next to the fragrant purple-blossomed paulownia tree. A vineyard of cabernet sauvignon, merlot and sauvignon blanc is in the works, and there's even a nature trail to explore. The four cottages nestled in the hardwoods feature fireplaces, whirlpool baths and private decks. Dinner served Tue–Sat at 7pm by reservation only. (800)581-3800. www.orchardinn.com

Turn L back onto Hwy 176 and travel 2 mi. Turn L at sign. Go up the drive for .1 mi.

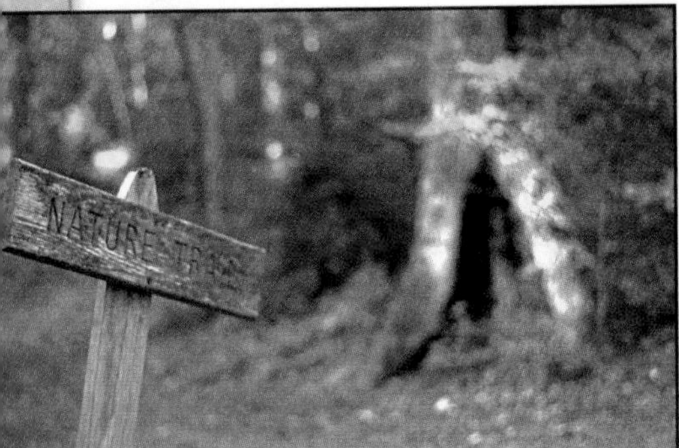

A culinary tip for the fresh vegetables from your garden: never soak diced vegetables in water before preparing them or they will lose their nutrients.

44 Sandy Cut Cabins PEARSON FALLS RD – If cabins are your cup of tea, stay in one of these two cozy one-bedroom/loft cabins at the Saluda entrance to Pearson Falls. Bordered by the Norfolk/Southern Railroad and the Pacolet River, you can hike and fish to the nostalgic sound of trains topping the Saluda Grade at Sandy Cut. Call Robert or Penny Phillips. (828)749-9555. www.vrbo.com/vrbo/4547.htm

Turn L back onto Hwy 176 and go approximately .6 mi to L on Pearson Falls Rd. Travel 2 mi down dirt road through tunnel to cabins on L.

The Road Goes On Forever

Side trips, tidbits, adventures, and treasure hunts

The Monarch Butterfly will only lay its eggs on the milkweed plant, and the milkweed is the only plant the caterpillars will eat.

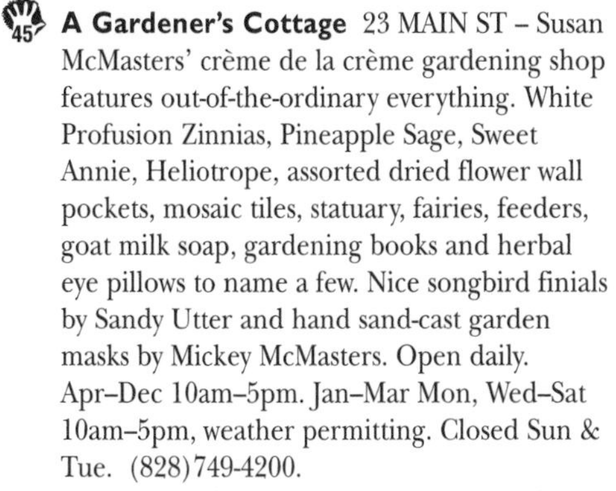

45 A Gardener's Cottage 23 MAIN ST – Susan McMasters' crème de la crème gardening shop features out-of-the-ordinary everything. White Profusion Zinnias, Pineapple Sage, Sweet Annie, Heliotrope, assorted dried flower wall pockets, mosaic tiles, statuary, fairies, feeders, goat milk soap, gardening books and herbal eye pillows to name a few. Nice songbird finials by Sandy Utter and hand sand-cast garden masks by Mickey McMasters. Open daily. Apr–Dec 10am–5pm. Jan–Mar Mon, Wed–Sat 10am–5pm, weather permitting. Closed Sun & Tue. (828)749-4200.

At intersection of Hwy 176 (Main St) and Pearson Falls Rd on L.

46 Saluda Forge CORNER OF MAIN AND PEARSON FALLS RD – Bill Crowell III says, "If you can dream it, I'll create it." In the garden realm it can be gates, fences, trellises, topiary pyramids or whatever you can conjure up. Mon–Sat 10am–5pm. (828)749-1713. www.saludaforge.com.

Just behind A Gardener's Cottage.

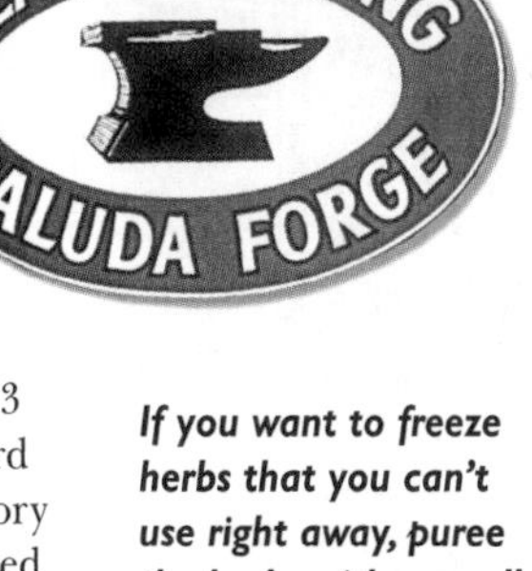

47 Good Thyme Café/Wildflour Bakery 173 E. MAIN ST – Should have been named Hard Time Café for having to decide between savory spinach quiche, smoked turkey on fresh baked cracked wheat bread, homemade granola with yogurt and fresh fruit and a number of other selections. There are even sticky buns, blueberry muffins, herb egg muffins and more for breakfast. Catering, special diets and take-out lunches available. Dining decisions Mon & Wed–Sat 7:30am–3pm. Sun brunch 9am–2pm. Closed Tue. (828)749-9224.

Next to A Gardener's Cottage.

If you want to freeze herbs that you can't use right away, puree the herbs with a small amount of olive oil then freeze in icecube trays. You can add the herb cube to your cooking as the need arises.

48 Charles Street Garden Suite 76 CHARLES ST – Prepare yourself for the magical world awaiting you in this secret garden with all the charm, mystique and romance of a fairy tale. A maze of green and growing things so vast that your peripheral vision will get a workout. The

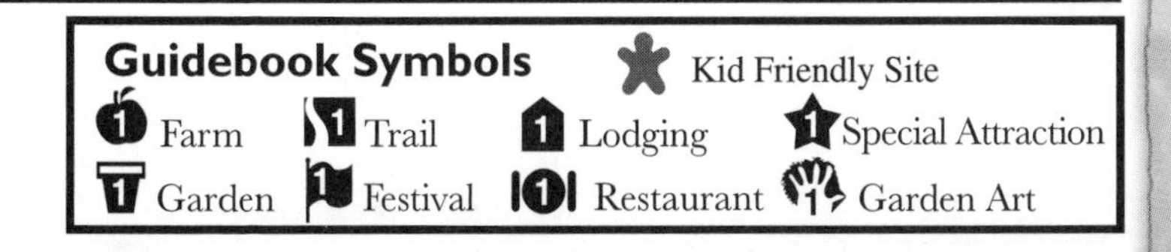

Make a wreath that's for the birds! Simply mix peanut butter, birdseed & suet. Spread the mixture on a pine cone or small grapevine wreath. Hang it in a tree for your fine feathered friends to enjoy nature's bounty.

guest suite overlooks this private garden guarded by a giant chestnut oak and no doubt, gnomes or fairies of some sort. If you can't believe in magic here, you need to give up the search. Half deposits required within five days of request. In order to insure privacy, gardens are only open to guests. Gardens are not handicapped accessible. (828)749-5846. www.saluda.com/charlesstreet

Continue on Main St into Saluda. Just past the school on the R, make the first R on Culliphen. Travel 1 block and turn L on Henderson and then an immediate R on Charles. Turn R into Episcopal Church parking and the Suite parking is just on the L.

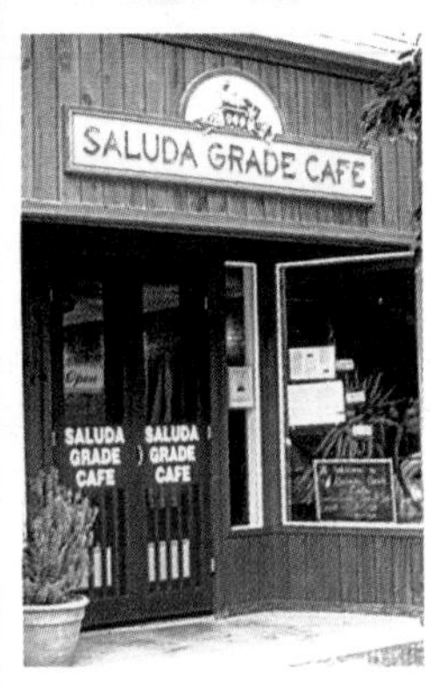

49 Saluda Grade Café MAIN ST – The steepest standard mainline railway grade in the US opened in 1878 with three miles cresting in this town. In honor of this high achievement, this café sets lofty standards with local produce such as fried goat cheese with sweet onion chutney and toasted foccacia chips, black and blue salad with mixed greens, blue cheese and blackened chicken, or cornmeal-fried trout with tomato corn tartar sauce. Shoot for the moon. Tue–Sun 11am–3pm & Wed–Sat 5pm–9pm. (828)749-5854.

Return to Main St and turn R. Just after first block on R.

Did you break your favorite flower pot? Don't throw it away, recycle it. Use the broken pieces to make a lovely wind chime with a bit of fishing line.

50 Heartwood Gallery 21 E. MAIN ST – Garden art abounds in Shelley DeKay's craft gallery with offerings such as Josey Sibold's rebar and concrete Wood Sprites, Richard Fisher's cast bronze bells, Carol Roeda's silhouette plant stands and Juana Pena's metal glazed garden stakes. Mon–Fri 10am–5pm. Sat 10am–6pm. Sun 12noon–5pm. (828)749-9365. www.heartwoodsaluda.com

Keep walking down Main St. On R.

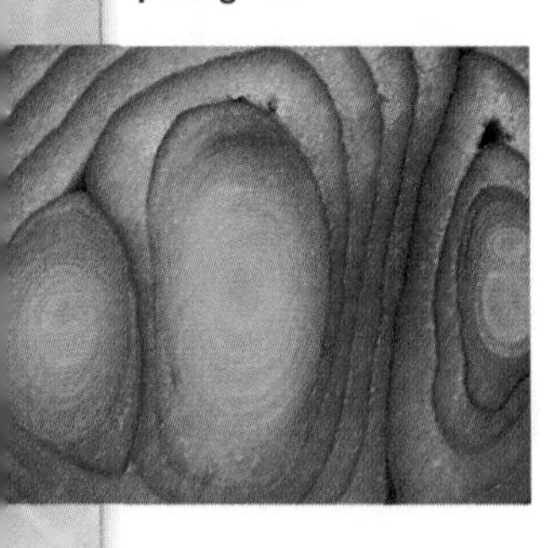

51 The Purple Onion 16 MAIN ST – One of the best things to ever put in your mouth is the pear and gorgonzola cheese, mixed greens, toasted walnut and balsamic vinaigrette salad in the local favorite café and coffeehouse of Stoney Lamar and Susan Casey. True to their

The Road Goes On Forever

Side trips, tidbits, adventures, and treasure hunts

During the Civil War, Union doctors used onion juice to clean gunshot wounds, and General Grant, deprived of it, sent a testy memo to the War Department : "I will not move my troops without onions!"

name, you'll find purple onions in many dishes such as the tabouleh, Greek salad, and roasted vegetable pizza. Mon–Tue & Thu–Sat 11am–3pm & 5pm–9pm. Closed Wed & Sun. Live regional music featured every Sat from 8pm–10pm. (828)749-1179.

52 **Spring Park** BEHIND THE PURPLE ONION – No, it's not big but this project of the Mountain Laurel Garden Club offers a downtown garden respite with its small, circa-1830 spring, once the only water source for Saluda, now surrounded by protective hosta, maidenhair fern and kenilworth ground cover spilling over well-worn stone steps. Think of it as Glastonbury on a budget. Open sunrise to sunset.

53 **The Summer House** 18 W. MAIN ST – While in an English state of mind, step inside this European style country store where you'll find potted angel vine plants, dried delphinium and sage, garden architecture, leaf chimes, hummingbird feeders and even a washboard fountain. Open Mar–Dec Tue–Sat 10:30am–4pm & Sun 1pm–5pm. Closed Jan–Feb & Mon. (828)749-1499.

54 **Coon Dog Day** MAIN ST – What do coon dogs have to do with gardens other than racing through them to tree a raccoon? Nothing, so far as we can tell. Still, the folks in Saluda are mightily proud of this all-day festival held the first Saturday after July 4th from 9am–12midnight. Arts, crafts, food, and music fill Main Street. Of course, there's a dog show at the school. And, don't miss the mountain street dance from 8pm–12midnight. For more info, call the City of Saluda. (828)749-2581.

Not sure if it will help keep the coon dogs out of your garden, but to keep the cats out, put chicken wire, or a decorative welded wire, flat on the ground in your garden.

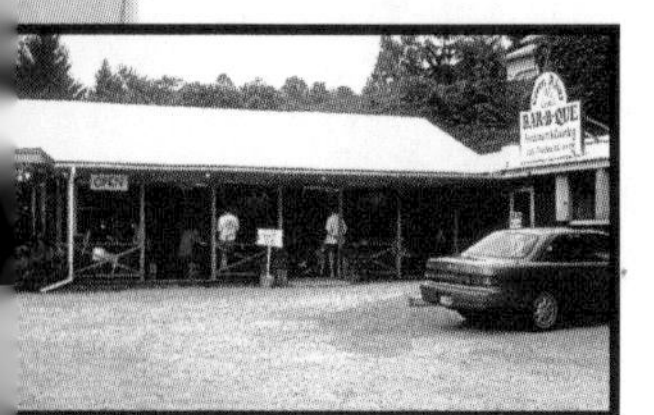

55 Green River Bar-B-Que HWY 176 – If you are seriously hungry, the gals at Green River know how to ease hunger pains. Pulled or sliced barbecue beef, pork and chicken, fried okra, collards and sweet potato fries for starters. Better save up some room for this indoor or outdoor dining experience. Tue–Thu 11am–8pm. Fri–Sat 11am–9pm. Sun 12noon–3pm. Closed Mon. (828)749-9892.

Continue on Main St on bridge over railroad tracks. Restaurant will be immediately on L.

56 The Oaks Bed & Breakfast 339 GREENVILLE ST – There's no rest for the wicker on the popular hardwood front porch at this cozy B&B. Brown-eyed Susans, azaleas, butterfly bushes and hydrangeas all vie for attention in the circular stone beds between the inn and Acorn Cottage. Lovely outdoor deck for dining. (828)749-9613 or (800)893-6091. www.theoaksbedandbreakfast.com

Head back on Main St and turn R on Greenville St (also says Mtn Page St) across from City Hall. Cross the railroad tracks and continue .3 mi to inn on R.

Here's an easy apple treat to make. Cut apples into chunks. Roll in mayonnaise then in a mixture of chopped bacon, nuts and grated cheese. Serve with toothpicks. Kids love it!

57 Apple Mill 1345 OZONE DR – Established in the early 1900's, Apple Mill is a family-operated processor and manufacturer of most things apple. While apple butter is the primary product, you can also find other jams, jellies and preserves made on-site, as well as a large selection of birdfeeders and statuary. Watch apples cook in a 200-gallon stainless steel kettle and see how an apple cider press works. Tour groups need to call ahead. Store is open daily year-round 10am–5pm. (828)749-9136.

Continue on Main St back through town to L on Ozone Rd. Go .8 mi to store on R just before intersection with Hwy 26.

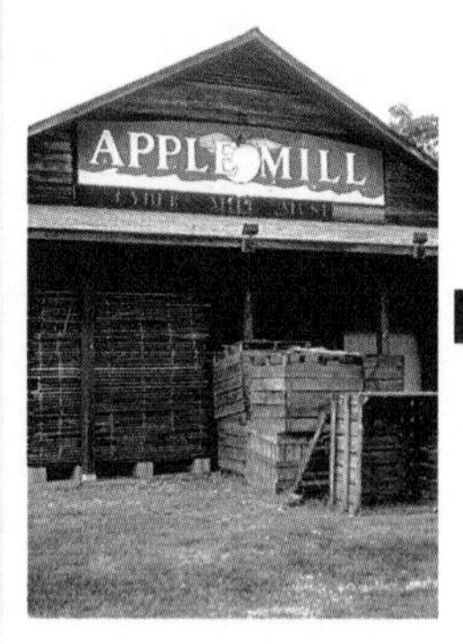

CHIMNEY ROCK VILLAGE

58 Esmeralda Inn & Restaurant HWY 74A – While the historic 1890 inn was destroyed by fire in 1997, the restoration, a special project of Preservation North Carolina, resulted in a beautifully accurate re-creation of the timber,

The Road Goes On Forever

Side trips, tidbits, adventures, and treasure hunts

SPOT IT

It's somewhere on this loop. Can you find it?

glass and stone of the original structure. An impressive waterfall attended by mosaic tile animal sculptures flanks the right side of the inn while a circular fountain bordered by hydrangeas graces the front. Chef Michael Okpych provides gourmet options to visitors and locals alike, including wild mushroom gratin with brie, Farmer's Market Tomato Salad, Roasted Tanglewood Farms Chicken with Hickory Nut Gorge Fig Reduction, asparagus corn pudding, and shrimp and grits. Lunch Mon–Sat 11:30am–2pm. Dinner Mon–Sat 5:30pm–8:30pm. Sunday brunch 11am–2pm. (828)625-9105 www.esmeraldainn.com

Take Hwy 26 E approximately 7.5 mi to intersection with Hwy 108. Travel N on Hwy 108 approximately 2.5 mi to intersection with Hwy 9. Turn N on Hwy 9 and travel approximately 9.5 mi to intersection with Hwys 64/74A at Lake Lure. Bear L alongside the lake through Chimney Rock about 2 mi to W side of town. Inn is on R.

59 The Old Rock Café HWY 74A – Pick up a picnic-to-go or enjoy a wide range of sandwiches, pasta and salads from the grapevine-covered deck overlooking the Rocky Broad River. Breezes carry the scent of potted miniature roses and basil while the river provides a bubbling flowing symphony. Later in the evening, apple orchard wood chips fragrantly smoke ribs, salmon and apple-roasted chicken. Mon–Thu 11am–8pm. Fri 11am–9pm. Sat & Sun 8am–11am breakfast & 11am–9pm lunch and dinner. (828)625-2329.

On R next to entrance to Chimney Rock Park.

60 Chimney Rock Park
HWY 74A – If you'd like to experience a day in the life of an eagle, stand at the top of the 500-million-year-old rock and view the world of Hickory Nut Gorge and beyond. Hike the Forest Stroll trail to a 404-foot waterfall through a

Apple Honey Shake

- ***1 quart chilled apple cider or juice***
- ***2 cups chilled orange juice***
- ***1/4 cup honey***
- ***2 tsp grated orange rind***

Combine ingredients and blend. Pour over ice in tall glasses. Garnish with mint sprigs, apple slices or long peels of orange. Makes 6 servings.

No bird soars too high, if he soars with his own wings.
– Blake

Guidebook Symbols
Kid Friendly Site
1 Farm | 1 Trail | 1 Lodging | 1 Special Attraction
1 Garden | 1 Festival | 1 Restaurant | 1 Garden Art

Come prepared for birdwatching at Chimney Rock Park.

"Birds of prey are an integral part of the area. The most exciting of these is a pair of Peregrine Falcons that has been present in the Park for the past few years. In 1990 they successfully fledged three chicks in Chimney Rock Park."

Information taken from the Chimney Rock Park Website. http://www.chimneyrockpark.com

dense forest of abundant and rare plant life and see the flora, fauna and natural beauty that attracted Dr. Lucius Morse to the region at the turn of the 20th century. The 1000-acre park, still owned by the Morse family, boasts a 26-story elevator inside the mountain, accessing the giant granite monolith, the Sky Lounge gift shop and snack bar and passage to the Skyline Trail, a 45-minute breathtaking hike to the top of Hickory Nut Falls. The Meadows make a great grassy stop to eat lunch and then lie back for some serious cloud study. Special events include rope and rock climbing demonstrations and guided bird and wildflower walks. New children's trails provide entertaining nature scavenger hunts. The Park is developing a future retail and wholesale nursery of native plants. Admission: Adults $11.95 & Children ages 4-12 $5.50. Discount rates for groups of 20 or more. Open daily 8:30am–5:30pm during Daylight Savings Time. Other times from 8:30am–4:30pm. Closed Thanksgiving, Christmas and New Year's Day. (800)277-9611. www.chimneyrockpark.com

Entrance on your R in the center of Chimney Rock Village.

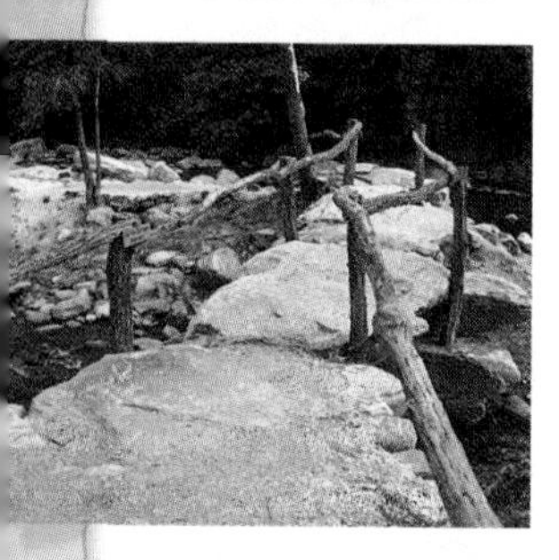

Rocky Broad River Walk in Chimney Rock Village HWY 74A – The Community Development Association of Chimney Rock added magical access to the Rocky Broad River with the 1998 construction of two natural rock bridges. Warning: your kids will want to live here forever. Open sunrise to sunset.

The park runs adjacent to Main Street (Hwy 74A) in Chimney Rock Village with the main access between Bubba O'Leary's Outfitters and Wolf Den on R just past entrance to the Park.

From fun to functional to just plain frivolous, you can find an array of garden gifts and accessories at Edie's. And, that's a good thing!

Edie's Good Things HWY 74A – Hot Lips Hilde, a Penland birdfeeder, adds a whimsical touch to other unusual offerings such as wooden flowers, flower candles, and a wide array of handmade baskets, clay, glass, metal and wood crafts. Open daily 9am–5pm. (828)625-0111. www.ediegoodthings.com

Down the street on the L.

The Road Goes On Forever

Side trips, tidbits, adventures, and treasure hunts

Volunteers in the tiny village of Chimney Rock work year-round to mantain and enhance the Rocky Broad Riverwalk. Everyone pitches in around their work schedules. Now, that's dedication.

63 **Riverside Park** HWY 74A – What a spot for the perfect picnic. Every table has an incredible view. Sunrise to sunset. (828)625-9000.
Just past Hickory Nut Gift Shop on R.

National Geographic has called Lake Lure, which is approximately 720 acres, one of the most beautiful man-made lakes in the world.

LAKE LURE

64 **Lake Lure Tours** HWY 74A –Just sit right back and you'll hear a tale, the tale of 21-mile long Lake Lure. This great water trail begins as you step on board a spacious, covered tour boat with a comfy seat. For one hour, you'll see the film location for the movie, "Dirty Dancing", hear the story of Snake Island, view the first home built on the lake, and delight in the legend of the church said to be in the center of the lake...100 feet down. Lots of flora and fauna to fawn over. Admission: Adults $9.50, Seniors ages 62 & up $8.50 & Children ages 4-12 $5.50. Open daily Mar–Nov 10am–7pm. (828)FUN4ALL.
Continue E on Hwy 74A/64 to the Lake Lure Marina on the L.

Photo courtesy of Lake Lure Tours

Created by stream erosion in solid rock, scientists can give no definite age for the Bottomless Pools.

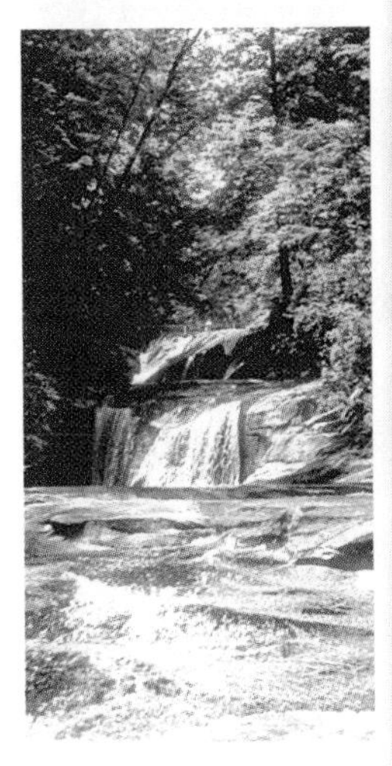

65 **Bottomless Pools** HWY 74A – An easy walking trail encircles the three enchanting pools carved for thousands of years by whirling water and re-circulating stones. Giant hemlocks, boulder overhangs and mossy banks with ferns and tiny red mushrooms decorate the edges of the path. If you become truly inspired by the bottomless pools in your beloved's eyes, there's a wedding chapel at the bottom of the trail. Admission: Adult $3 & Children ages 7-12 $1. Open daily 10am–5pm. (828)625-8324.
Just past the marina, look for sign on R.

66 **Lodge at Lake Lure** 361 CHARLOTTE DR – Step through the ivy arch at the front of this elegant inn and enter a haven of mountain and lake views. Off the stone terrace, you'll find trails down to the lake, boathouse, and two

"Chimney Rock Park is located on the south side of Hickory Nut Gorge, a deeply cut valley in the northwest corner of Rutherford County, North Carolina. Due to great variations in environmental conditions, such as topography, rocks, soils, availability of moisture, and exposure to sunlight, the Park has a very diverse plant life. More than 550 species of vascular plants, including 32 ferns and fern allies, have been identified. Several species are on the list of North Carolina's Endangered, Threatened and Candidate Plant species. One plant is included in the Federal list of Endangered and Threatened Wildlife and Plants."

Information taken from the Chimney Rock Park Website. http:// www.chimney rockpark.com

beautifully-furnished homes to vacation in. (800)733-2785. www.lodgeonlakelure.com

Continue on Hwy 64/74 around the lake past the intersection with Hwy 9. Travel .5 mi and turn L onto Charlotte Dr. Continue up Charlotte Dr for .2 mi to lodge.

67 **Point of View Restaurant** BUFFALO SHOALS RD – Everyone's point of view matches perfectly gazing at the vista of Lake Lure from this elegant restaurant. The mountain trout should not be missed. Open daily year-round. 5pm–9pm. (828)625-4380.

Return to Hwy 64/74A and turn L travelling approximately .3 mi to intersection with Buffalo Shoals Rd. Restaurant is on L.

68 **Ivivi Lake and Mountain Lodge** 161 WATERSIDE DR – The people of South Africa begin each day saying, "Ivivi," as they bow to the sun and express their belief that each day is the beginning of their life. This luxurious, contemporary bed & breakfast features beautiful views from each of the seven guestrooms and romantic sunset cruises on the lake. Specialize in retreats for groups. (828)625-0601 www.ivivilodge.com

Continue on 64/74A to L on Bill's Creek Rd. Travel 2 mi to L on Buffalo Creek Rd. Then 1.8mi to L on Noblitt Ct. Drive is on L.

69 **The Cottages at Spring House Farm** 219 HAYNES RD – The restored 1826 historic house of Albertus Ledbetter, a Scottish immigrant, sits amidst 92 pristine acres of woodlands, walking trails, creeks and streams. Arthur and Zee Campbell added four unique and private cabins on the property where you can rediscover nature and reconnect with yourself via a spot by the fireplace, in the hot tub or in a sunbeam on one of the trails. Listed on the National Register of Historic Places, this eco-retreat is open year-round to guests of the B&B. For tour only, call ahead for appointment. Admission is $5pp. (828)738-9798 or 877-738-9798. www.springhousefarm.com

Take Buffalo Creek back to Bill's Creek Rd . Turn L. Travel N for approximately 7.1 mi to L on Cove Rd for .5 mi. Turn L on Ham Creek Rd for .8 mi and then L on Haynes Rd. Retreat is on L.

The Road Goes On Forever
Side trips, tidbits, adventures, and treasure hunts

Nearly 90% of the world's plants depend on bees and other pollinating insects to reproduce seed and perpetuate the species.

OLD FORT

70 Painter's Greenhouse PINE COVE RD – Steve and Susie Painter welcome you to their enormous greenhouse full of hanging baskets, bedding plants, annuals, and some of their specialties: herbs, vegetables, combination pots, perennials and wedding ferns. Mar Mon–Sat 9am–3pm & closed Sun. Apr–May Mon–Fri 9am–6pm, Sat 9am–4pm & Sun 12noon–4pm. June Mon–Fri 9am–4pm & Sat 9am–3pm. Closed Sun. Closed July–Feb except by appointment. (828)668-7225.

Backtrack to intersection of Haynes and Ham Creek (also named Greasy Creek Rd). Go 1.5 mi and turn L on Sugar Hill Rd. Go 3.1 mi (past Woody's Trout Farm at 2 mi) to L on Old Fort Sugar Hill Rd at general store. Travel approximately 8 mi to L on Bat Cave Rd. Go 1.9 mi to R on Pine Cove Rd. Go 2.1 mi and turn L on Roy Moore Rd. Greenhouse is on immediate L.

The Mountain Gateway Museum is an official branch of the North Carolina Museum of History.

71 Mountain Gateway Museum CATAWBA AVE – Mary Virginia "Binkie" Adams, age 86, carries a business card that says, "Ask me about Old Fort." If you're lucky, you'll meet her at this museum, a regional affiliate of the NC State Museum of History in Raleigh. Located at the former site of Davidson's Fort, an old frontier fort, hence the town name, the museum boasts two log cabins from the 1800's as well as exhibits, programs and living-history demonstrations depicting life in the settlement period and into the twentieth century. The museum building was built in 1936 as a Works Progress Administration project by the folks in Old Fort who hauled and laid the river rock for the mid-Depression grand salary of $3.50 a week. But we're "getting above our raising" since Binkie knows far more about these here parts than anything we could ever tell you. Picnic area and amphitheater. Open year-round Mon 12noon–5pm, Tue–Sat 9am–5pm & Sun 2pm–5pm. (828)668-9259.

Backtrack to intersection of Catawba Ave (Bat Cave Rd) and Old Fort Sugar Hill Rd. Travel .8 mi on Catawba Ave back towards Old Fort, under Hwy 40 and turn R onto Water St. Museum is immediately on R.

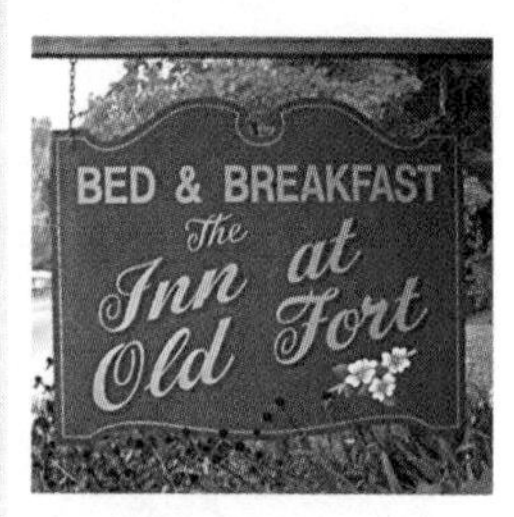

72 The Inn at Old Fort 38 W MAIN ST (HWY 70) – An English garden, moon garden, herb garden, vegetable garden and winter shrub garden await your enjoyment at this Victorian country cottage, circa 1880. There is also a Midsummer Night's Dream garden and blue perennial garden surrounding the garden shed. At breakfast, delight to the tastes of peaches, apples, blueberries, strawberries and raspberries from the gardens with fresh baked sweet breads and muffins. Afterwards, you can retire to the reading grotto in the antique rock fish pond. (828)668-9384.

Turn R off of Water St onto Catawba Ave for .1 mi and turn L onto W Main St. Inn is just on R across from the historic arrowhead monument and railroad depot.

73 Pisgah National Forest Picnic Area OLD US HWY 70 – No, there's not much to do at this lush green picnic park besides frolic with the monarch butterflies and splash in the mountain creek with your children and your own playful self. Oh well. (828)652-2144.

Go .2 mi and turn R on Old US Hwy 70. Travel 2.4 mi to park on L across from Pisgah National Forest Picnic Area sign.

ANDREWS GEYSER

74 Andrew's Geyser MILL CREEK RD – To mark the railroad gateway to the Blue Ridge Mountains and in honor of the man who mapped out the route, a gravity-forced geyser was constructed in 1885. Don't you know his mama was proud! The reservoir for the geyser is controlled by the Inn On Mill Creek up on the mountain above via a six-inch galvanized steel pipe that falls 500 feet in elevation through forest and valley to create a geyser by day and a waterfall at the inn at night. Open year-round sunrise to sunset. (828)668-7223.

Turn L back onto Old US Hwy 70 and then immediately R on Mill Creek Rd at sign. Continue 2 mi to geyser on L.

Shortia

In 1878, nationally renowned botanist M.E. Hyams rediscovered a sparkling plant named shortia on the banks of the Catawba River in McDowell County. When Hyams discovered Shortia galacifolia, it hadn't been gathered for many decades, and was thought to be extinct. Botanist Andre Michaux placed one single cluster, in fruit only, in the Herbarium of the Jardin des Plantes in Paris 75 years before Hyams rediscovered it.
Taken from Mountain Treasures, McDowell County Tourism, P.O. Box 1028, Marion, NC 28752.

The Road Goes On Forever

Side trips, tidbits, adventures, and treasure hunts

The Inn on Mill Creek MILL CREEK RD – It's a wonderful life at Jim and Aline Carillon's luxurious seven-suite inn, the perfect place to rest your head after a day of walking their pick-your-own five-variety apple orchard. Peaches, apricots, grapes, blueberries and blackberries also await sampling before trout-fishing in a one-acre lake, the headwaters of Andrews Geyser. Open year-round. (877)735-2964 or (828)668-1115. www.inn-on-mill-creek.com

Continue N on Mill Creek under railroad pass for approximately .5 mi and turn L on gravel road where Mill Creek continues at intersection with Graphite Rd. Go 1.5 mi and under second railroad overpass. Inn will be immediately on L and orchard is on R.

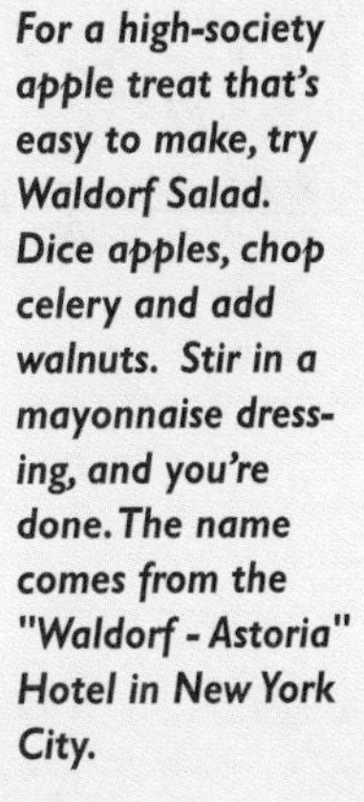

For a high-society apple treat that's easy to make, try Waldorf Salad. Dice apples, chop celery and add walnuts. Stir in a mayonnaise dressing, and you're done. The name comes from the "Waldorf - Astoria" Hotel in New York City.

A Warp in Time 4366 GREENLEE RD – Go back in time to the 1700's with Anne and David Allison at their log cabin where they weave, spin, and naturally dye coverlets, linens, shawls and special order yardage. Colorful flower beds and a prehistoric tree surround their anachronistic domain. Sat & Sun. Evenings after 5pm and by appointment. (828)668-4885.

Take Mill Creek back to Old US Hwy 70 and turn L on Main St. Travel 2 mi to R on Greenlee Rd. Go about .5 mi to sharp curve and then another .2 mi to drive on L. Proceed .2 mi up gravel drive.

Historic Carson House HWY 70 W – What began as an Irish immigrant's walnut log cabin in 1790, transformed into a stagecoach inn that hosted the likes of Davey Crockett, Sam Houston and Andrew Jackson. Learn about the legends Tue–Sat 10am–5pm & Sun 2pm–5pm. Closed Mon. (828)724-4948.

Turn L on Greenlee Rd and continue for 4.3 mi to R on Hwy 70. Travel 4.1 mi to historic site on R just past intersection with Hwy 80. Look for sign.

MARION

Mountain Pride Produce HWY 70 W – Look for the baskets of vibrant red tomatoes and strawberries at this roadside

stand perched proudly in front of Mike Layman's vast strawberry fields. All produce picked fresh daily. May–Oct Mon–Sat 9am–6pm. Closed Sun. (828)652-9899.

Continue E on Hwy 70 for 1.1 mi to produce stand on L just before Walmart.

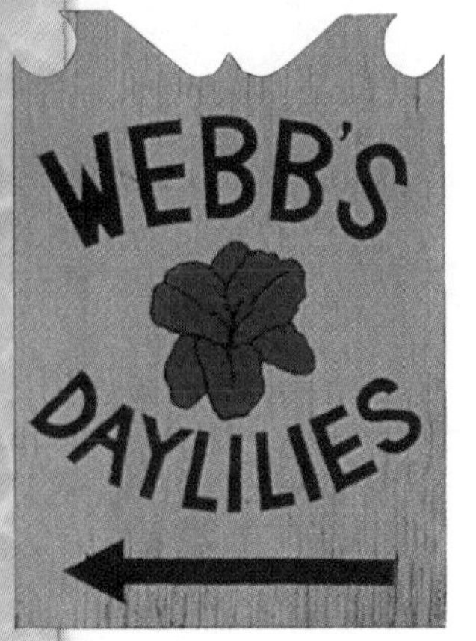

79 **Webb's Daylily Gardens** 385 LUCKY ST – It's a safe bet that Betty Webb's gardens are a holiday stop for nature spirits, given the over 125 varieties of daylilies that she grows. With lily names like Raspberry Pixie, Peach Fairy, and Irish Elf, best be on the lookout for Tinkerbell. Garden sales Apr–Oct. Peak bloom season June–July Wed–Fri 10am–5pm. (828)652-3636. (The Visitor Center nearby provides a great restroom stop.)

Continue on Hwy 70 for .2 mi to R on 221 S (bypass). Go 1.9 mi to Tate St Exit. Turn immediately R on Old Hwy 10. Go .1 mi to L on Lucky St. Go .4 mi to gardens on L.

80 **Josephine's Café at Lone Beech** 64 HILLCREST DR– A restored historic Greek Revival mansion completed in 1905 provides the perfect setting to enjoy homemade soups, freshly baked breads and desserts while

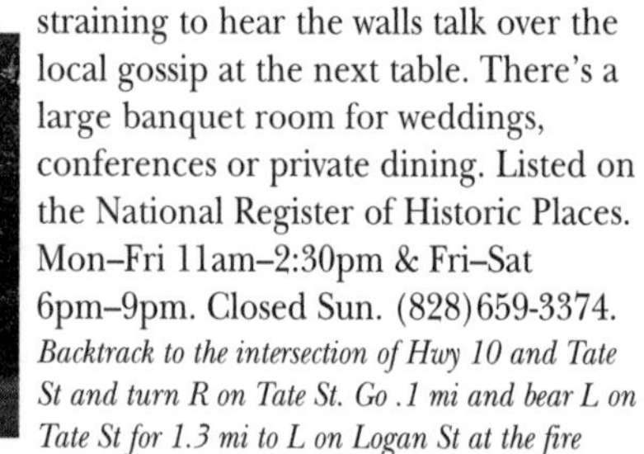

straining to hear the walls talk over the local gossip at the next table. There's a large banquet room for weddings, conferences or private dining. Listed on the National Register of Historic Places. Mon–Fri 11am–2:30pm & Fri–Sat 6pm–9pm. Closed Sun. (828)659-3374.

Backtrack to the intersection of Hwy 10 and Tate St and turn R on Tate St. Go .1 mi and bear L on Tate St for 1.3 mi to L on Logan St at the fire department and library. Travel .1 mi to L on Hillcrest and proceed 300 yards to restaurant on R.

Recycle your baskets! If you purchase cherry tomatoes at the market, save the plastic baskets to dry your flowers and herbs.

81 **P&R Garden Center and Produce** 1033 & 1200 RUTHERFORD RD (HWY 221 S) – Take a load off in an Adirondack chair beside the fountain amongst miniature roses, shrubs, gazing balls, statuary, locally made cypress furniture and seasonal plants. The log cabin holds specialty garden items and clothing.

The Road Goes On Forever

Side trips, tidbits, adventures, and treasure hunts

The zucchini was introduced to the United States in the mid-1900's by the Italians and is now grown by more gardeners than any other squash.

Down the street you'll see the produce stand full of fresh vegetables, jams and jellies. Mon–Sat 8am–8pm & Sun 8am–6pm. Closed at Christmas. (828)652-9951.

Backtrack to library and fire department. Turn L on W Court St. Take the first R on Main St and go .4 mi to merge with Rutherford Rd. Continue .5 mi to the garden center on R just past the Hook and Anchor Restaurant. The produce stand is down the road close enough to throw a rock at (but don't).

Side trip...

82 **We-Du Nurseries** 2055 POLLY SPOUT RD – Near the border of McDowell and Rutherford counties, numerous stock beds and 12 greenhouses are home-sweet-home to an enormous variety of nursery-propagated natives and collector herbaceous perennials and woody ornamentals. Dennis Niemeyer and Joani Lawarre successfully mail order to customers in 42 states. Specimen trees such as the Franklin Tree discovered in coastal Georgia in the 18th century, many native azaleas, wildflowers, vines, ground covers and ferns provide a procession of flower and foliage color throughout the year. Check website for catalog information. Open Thu & Fri plus Sat in Apr–May & Sep–Oct. Visitors may wander the nursery on other days but it is best to call ahead as shipping days in the spring & fall can be very busy. (828)738-8300. www.we-du.com

Continue S on Hwy 221 through the intersection with Hwy 226 and cross over Interstate Hwy 40. From I-40 it is 5.5 mi to Polly Spout Rd. Turn L and continue 2.5 mi to nursery on R.

83 **Don Balke Wildlife Gallery** 754 VEIN MTN RD – The home of the locally and nationally famous wildlife painter is a great stop for inspiration. Open Nov–Dec. Other times, call ahead for appointment. (828)652-2703. www.balkeart.com

Continue N on Polly Spout Rd for .2 mi to R on Vein Mtn Rd. Pass through one-lane tunnel with a creek running beside the road for 5.5 mi to the gallery on the L.

Continue 1.2 mi to L on Hwy 220 at Dysartsville. Travel back to Marion and to the intersection with Hwy 70.

Brown Mountain Lights

The region's most popular mystery! On certain clear evenings, small but brilliant spherical lights or orbs can be seen bobbing up and down, disappearing and reappearing. This mystery has attracted thousands of curiosity seekers over the centuries. Extensive scientific research has failed to explain the phenomenon. There are several vantage points along NC 181, N of Morganton, and Wiseman's View on the Kistler Memorial Highway (SR 1238), near Linville Falls. (828)652-1103. Taken from Mountain Treasures, McDowell County Tourism, P.O. Box 1028, Marion, NC 28752.

Guidebook Symbols

Kid Friendly Site

1 Farm · 1 Trail · 1 Lodging · 1 Special Attraction

1 Garden · 1 Festival · 1 Restaurant · 1 Garden Art

Lake James is 1,200 feet above sea level. It was created from 1916 to 1923 after the construction of dams across the Catawba River, Paddy Creek and Linville River. The lake is a 6,510-acre body of water. It is named for James B. Duke, founder of Duke Power.

...Meanwhile, back on the trail

84 **Lake James State Park** 2785 NC 126 – The hiking trails get lots of foot traffic with nature programs on reptiles, bird and wildflower hikes available mid-March–November. Good place for fishing with the kids and great views of Linville Gorge across the lake. Open daily. Apr–May & Sep 8am–8pm. June–Aug 8am–9pm. Oct & Mar 8am–7pm. Nov–Feb 8am–6pm. Closed Christmas. (828)652-5047.

Travel back to Marion to the intersection of Hwy 70 and Hwy 226/221. Turn R on 70 E and go approximately 5 mi to L on Hwy 126. Follow signs to the park.

LINVILLE FALLS

85 **Linville Caverns** HWY 221 N – The inner beauty of Humpback Mountain was discovered in 1822 when fishermen noticed trout swimming in and out of the mountain. At North Carolina's only show cavern, a guide will take you along the well-lit, smooth trail into the mountain pointing out interesting formations such as draperies, canopies and tobacco leaves. Admission: Adults $5, Children ages 5-12 $3 & Seniors ages 62 & up $4. Special group rates for more than 25. Open daily. Nov–Mar 9am–4:30pm. Apr–May & Sep–Oct 9am–5pm. June–Labor Day 9am–6pm. Dec–Feb weekends only. (800)419-0540. www.linvillecaverns.com

Travel back to Marion on Hwy 70 W to the intersection with Hwy 226/221. Turn R and head N on Hwy 221 for approximately 18 mi to this natural attraction on L.

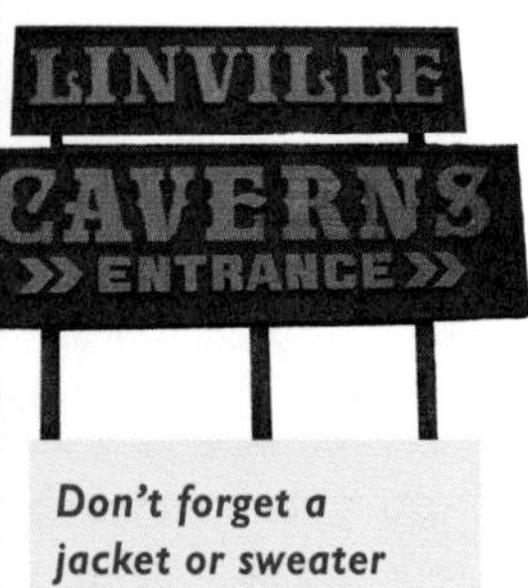

Don't forget a jacket or sweater for your excursion into Humpback Mountain's Linville Caverns. It's chilly inside, even in the summer.

86 **Famous Louise's Rock House Restaurant** US 221 & NC 183 – The fastest and tastiest way to travel from Burke County to Avery County to McDowell County is to dine in the restaurant that sits on the corner of all three counties. Your food will be cooked in Avery County, picked up by your waitress in Burke County and usually served just over the line in McDowell County. Fri & Sat 6am–8:30pm. Sun 6am–7pm. Mon, Wed & Thu 6am–8pm. Closed Tue. (828)765-2702.

Continue N on Hwy 221 for 3.3 mi to restaurant on L.

87 Linville Falls Lodge and Cottages/Spear's Restaurant INTERSECTION OF US 221 & NC 183 – Linville Gorge Wilderness Area and Linville Falls are within walking distance of your lodge room or fully furnished cottage. The world-famous restaurant knows how to slow cook barbecue, and grill mountain trout, black angus steak, and salmon so well that you may need to walk all the way home at the end of this trail. (828)765-2658 or (800)634-4421.

Just across the street from Famous Louise's.

88 Linville Falls HWY 183 – Begin your new exercise regimen at the most popular waterfall in the Blue Ridge. If the one-mile round-trip moderate trail doesn't leave you breathless, the three-tiered waterfall plunging into the Linville Gorge, the "Grand Canyon of the Southern Appalachians," ought to do the trick. Sunrise to sunset. (828)765-6082.

Turn R on Hwy 183 off of Hwy 221 and travel .7 mi to falls entrance on R.

Linville Gorge Wilderness is part of Pisgah National Forest and includes 10,975 acres. In 1951, the Chief of the Forest Service designated it as a wilderness area. When the Wilderness Act of 1964 was signed, the Gorge became one of the original components of the National WIlderness System. The walls of Linville Gorge enclose Linville River for 12 miles and elevations range from 1,300 feet on the Linville River to 4,120 feet on Gingercake Mountain.

Waldensian Wines

In their homeland in the Northern Italian Alps, each Waldensian family had its own small vineyard to produce wine for home use. French-speaking Italians who were persecuted for their religious beliefs for centuries before the Reformation, the Waldensians were "an agrarian people—sheep herders, cheese-makers."

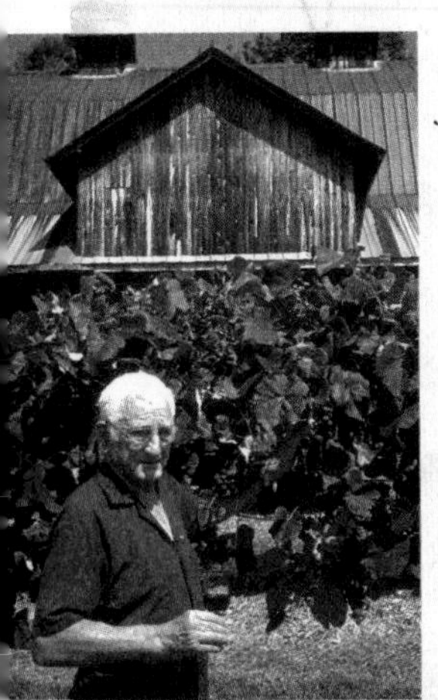

"Wine making is part of our heritage," says Joel Dalmas, vice president of Waldensian Heritage Wines. Dalmas calls the Valdese winery, headquartered in what was once the Dalmas family's dairy barn, "a great big overgrown homemade operation."

Waldensian Heritage Wines produces more than 4,000 gallons each year, from "Vitis Lambrusca,"—bunch grapes whose cultivars include Catawba, Concord, Delaware and Niagara. Waldensian is the only North Carolina winery to use Lambruscas, which impart a distinctively intense, fruity "taste of the grape" to the wines derived from them. To sample Waldensian's wares, you pretty much have to visit the winery, since it sells "99.5 percent" of its product on site.

And, what a treat it is. Almost before you've closed the barn door and entered the cool downstairs social hall, someone is offering you a sample of a full-bodied semi-dry Burgundy Valdese, a delicate Blanc Royal, or a sweet Piedmont Rose. An hour's tour of production and storage facilities develops your taste for Waldensian thrift and ingenuity. Their homemade equipment cuts cost, not quality.

Most of the 25 tons of grapes the winery uses each year come from farmers in New York's Finger Lakes region.

Although a demonstration vineyard next to the barn—about the size of a family vineyard in the Old Country—now produces 150 to 200 gallons annually. Recently, the winery began experimenting with grapes grown by a former Stokes County tobacco farmer.

A first-generation American who didn't start speaking English until he entered elementary school back in the 1920s, Dalmas relishes recounting Waldensian (and the winery's) history. He and a small group of friends began the operation shortly after they returned from serving in World War II. They found the gambrel-roofed stone and wood barn standing empty and put it to use. They formed a winemaking cooperative "to preserve the heritage." It "went commercial" in the late 1980s.

The vintners couldn't be more serious about the quality of their product. "We've never had a bottle of wine come back on us," Dalmas says. But a hint of a smile plays around his mouth when he describes the "bottling parties" the cooperative holds whenever the stock runs low. They're convivial social events of the sort that agrarian communities—from the Alps to the Appalachians—have always enjoyed.

"When we're bottling, we take coffee breaks," Dalmas says, "but we never serve coffee."

Water Ways Trail

Striped umbrellas bow to brimming baskets of Beefsteaks and Big Boys at a roadside stand. Brash black-eyed Susans, airy Queen Anne's lace and Joe-pye weed compete for attention with saucer-sized blooms of hibiscus, along these winding roads. ≋ Water has a way with land. It carves and caresses, falls and floods. From the trailhead town of Franklin, where the Little Tennessee slides past Indian mounds and through prehistoric fish weirs, follow its flowing signature as it alternately sculpts and smooths a bounteous landscape. ≋ How better to begin than by navigating the high road to Highlands? Partake of the cascading Cullasaja drawing its bridal veil across a hemlock-fringed gorge. Then buzz around Highlands, a beehive of activity on a summer afternoon. On its outskirts, explore a botanical garden. ≋ Downscale to Dillard; cart your cooler into Otto. At a roadside creamery, tickle your taste buds with pralines and cream or a chocolate malt while you weigh which treasures to carry away: cottage cheese, butter, golden milk, or a dozen brown eggs. Visit a retired educator who sows the seed of native azalea and mountain laurel collected from Whiteside Mountain and Wayah Bald. Watch a swallowtail steal nectar in a shade-cloth-covered hoophouse, a perennial paradise for green thumbs. ≋ At a hideaway lodge, sip morning coffee amid the treble zing of contending little hummingbirds while your host picks blackberries to garnish peachy three-cheese crepes. On the road west toward Chunky Gal, a farm stand's lure—"local grown, taste the difference"—

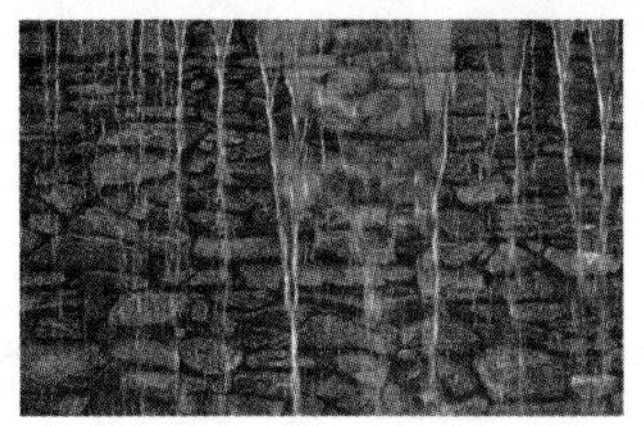

When in still waters, be content to just float.

Follow the Water

tempts travelers. ≋ Hayesville's quilt square, centered by a ruddy brick courthouse of Clay, invites a leisurely stroll. Wet your feet in a water garden, where foil-like fish fin through pond-sized pools. At a folk school, sing behind the plow, dance, build a banjo, smith iron, turn wood. An heirloom garden keeps hunger at bay. ≋ Glide along the Hiawassee to Murphy, its blue marble courthouse the hub of Cherokee County. Approach Andrews through a maze of corn. Handsome old residences that bloom along the railroad tracks serve as 21st century B&Bs. Behind a stagecoach inn, find a foretaste of the tremendous trees of Joyce Kilmer Forest—an ancient gingko and many-centuried oaks. ≋ Head up the Valley Peak at Topton, near Nantahala, land of the ne'er seen sun. Then ramble through Robbinsville. ≋ Bide awhile at a hidden farmstead, where Jersey cows bear flowery names: Goldenrod, Trillium, Flame Azalea and Violet. Watch a potter transform clay to vessel. Then forge on to Fontana to consider the concrete and steel it takes to harness water's rush. ≋ Retreat to Stecoah to study the spin and weave of an old stone school with a future. A room full of looms and a shop stocked with woven table linens, glowing beeswax and pieced quilts speaks to a community's crafted dream. ≋ Take a back road to Franklin along a ridge and descend to pastures of plenty in the valley of the little Tennessee. Kingfishers, frogs and dragonflies are natural ornaments amid a sea of lotus and lilies that awaits you here. Before you're sun struck or water 'witched, you'd better paddle on home. ≋

Water Ways Trail

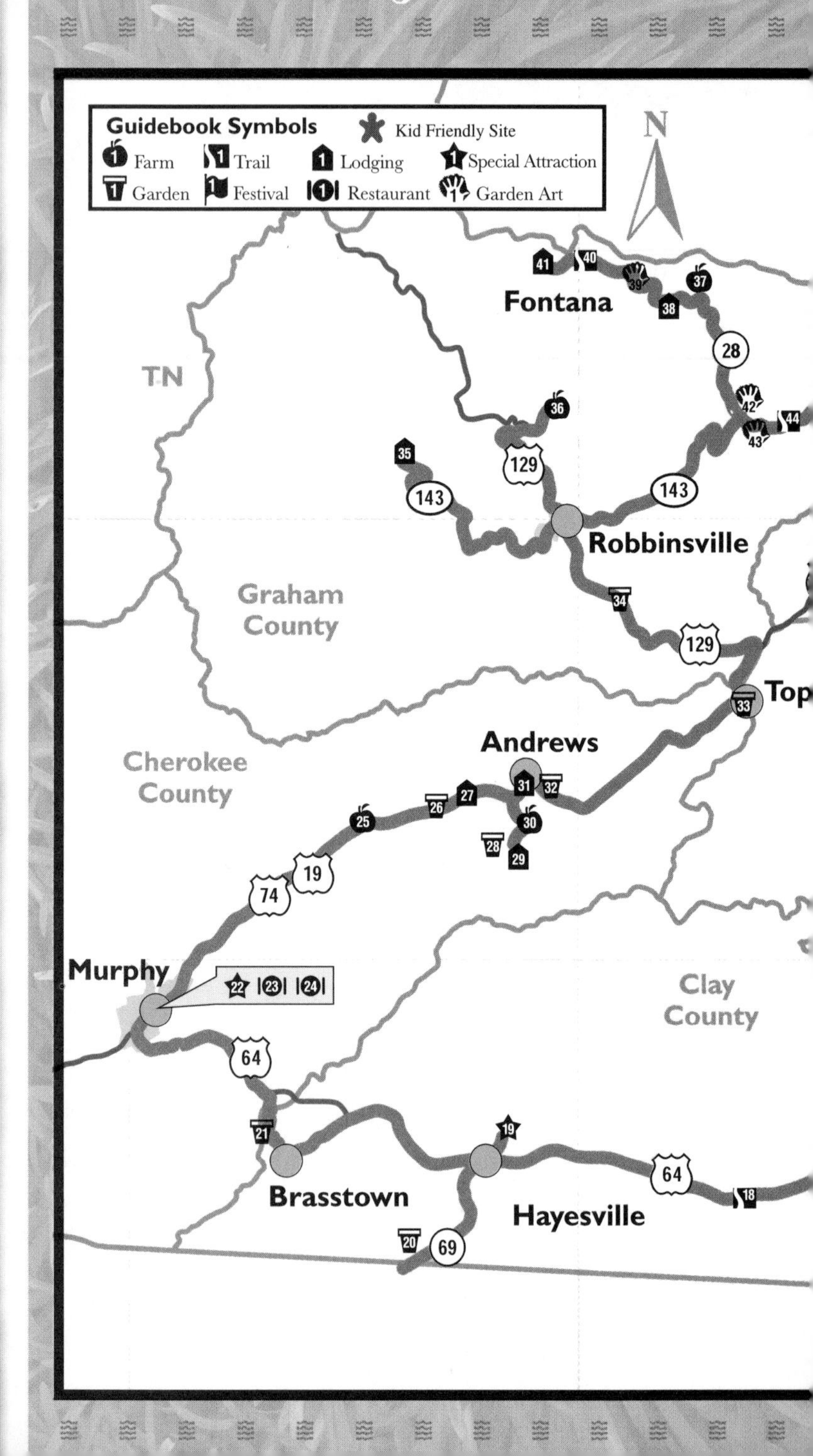

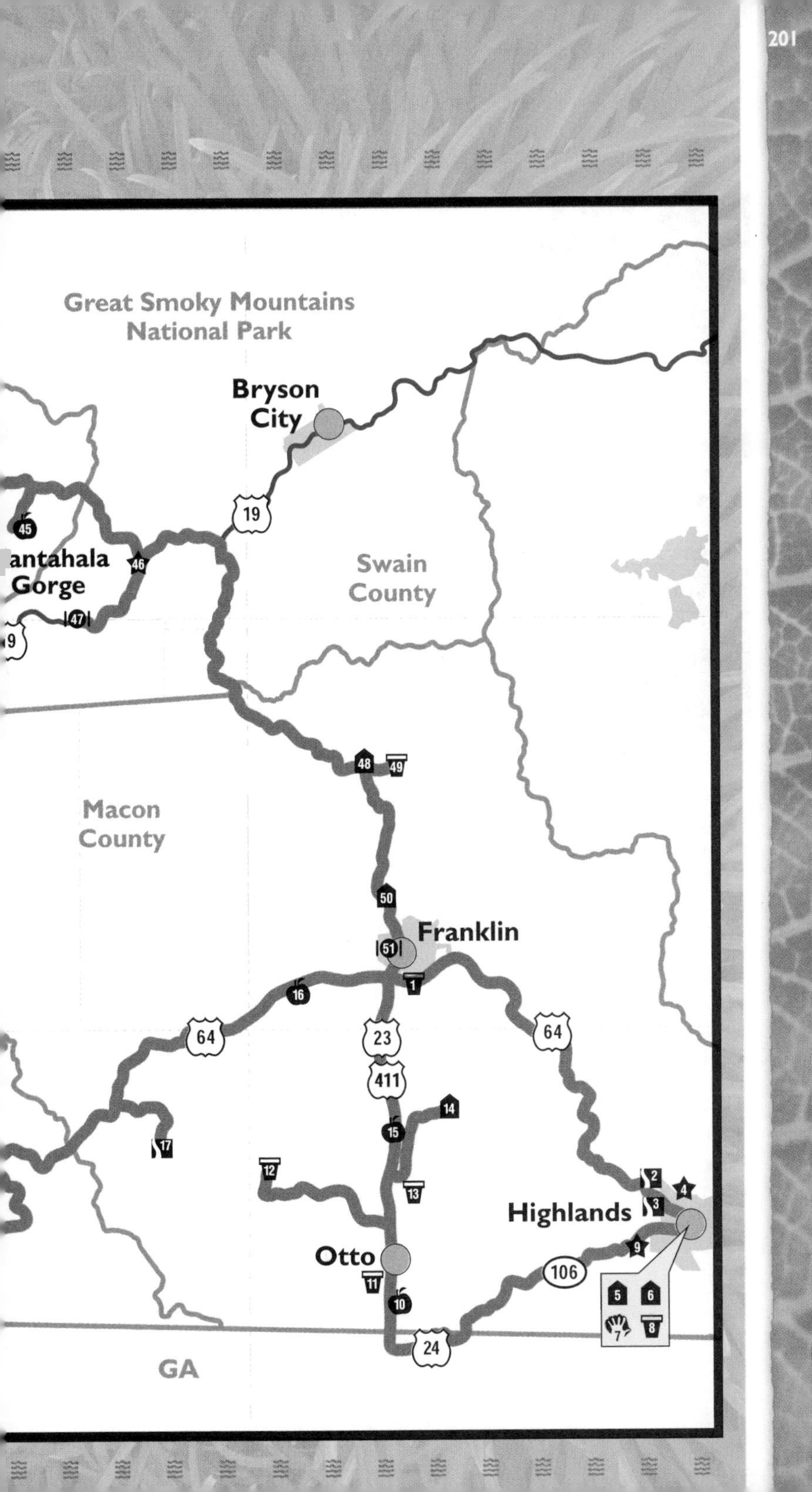

Great Smoky Mountains National Park
Bryson City
19
45
antahala Gorge
46
47
9
Swain County
48
49
Macon County
50
Franklin
51
1
16
64
23
411
64
14
15
17
12
13
2
4
3
Highlands
9
Otto
11
106
10
5
6
7
8
24
GA

The Inn at Half Mile Farm, Highland's newest country inn, features a recently renovated 1877 farmhouse. The inn's grounds also include a six-acre lake, two fishing ponds, streams, and a heritage fruit orchard. Try one of the cooking and garden theme weekend packages. Call Beth and Jack Henry for more information or reservations. (800)946-6822. www.innathalfmile farm.com

FRANKLIN

1 **Spring Valley Nursery** 57 SAUNDERS RD – Wander about at leisure on five acres of daylilies, ferns, ornamentals, hosta, mountain hardy shrubs and trees, evergreens, extensive sun and shade perennials, grasses, bog plants, and herbs. You'll find a colorful stroll awaiting you on the path through several hundred varieties of daylilies. Most of Jake and Marian Bridges' stock is grown and climatized on-site by their hardy band of horticulturists. Open Mon–Fri year-round. Apr–Oct 8am–6pm. Nov–Mar 8am–5pm. (828)369-9778.

Starting from the US 441 and Hwy 64 intersection in Franklin, turn E on Hwy 64/28 towards Highlands for .9 mi. Nursery will be on L.

2 **Cliffside Lake & Van Hook Glade Recreation** HWY 64/28 E – Take a scenic journey under the cover of magnolias, rhododendron and azaleas through the one-mile Van Hook Glade to the lake at this recreation area. Swimming or fishing available. Entrance fee $3. Camping fee $10 or $5 for Seniors with Golden Pass. (828)526-5918.

11.4 mi S on Hwy 64/28. Turn L at sign.

3 **Dry Falls** HWY 64 E – The second largest single drop on the Cullasaja River features a walkway allowing visitors to walk behind the falling waters. Admission is charged.

Approximately 1 mi past the Cliffside Recreation Area on the R.

4 **Bridal Veil Falls** HWY 64 E – You can drive behind these lacey-white falls on your way through waterfall country.

From Dry Falls, continue .8 mi E to falls on the L.

HIGHLANDS

5 **Colonial Pines B&B** 541 HICKORY ST – Iris beds, ragged gardens and two acres of rhododendron, hemlock, maple and oak trees may be enjoyed from the vantage point of an Adirondack chair at this quiet country guest

house. You'll reap rewards from the berry gardens at breakfast. (828)526-2060.

Continue 2.3 mi into Highlands to red light. Continue on Main St for .4 mi to L on Hwy 64 towards Cashiers. Travel .5 mi. to R on Hickory St. Fourth drive on R.

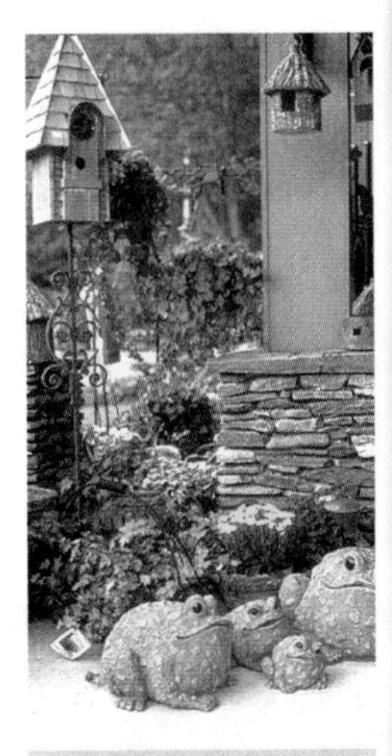

6 Highlands Inn/Kelsey Place 4TH & MAIN STS – This inn that dates back to 1880 offers a bird's eye view of Main Street. Relax in one of the many rocking chairs and reflect on the marvelous culinary creations that await you at the Kelsey Place. Traditional Southern fare finds itself intertwined with gourmet offerings such as Mountain Corn Chowder with Cheddar Spoon Bread. (800)964-6955.

Turn R and then L onto Hwy 64 to return to Highlands. Turn L on Main to L at corner of 4th St (Hwy 64 West).

7 The Bird Barn MAIN ST – Exuding the same charm as its sister store in Cashiers, this downtown shop is full of garden treasures. With bird feeders for every taste, from locally made twig feeders to the squirrel-proof variety, you're bound to take one home with you. Mon–Sat 10am–5pm. (828)743-3797.

Continue on Main St through one light on R.

8 Highlands Nature Center and Botanical Garden HORSECOVE RD – Don't be surprised to hear 10-year-old experts explaining to the younger, less experienced visitors about cardinals and copperheads. The center offers numerous children's programs and a playroom. This hands-on experience includes botanical gardens and lectures. Memorial Day–Oct. Pick up a listing of events at the Center. Mon–Sat 10am–5pm. (828)526-2623.

Continue on Main St for .5 mi. Center will be on L. Parking on R.

If you're impressed with the scenic Scaly Mountain area outside of Highlands, call Fire Mountain Inn, Cabins & Treehouses where a fireplace, Jacuzzi and hot tub will warm your body while the magnificent mountain views warm your heart. By reservation only and property is exclusively for guests. (828)526-4446. www.firemt.com

9 Highland Safari Tours 2 TURTLE POND RD – Explore uncharted waterfalls and search for wild

Guidebook Symbols

Kid Friendly Site
1 Farm | 1 Trail | 1 Lodging | 1 Special Attraction
1 Garden | 1 Festival | 1 Restaurant | 1 Garden Art

Your yard might not be a rain forest, but if some areas seem too wet for most plants, try these:

Fingerleaf rodgersia
Four-o'clocks
Siberian Bugloss
Turtlehead
Yellow flag

turkey in a Land Rover through the rain forest area of the Nantahala Forest. Open daily. 9am and 1pm for three-hour tours. Adults $65 & Children under age 13 $45. Call for ahead for advance reservations. (877)945-3484. www.highlandsafari.com.

4 mi S of Highlands on Hwy 106 (Dillard Rd) on R.

OTTO

10 **Spring Ridge Creamery** 11856 GEORGIA HWY – You'll scream for the ice cream at this Jersey dairy farm with fresh milk, eggs, butter, cheese and many flavors of to-die-for ice cream. Tours available with appointment. Mon–Sat 8:30am–6:30 pm. Sun 11am–6:30pm. (828)369-2958.

Continue on 106 S for about 10 mi to Hwy 246 into Dillard, Ga. Turn R onto US 441 N towards Franklin. Continue on 441 N for 1 mi to creamery on R.

11 **Huffman Native Plants** HWY 441 NORTH – John Huffman, a retired educator, knows native plants like the back of his hand. Dog hobble, Henry's garnet, columbine, bald cypress, flame and pink shell azaleas, deciduous Leucothoe, ginseng, bottlebrush buckeye, Hummingbird Clethre, grey and silky dogwood yield to the magic of this green thumb. Open year-round usually from 8am–dark. (828)524-7446.

Continue on 441N about .25 mi. Turn L on dirt road at sign.

12 **Coweeta Hydrologic Lab** 3160 COWEETA LAB RD – The Forest Service maintains this research station to study tree growth, watershed and weather patterns. Come out and explore on your own or call for more information. Mon–Fri 7:30am–4pm. (828)524-2128.

Go about 2 mi further on 441N. Make a L on Coweeta Lab Rd and travel 3 mi to lab on R.

If you are looking for some self-sowing perennials for your garden, check Mostly Herbs for these varieties:

Columbine
Golden Marguerite
Lady's-Mantle
Lance-Leaved Coreopsis
Rose Campion

FRANKLIN

13 **Mostly Herbs** 67 MY PLACE LANE – Marian Ernst is "mostly mad" about herbs but also provides an extensive selection of perennials such as pulmonaria, echinacea, sedum,

"Plant sweet corn in the spring when the leaves of the white oak tree are as large as a mouse's ear or when the soil feels warm to your bare bottom." – The Garden Diary and Country Home Guide published in 1908.

hellebores, hibiscus and daylilies. Herb farm and gift shop hours are Wed–Sun 8am–6pm. (828)369-5274.

Continue on 441N for approximately 2.8 mi. Turn R on Riverside Rd. Turn R on Hickory Knoll Rd. Go 1.4 mi to My Place Ln on R.

Information on rare plants and the ginseng trade in NC is available from the NC Department of Agriculture, Plant Industry Division. Check out the department's website, www.ncagr.com/plantind/plant/conserv or call (919) 733-3610, and ask about the Plant Conservation Program.

14 **Hummingbird Lodge** 1101 HICKORY KNOLL RIDGE RD – True to its name, you can watch a number of these little birds drinking nectar from the hanging fuchsia baskets on the deck overlooking lush woodland, a pond and the ragged gardens below. The log retreat with three rooms is surrounded by peaceful quiet and numerous hiking trails. (828)369-0430.

Turn L back onto Hickory Knoll Rd. Continue past intersection with Riverside to the Y intersection. Bear R at the church and continue on a gravel road for 1 mi past pond. Go L on Hickory Knoll Ridge Rd up the mountain 1 mi.

15 **Bateman's Produce** 5967 HWY 441 – What you need to do first is grab a pint of blackberry cider to sip as you stroll through this extensive roadside market. Twig furniture, hanging baskets, rhododendron, roses, and shrubs intermingle with hundreds of varieties of canned produce, jams, jellies and local honey. Macon and Jackson County Christmas trees make a show every holiday season. Open daily Apr–Dec 8:30am–6:30pm. (828)524- 8497.

Take R back onto 441 N. Market is .1mi on L.

16 **Kirkland Farm Produce** HWY 64 W – If you had to be stranded on a deserted island, you'd do well to take along Ted and Vivian Kirkland. At least you'd have tomatoes, beans, corn, okra, watermelon, eggplant, peppers, cantaloupes and strawberries. A far cry better than Gilligan's gang made out. All the fruits and vegetables are locally grown at the couple's farm nestled against the nearby Chunky Gal mountains. Mon–Sat 8am–6pm. (828)369-8530.

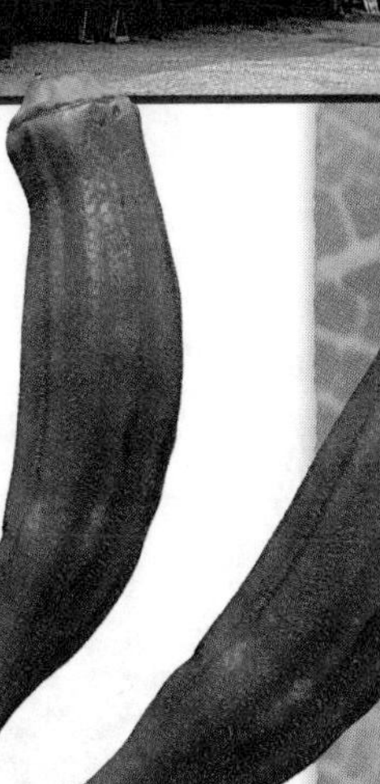

Take Hwy 441 for 5.1 mi into Franklin and exit onto Hwy 64W (Murphy Rd). Travel 4.2 mi to produce stand on L.

Guidebook Symbols Kid Friendly Site
Farm · Trail · Lodging · Special Attraction
Garden · Festival · Restaurant · Garden Art

The Little Tennessee River Greenway

In tribute to the Little Tennessee River, known to the Cherokees as Yu'nwi Gunahita or Long Man, the town of Franklin has blazed a six-mile trail along the banks of the river through town. Threatened species thriving in or near the Little Tennessee River include Appalachian Elktoe Mussel, Hellbender Salamander, and Cooper's Hawk. The trail begins in southeast Franklin and runs north to its convergence with Lake Emory. Plans for the trail include beginning it at the Macon County Recreation Park. One access is at the intersection of Main Street and Henson Bridge. (828)369-7331.

17 **Standing Indian Recreation Park** HWY 1448 – For outstanding hiking and horseback riding trails, you can't do better than this park which also features trout fishing and beautiful scenic driving.

Continue W on Hwy 64 for 7.3 mi to L at Wallace Gap on Old Murphy Rd. Drive 2 mi to USFS RD 67 and turn R into the recreation area.

HAYESVILLE

18 **Chunky Gal Stables** HWY 64 W – Take a trail ride through rich cove forests with rare plant species such as dwarf ginseng, American Columbo, yellowwood, Goldie's fern and glade fern. Unusual geology supports the existence of unusual plant communities called serpentine barrens as well as Southern Appalachian bogs. This eight-mile ridge that runs between the Appalachian Trail and US 64 is named after the Cherokee legend of a plump Indian maiden who fell in love with a brave. When he was banished from camp, she loyally followed him over the mountain. Look for their trail with these outfitters. Riding reservations required a few days ahead. Call for costs. Open year-round 8:30am–5pm. (828)389-4175.

Continue W on Hwy 64 for 9.8 mi. Stables on R and look for sign.

19 **Clay County Historical & Arts Council Museum** DAVIS LOOP – It's a pretty safe assumption that Gertrude Price never knew her early 1900's farmhouse kitchen would become immortalized in this museum preserving local history and native arts and crafts. Talk about an incentive for keeping the kitchen floor clean! Native American artifacts, farm equipment, an old loom and the county doctor's office from the early 1900's also featured. Contributions accepted. June–Aug Tues–Sat 10am–4pm. (828)389-6301.

Return to Hwy 64W and continue 10.2 mi to first red light. Continue through for .5 mi to intersection with Bus

The Road Goes On Forever

Side trips, tidbits, adventures, and treasure hunts

While in Brasstown fill up your tank at Clay's Corner convenience store, the self-proclaimed "possum capitol" of the universe. Gaze upon memorabilia celebrating the planet's most under-rated marsupial.

Hwy 64 across from First Citizens Bank and turn R. Go .7 mi and turn L onto Davis Loop to this site which was once the old county jail.

20 **Hayesville Water Gardens** 1687 MATHESON COVE RD – Ted Williams and Joe Stevens are the father and son team who operate this aquatic nursery and water garden supply. There are nice display gardens along with water lilies, irises, ferns, tropical plants and Japanese maples. Statuary, pumps, installation information and more. Tue–Sat 9am–5pm. (828)389-0914.

Return to 64/69 intersection and go through light to Hwy 69 S. Travel 3 mi to R on Matheson Cove Rd. Nursery just on R.

BRASSTOWN

21 **John C. Campbell Folk School** 1 FOLK SCHOOL RD – Amongst fields of gold and rolling green meadows sits the renowned school of crafts, music, dance, cooking and gardening founded in 1925 and based on the Scandinavian "people's schools." Vegetable, herb, flower and dye-plant and fiber gardens are part of the teaching program. The exhibits at the history center celebrate agriculture, crafts, music and community. The 380-acre campus is listed on the National Register of Historic Places. Nature trails including streamside interpretive park. Craft shop open Mon–Sat 9am–5pm & Sun 1pm–5pm. Call for workshop schedule. (828)837-2775 or (800)FOLKSCH.

Return to Hwy 64. Turn L on 64W. Travel approximately. 7 mi to L on Settawig Rd. Look for sign. Go 2.3 mi to R on Old US 64. Go .1 mi to L on Brasstown Rd for .2 mi to school on L.

MURPHY

22 **Cherokee Historical Museum** 87 PEACHTREE ST – Farm implements, blacksmith tools, a cobbler's bench and early pioneer settler items serve as evidence of the blood, sweat and tears that built up this region. Native American artifacts attest to the laborious and courageous lifestyle

It's said that lemon grass tea has a soothing effect on the nerves and helps to keep skin clear.

Guidebook Symbols

Kid Friendly Site

Farm | Trail | Lodging | Special Attraction

Garden | Festival | Restaurant | Garden Art

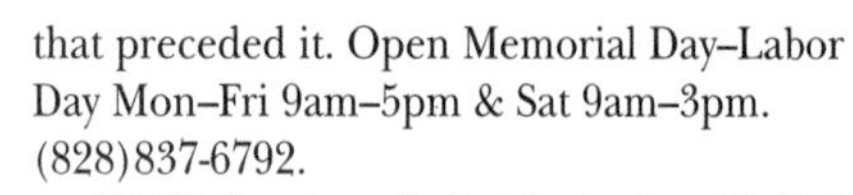

that preceded it. Open Memorial Day–Labor Day Mon–Fri 9am–5pm & Sat 9am–3pm. (828)837-6792.

Return to Old US 64 and turn L. Go 1.9 mi to L on US 64. Go 4.5 mi To junction with Hwy 19/74 and continue through light. Continue on Terrace Rd for .4 mi merging with Peachtree. Museum is on R next to the courthouse.

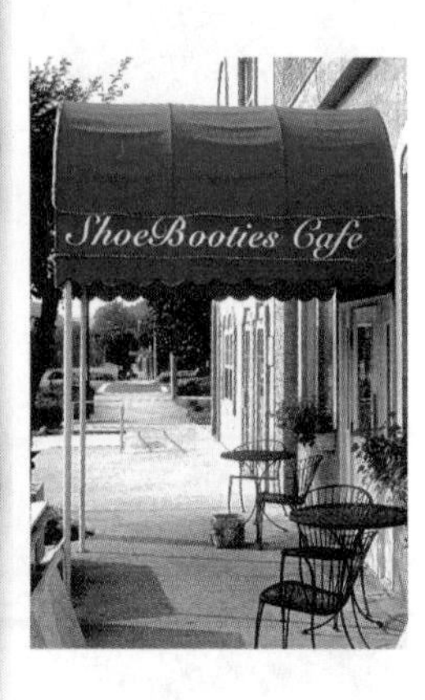

23 **Shoe Booties Café** 107 PEACHTREE ST – Fried zucchini, baked trout and home-baked goods like Key Lime Pie and Caramel Fudge Pecan Cake will tickle your taste buds at this combo café/deli/bakery. Mon–Sat 11am–3pm & 5pm–9pm. (828)837-4589.

Located just down the street on the R next door to the County Extension Office.

24 **No Name Deli and Ice Cream Parlor** 16 OLD RANGER RD – Return to a bygone era at an old-fashioned ice cream parlor originating in 1928 as Shields Mercantile. After you fuel up on a cold or hot sub, lasagna, salad and ice cream, you'll need to walk it off at the adjacent Hiawassee River Garden. Deli hours: Mon–Fri 11am–3:30pm & Fri 5pm–9pm. (828)837-9138.

Take L onto Hiawassee St. Deli is .5 mi on R just after the river and beside McDonald's.

ANDREWS

25 **Wood Farm and Corn Maze** HWY 74 – If Dorothy had had a corn maze like this to romp through, she may have been content to stay in Kansas. The corn, soybean, pumpkin and tobacco farm comes to life in July when the maze opens to the public. It stays open through the end of October when spooks and goblins "stalk" the maze. Admission: Adults $6, Children ages 5-11 $4 & Children under 5 free. (828)321-5032. www.cornfieldmaze.com

Continue N on Hwy 129/74/19 for 13 mi. Turn L into field just past airport. Sign will be on the R.

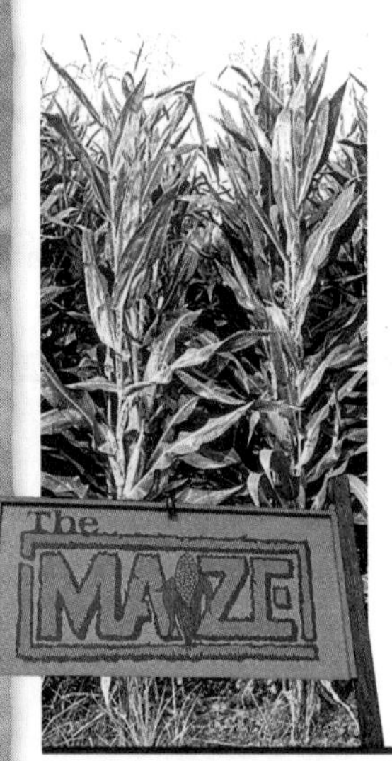

26 **Annie Martin Stover Wildflower Garden** MAIN ST – The late civic leader and conservationist is immortalized in the garden

The Road Goes On Forever

Side trips, tidbits, adventures, and treasure hunts

Only about 10% of the corn grown in the U.S. ends up on the dinner table. Over 50% of it is used for livestock feed, and the rest of the crop is used to make everything from syrup and starch to whiskey and oil.

created by Mildred Johnson and Brenda Forbes, Stover's daughter. Trillium, butterfly weed, doll's eye, great Solomon's seal, turkey mustard, blue stars, green dragons, pink and yellow lady's slippers, bee balm, and some 150 other varieties grow on the west bank of the Andrews Library. Open daily. (828)321-5845.

Continue N on Hwy 129/74/19 for 1.2 mi to R on Bus. 19 (Main St). Library will be on your L.

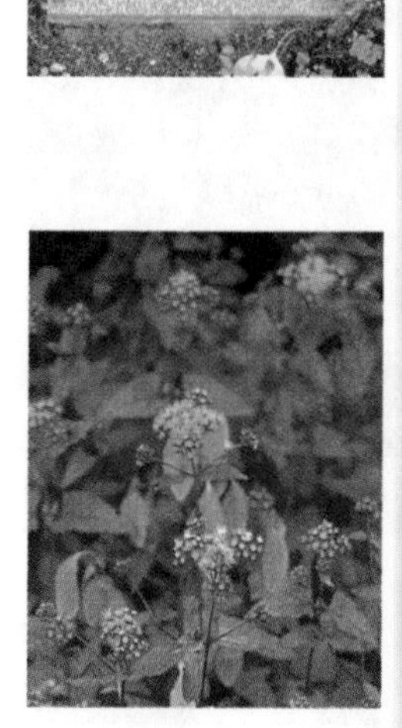

27 **Bradley Inn** 983 MAIN ST – Step back in time on one flight of stairs at this turn-of-the-century bed and breakfast. Downstairs, enjoy the locally made crafts and desserts in the coffee and garden gift shop. Nice selection of birdhouses and garden items. Open daily 8am–5pm serving breakfast and lunch. B&B open year-round. (828)321-2391.

Turn L back onto Main St and go .8 mi. Inn will be on your L.

28 **Hillside Nursery** 357 BRISTOL AVE – What a great stop for bedding plants, (annuals and some perennials), mixed containers, and unique custom design planters! But don't take your shoes off. They're liable to fill'em with dirt and plant something in them such as hen and chicks. Mar–Dec Mon–Sat 8:30am–5pm. (828)321-4377.

Continue down Main St to intersection with Cherry St. Turn R on Cherry St which will become Bristol Ave. Nursery will be on your L.

29 **Hawksdene House** 381 PHILLIPS CREEK RD – "Hawke" and "Dene", two of the resident llamas say, "Lunch or dinner is on us," as they carry your meal on a trek into the Nantahala National Forest. Search for a hidden waterfall and salivate over Master Gardener Daphne Sargent's lush English and water gardens. This B&B also features two- and three-bedroom cottages and an on-site stream for gold panning. (828)321-6027.

Continue on Bristol Ave away from Andrews for 2.7 mi. Turn L on Phillips Creek Rd. Retreat will be .4 mi on L.

Vines That Need No Trellis:

Boston Ivy
Climbing Hydrangea
English Ivy
Trumpet Creeper
Wood Vamp

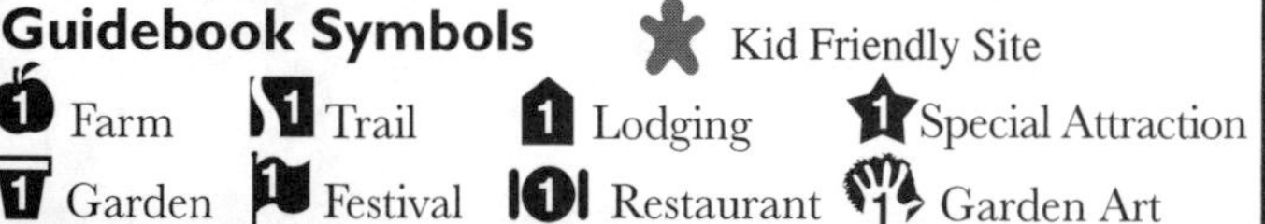

If you want to feed your family chemical free food, buy organic and do the canning yourself.

30 Darlene's Mountain Fresh Produce MAIN ST – For all we know, this nice variety of fruits and vegetables just rolled down the hill from the looming Snowbird Mountains. Tall tales and plants also await you at this friendly road-side stand. Mar–Dec 8:30am–9pm.

Return to Main St and turn R. Stand is .5 mi on R.

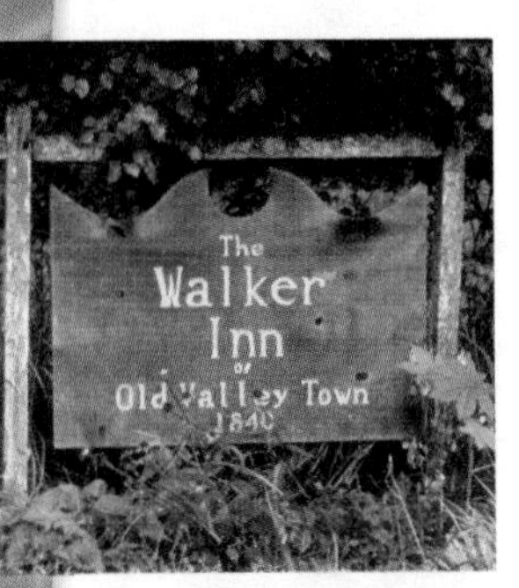

31 Walker Inn 385 JUNALUSKA RD – Keeping watch over the strawberry garden, herb garden and vegetable garden with everything from asparagus to zucchini is North Carolina's largest recorded gingko tree. Blackberry and raspberry bushes, peach trees and grapevines thrive near a grove of ancient white oaks, some over 400 years old. The historic stagecoach inn is open Apr–Nov. (828)321-5019.

Take Main St out of town for .5 mi to Y intersection. Bear R onto Junaluska Rd. Inn will be .5 mi on L.

32 Seven Springs Nursery OLD ANDREWS RD – Ferns, foxglove, Moonlight Scotch broom and other natives live quite happily but not ever after (judging by the booming business) at this extensive nursery. Workshops on landscaping are also offered. Mon–Sat 9am–5pm. (828)321-2234.

Travel back to Y intersection and turn R onto Old Andrews Rd. Travel .3 mi and nursery is on R.

A Selection of Non-Pruning Shrubs:

'Compactum' Oregon Grape Holly
Dwarf Fothergilla
'Green Gem' Hybrid Boxwood
'Hancock' Chenault Coralberry
'Henry's Garnet' Virginia Sweetspire
'Ivory Halo' Tatarian Boxwood
'Nordic' Inkberry
'Palibin' Meyer Lilac

TOPTON

33 Nelson's Nantahala Hideaway HWY 19/23 &74 – You'll want a cozy, rustic cabin to relax in after exploring the trails and enjoying some of the outdoor activities offered in the surrounding Nantahala Forest. Campsites and RV sites available too. (828)321-4407.

Continue down Old Andrews Rd to Hwy 19/129. Travel 6.3 mi into Topton. Cabins are on R after post office.

ROBBINSVILLE

34 Taylor's Greenhouse HWY 129 AT SWEETGUM – Fairies must work overtime to keep the growing things here so vivid and thriving. Sweet potatoes co-exist with roses, herbs,

The Road Goes On Forever
Side trips, tidbits, adventures, and treasure hunts

SPOT IT
It's somewhere on this loop. Can you find it?

painted daisy, foxglove and assorted bedding plants, shade and fruit trees under the care of Jean Taylor and her talented staff. Mon–Sat 9am–5pm. Mar–June 8am–5pm. (828)479-8675.

Continue on Hwy 19/129 for .2 mi to L onto Hwy 129 (Tallulah Rd) toward Robbinsville. Travel 7.9 mi to Old Tallulah Rd. Turn R and greenhouse is immediately on R.

To control weeds in herb gardens, use mulch. It will not only control the weeds, but it will help keep foliage clean and hold moisture in the soil.

35 **Snowbird Mountain Lodge** 275 SANTEELAH RD – In the land of the Cherokee, skirting the sapphire-fingered Santeelah Lake, and nestled on almost 100 acres of pristine mountaintop, this lodge boasts interior paneling, beams and furniture of wild cherry, maple, butternut and chestnut crafted by local artisans. The rustic cuisine includes mountain trout with grilled vegetable salsa and sorghum–marinated rib eye with grilled red onion. Chef Mark Crim sees to it that the herbs, produce and fish come from nearby farms. The Joyce Kilmer Memorial Forest nearby provides sublime sanctuary for those seeking solace with nature. (800)941-9290. www.Snowbirdlodge.com

Travel 3.2 mi into Robbinsville on Hwy 129 and pick up Hwy 143 (Tapoco Rd). Go 1 mi and bear L on Hwy 143. Travel 3.2 mi to R on 143 West (Snowbird Rd). Go 2 mi and bear R on Santeelah Rd. Continue for 4.5 more mi and lodge is on L.

Fruit vinegars add an interesting flavor to salads and sauces. They also make great sore throat and cold soothers. Simply add one tablespoon of vinegar and one tablespoon of sugar to a mug of hot water. A bit of brandy added may cure you even faster, but we would suggest you consult your doctor first.

36 **Stony Hollow Farm** 940 OLLIES CREEK RD – Blueberries, blackberries and raspberries will have you smacking your lips at the farm of Scott and Melissa Boxberger. Cut flowers such as zinnias, delphinium and yarrow scent the air and add color amongst the jars of honey, homemade jams and jellies. Apr–Oct Mon–Sat 9am–5pm. Sunday is self-serve on an honor system. (828)479-9092.

Travel back to Robbinsville and turn L on Hwy 129 toward Knoxville. Go 3 mi and turn R on E Buffalo Rd just before the Ted Jordan bridge. Go about .9 mi to L on Ollies Creek Rd. Farm is .7 mi on L.

37 **Yellow Branch Pottery and Cheese** 136 YELLOW BRANCH CIRCLE – A sample of the farmstead or jalapeno cheese at this Jersey cow

Fontana Dam

There must be somewhere to cool off aching and trail-weary feet near this gigantic hydroelectric dam. Crossing over it is a milestone for many Appalachian Trail hikers. Picnic tables, camping and hiking are all available near the interpretation center of the highest concrete dam east of the Mississippi. (800)467-1388.

farm will have you digging out the crackers you packed in the backseat with the kids. One of only a few licensed cheese facilities in Western North Carolina, Yellow Branch is also home to a working pottery studio with functional pieces such as say, cheese platters. Cinnamon fern, bamboo and iris abound to admire as you munch. Apr–Oct Tue–Sat 2pm–5pm. (828)479-6710. www.yellowbranch.com

Return to Robbinsville via Hwy 129 and turn L onto Hwy 143N. Continue 9 mi N on Hwy 143 to intersection with Hwy 28N. Turn L and travel 3.6 mi to R on Old Yellow Branch Rd. Go 1 mi to R on Yellow Branch.

38 **Mountain Hollow B&B** POSSUM HOLLOW RD – Two large barns covered in Virginia creeper, one of which is the workshop of wood-turner Robert Woods, greet you on the winding road up the field to this inn. Nice views and soft beds at this country Victorian with four rooms and a large covered porch overlooking the 35-acre valley. First dibs goes to the suite with a fireplace and Jacuzzi. (828)479-3608. www.mountainhollowbb.com

Continue back up Yellow Branch Rd .1 mi to R on Possum Hollow Rd.

39 **Mountain Memories/Bloomin' Baskets** HWY 28 NORTH – Birdhouses, woven backpacks, carved gourds, handmade baskets, beeswax candles and grapevine wreaths are the stars at Virginia Spitzer's crafts and antiques shop. Homemade grape, blackberry and other assorted jams and jellies. June–Oct Mon–Sat 10am–4pm. Off season Thu–Sat 10am–4pm. Closed Jan–Feb. (828)479-2940.

Continue N on Hwy 28 for 3 mi. Shop is on the R.

40 **Lewellyn Cove Walk** HWY 28 N – The USDA Forest Service maintains this 3-mile trail of wildflowers and native plants. If you're short on time, there's a one-mile nature walk you can take as well.

Continue 6.6 mi N on Hwy 28 towards Fontana Village. Trail will be on L.

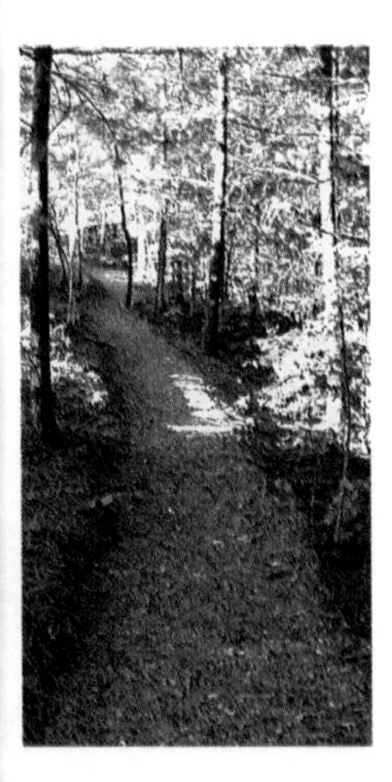

The Road Goes On Forever

Side trips, tidbits, adventures, and treasure hunts

A hummingbird will feed at over 1,500 flowers in an average day.

Fontana Village HWY 28 NORTH – Nestled between the Great Smoky Mountains and the Nantahala Mountains, you'll find a world unto itself at this resort village featuring 15 miles of hiking and biking trails, trout pond fishing, and pontoon and fishing boat rentals/outfitting. The all-recreation facility also sports varied accommodations such as a lodge, cabins, cottages and condos. An on-site store, post office and laundromat add comfort to this remote destination. Explore life in 1872 at the Jesse Gunther Cabin. Open year-round. (828)498-2211.

Continue on Hwy 28N 1 mi.

Did you know you can burn approximately 100 calories in half an hour of gardening?

Stecoah Valley Center SCHOOL HOUSE RD – Mayberry should have had an arts and crafts community center like this one. Local artists revitalize the old school with the dried floral and herbal wreaths of Janet LeZurre, turned-wood bowls by Robert Woods, face jugs by Linda Corn and A. John, Medieval World hand-built pottery, Theresa George nature photography, and an assortment of stepping stones, garden stakes, and plant rooters. Educational tours of the on-site weaving room. The Azalea Trail around the school provides just enough exercise to justify a smidgen of the local Aunt Bee-wanna-be's lemon pound cake. Picnic tables to boot. Open year-round Mon–Fri 1pm–5pm.

Go S on Hwy 28. Travel .9 mi past Hwy 143 intersection to R onto Stecoah Rd. Continue .2 mi and cross Cody Branch Rd onto School House Rd. Center is .1 mi on L.

Bee Global SCHOOL HOUSE RD In the Stecoah Valley Center, Jeff and Crim Bassett produce 100 percent natural beeswax candles without the use of molds. Flora from the local mountains decorate these illuminating lanterns that will light up your heart. Mon–Sat 9am–5pm but best to call ahead. (828)479-8284. www.beeglow.com

Saving seeds from the blooms you love? The most important thing is to keep the seeds dry. You can refrigerate them, but make sure they are dry before you put them in an air-tight container.

Appalachian Riding Outfitters GUNTER GAP RD – Jump in a blazing saddle on the back of a Quarter horse or Paint to experience the Great Smoky Mountains from a higher vantage point. Three- and four-hour rides as well as four-day overnight rides available. Handicapped children ride free but give at least a week's notification. Rides daily. Call for cost information as well as reservations, which are required. (888)414-2122.

Turn R on Stecoah back to Hwy 28 S. Continue S on Hwy 28 for 1.1 mi and turn R at Wolf Creek General Store (rides depart from store).

45 **Tumbling Waters Campground & Trout Farm** 1612 PANTHER CREEK RD – The trout don't fall out of the sky but pretty close to it with this stocked lake and Panther Creek running beside it. Campground and cabin provide lush green setting to fall asleep with dreams of rainbow and salmon trout. Open year-round. (828)479-3814. www.geocities.com/tumblingwaterscg

Continue S on Hwy 28 for 3.5 mi and turn R at camping sign onto Panther Creek Rd. Go 1.7 mi to campground behind cottage.

NANTAHALA GORGE

46 **Nantahala Village** 9400 HWY 19W – Originally established in 1948, this retreat offers over 50 cabins and a beautiful newly-constructed lodge with lots of opportunities to meet, eat, hike and bike. On-site restaurant features such enticing dishes as spinach mushroom strudel, wild forest pasta with mushrooms and artichokes and fresh local mountain trout that you can enjoy by a stone fireplace in the black walnut–floored and wormy chestnut-paneled dining room or in the great outdoors on the dining deck. (800)438-1507. www.nvnc.com

Continue S on Hwy 28 through the Almond community for 5.2 mi. Turn R onto Hwy 19/74. Travel approximately .6 mi to resort on R.

People love chopping wood. In this activity one immediately sees results.
– Albert Einstein

Relia's Garden 13077 HWY 19 W – The "restaurant on the hill" at Nantahala Outdoor Center is named for Aurelia Kennedy, creator of the original restaurant and the plentiful organic garden. Herbs, flowers and spices mesh freshness to end up as signature dishes such as portobello tower, sherry cream pasta, and chili, garlic and lime marinated chicken breast. Apr 6–Oct 28 Sun–Thu 4pm–9pm & Fri–Sat 4pm–10pm. Call for hours in off-season. (800)232-7238.

Continue S on Hwy 19/74 for 3.4 more mi. Nantahala Outdoor Center Outfitter's Store will be on the L but turn R across bridge and up the hill for .1 mi.

Sunflower seeds are a healthy snack for both people and their fine-feathered friends. Harvest sunflower heads when 2/3 of the seeds are ripe. Leave about one foot of the stem attached. Hang in a warm, dry and well-ventilated place to dry.

FRANKLIN

Snow Hill Inn 531 SNOW HILL RD – From this beautifully renovated B&B, you can catch gorgeous views of the Nantahala game lands and distant Cowee Mountains. Of course, the best view may be from the Rapunzel tower on the front lawn. Open year-round. (828)369-2100.

Return to 28/19/74 intersection and continue straight to follow Hwy 28. Travel 2.9 mi to R onto Hwy 28S to Franklin. Continue 13.5 mi to L on West Mills Rd. Turn L on Snow Hill Rd and Inn will be on your R.

Moss makes a great ground cover for shaded areas with wet or infertile soil. Add a birdbath to the area and let the splashing birds keep your moss garden moist.

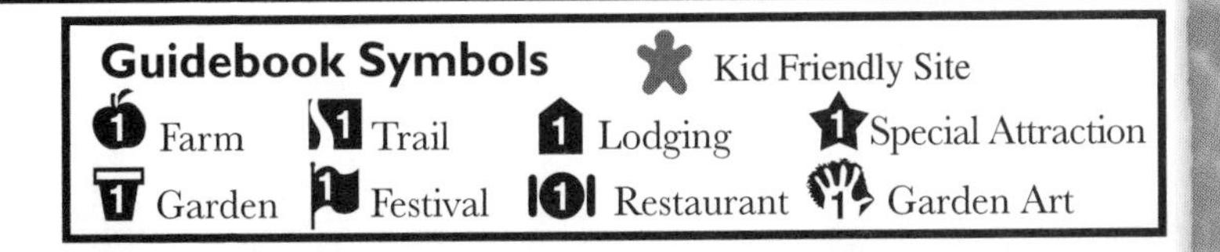

If you are inspired to create your own water garden after visiting Perry's, we recommend starting with the following books:

Kathleen Fisher, *Complete Guide to Water Gardens*, Creative Homeowner Press, 2000

Judy Glattstein, *Waterscaping: Plants and Ideas for Natural and Created Water Gardens*, Storey Books, 1994

Bill Heritage, *Ponds and Water Gardens*, Cassell Academic, 1994

Eleanore Lewis, editor, *Better Homes and Gardens Water Gardens*, Better Homes & Gardens Books, 2001

Helen Nash and Steve Stoupe, *Plants for Water Gardens: The Complete Guide to Aquatic Plants*, Sterling Publications, 1999

Peter Robinson, *American Horticultural Society Complete Guide to Water Gardening*, DK Publishing, 1997

Peter Robinson, *Water Gardens in a Weekend: Projects for One, Two or Three Weekends*, Sterling Publications, 2001

Peter D. Slocum with Peter Robinson and Frances Perry, *Water Gardening: Water Lilies and Lotuses*, Timber Press, 1996

Anthony Archer-Wills and Helen Woodhall, *Designing Water Gardens*, Sterling Publications, 2000

The Road Goes On Forever

Side trips, tidbits, adventures, and treasure hunts

49 Perry's Water Gardens 136 GIBSON AQUATIC FARM RD – Now we know where Monet went when no one could find him and where Daniel Webster determined the definition of "exotic." Thirteen acres of walking trails offer a fascinating study of thousands of blooms at the largest aquatic nursery in the United States. Free admission. May 20–Labor Day Mon–Sat 9am–12noon & Sun 1pm–5pm. Store closed 2nd week of Dec–2nd week of Jan. (828)524-3264.

Go back toward Snow Hill Rd and turn R. Go .5 mi to R on Leatherman Gap Rd. Gardens are .25 mi on L.

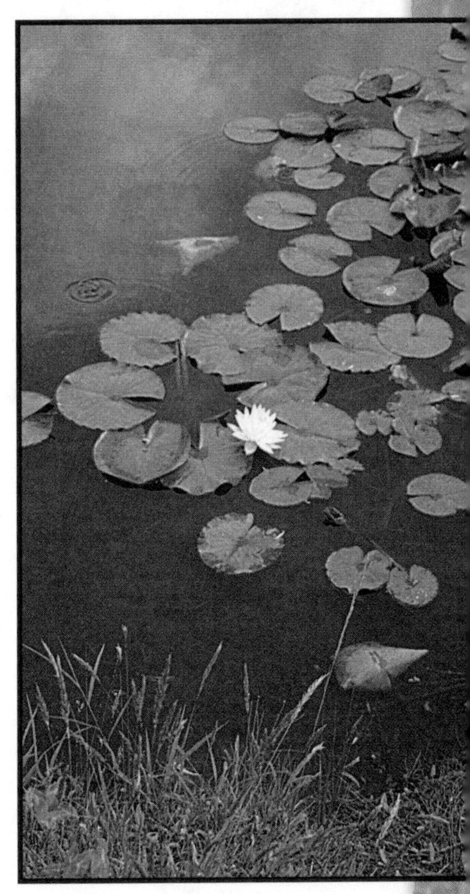

50 Franklin Terrace
159 HARRISON AVE – Originally built in 1887 as a school, this inn is listed on the National Register of Historic Places and bespeaks the Southern hospitality of an earlier era. Relax in a rocking chair under fern tendrils on the extensive screened-in porch. Apr 1–Nov 15. (828)524-7907. www.franklinterrace.com

Return to Hwy 28 and continue S for 6.9 mi to Franklin. Hwy 28 becomes Harrison Ave. Inn will be immediately on L.

Can't you just smell the apple pie?

51 The Gazebo 44 HERITAGE HOLLOW – An open-air creek side café offers a romantic setting to feast upon chicken framboise, stuffed tomatoes and fresh baked chunky apple pie. Open year-round. Sat–Mon 10:30am–4pm & Tues–Fri 10:30am–8pm. (828)524-8783.

From Harrison Ave, turn R onto Main St and then L onto Palmer. From Palmer St head E to R on Porter St. Café is on L.

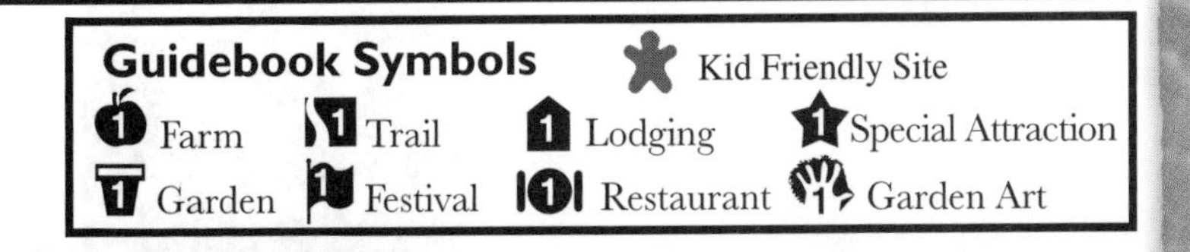

John C. Campbell

The Gardens of John C. Campbell Folk School.

Amid rolling pastureland and meandering creeks, John C. Campbell Folk School hugs a hillside where field and forest meet. Imagine it as a tapestry, where agriculture, gardening, craft and community are expertly interwoven. Among the rustic structures erected or retrofitted since Olive Dame Campbell and Marguerite Butler founded the school in the mid-1920s, a dairy barn rings with the music of hammer and anvil. The sturdy little farmhouse that commanded a view of the surrounding countryside when Campbell and Butler first set eyes on Brasstown—and served as their first classroom—is now a student dorm. Festivals are staged in an old open-air milking parlor.

It's fitting that a school whose motto is "we sing behind the plow" teaches homestead arts: gardening, cooking, dyeing and spinning. Natural that painters, poets and photographers find inspiration in the multitude of gardens that ornament the 380-acre campus. Appropriate that all who break bread together in the dining hall should enjoy the fruits—and vegetables—of resident gardener Tim Ryan's labors.

A one-acre homestead garden is Tim's eminent domain. Planted on the site of the school's original garden, it keeps cooking classes in raw materials (its superabundance feeds the dining hall). The garden's a throwback to a time when folks saved seeds and shared them, when fertilizer came, not in bags, but from barnyards.

The not-so-secret ingredient in Tim's compost mix is three truckloads of donkey doo hauled in weekly. "They laugh at me about my donkey manure," Tim says. But the proof's in the pudding the garden serves up—Paul Bunyan-sized eggplants, cauliflower, cabbage, chard, leeks, and the sweetest, straightest carrots a body could yearn for.

When a third-generation woodworker donated seed from 14 varieties of heirloom peppers and tomatoes and two kinds of okra that had been in his family for four generations, Tim "felt like someone was giving me rubies." Among the gems: a green keeper tomato you can wrap in newspaper to unwrap on Christmas Day, a "Cherokee purple" that's better than a Brandywine, and a prime pink Oxheart for canning. Also gleaned from local sources: yellow and white "Dent Corn" and "Turkey Craw Beans." These last supposedly derive from beans a hunter removed from the gullet of a Tom he'd bagged.

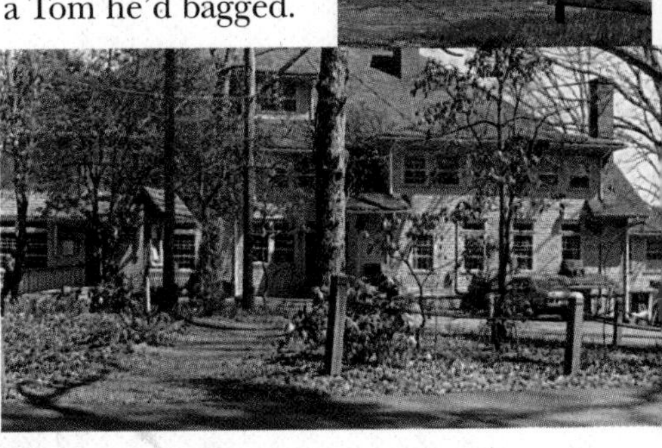

Craft and herb gardens encircle a kettle fountain. Perennial and cutting gardens light up hillsides. New gardens transform once-barren ground outside enameling, clay, jewelry and woodcarving studios. Planned and planted by a class in landscape design, they became a powerful force for collaboration the week they went in. Wooden mushrooms sprang up overnight, a gift from wood turners. Blacksmiths forged poles for hummingbird feeders. Wood carvers chiseled a sign. A French cooking class catered the gardens' dedication and poets held a reading. What happened that week harkens back to the school's beginnings, when local residents' pledges of land, logs and labor convinced a couple of outlanders that, in Brasstown, they'd found their field of dreams.

Index

Abbington Green 91, 107
Abbott, Stanley W. 120
Acorn Cottage 184
Ad Tate Knob 132
Adams, Mary Virginia "Binkie" 189
Alan's on Main Street 150
Albemarle Inn 107
Alderman, Cheryl 116
Alderman, Red 49
Allison, Anne and David 191
Allison-Deaver House 140
Alpaca Corner 36
Altavista Gallery/B&B 30
Alvarez, Jean 131
Andrew's Geyser 190
Andrews 199
Angelica's 35
Annie Martin Stover Wildflower Garden 210
Antique Station and Serendipitea 26
Anvil Arts Studio and Sculpture Gardens 22
Appalachian Riding Outfitters 214
Appalachian Cultural Museum 37
Appalachian Natural Soaps 104
Apple Blossom Trail 115
Apple Hill Orchard & Cider Mill 168
Apple House 117
Apple Inn, The 107
Apple Mill 184
April's Flowers 23
Arbor, The 38
Arrington, Benny and Jane 129
Arrowmont Stables and Cabins 149
Arthur Morgan Elementary School 71
Asheville 82, 88, 103
Avery County 18, 24
Avery County Agricultural and Horticultural Fair 24

B

B.B. Barns 90
Bakersville 72
Bakersville Creekwalk 74
Bald Knob Farmhouse 45
Balsam 125, 128
Balsam Mountain Inn 124, 128
Banner Elk 18, 25
Banner Elk Inn 25
Banner Elk Stables 25
Barber's Orchards Fruit Stand 128
Barefoot Gardens 93
Barnardsville 82, 100
Barnwell's Orchard 102
Bartlett, David 40
Bartram, William 51
Bassett, Jeff and Crim 213
Bateman's Produce 205
Beaufort House 111
Beaver Lake Bird Sanctuary 96
Beaverhorn Elk Ranch 33
Bee Global 213
Bell, Michael 42
Belle Mead Hot Glass Studio 84
Benefit Daylily Sale 116
Berry Nice Blueberry Farm 116
Bethel 33
Beverly Hills Nursery 70
Big East Trailhead 138
Big Lynn Lodge 77
Billy Laughter Orchards 117
Biltmore Cast Stone 90
Biltmore Estate, The 82, 92, 118, 119
Biltmore Station Farmer's Market 107
Biltmore Tailgate Market 107
Bird–n–Garden Barn Bird Barn'n Garden, The 148
Black Mountain 82, 83, 86, 106
Black Mountain Bakery 87
Black Mountain Gallery 86
Black Mountain Inn 87
Black Mountain Iron Works 86
Black Mountains 53, 71
Black Walnut Inn 111

Blake House Inn 111
Bloomin Baskets 212
Blowing Rock 38
Blue Ridge Barbecue Festival 179
Blue Ridge Corn Maze 141
Blue Ridge Parkway 43, 120
Blue Ridge Soap Shed 78
Boone 35
Boone Area Home and Garden Tour 37
Botanical Gardens at Asheville 103, 118, 119
Bottomless Pools 187
Bow-legged Scarecrow, The 69
Boxberger, Scott and Melissa 211
Boyd Mountain Log Cabins 133
Boyd, Betsy and Dan 133
Bracken Mountain Bakery 141
Bradley Inn 209
Brasstown 207, 218
Brevard 124, 140
Briar Rose Farm 59
Bridal Veil Falls 202
Bridge Street Café and Inn 62
Bridges, Jake and Marian 202
Brown Mountain Lights 193
Brown Trout Mountain Grille 146
Brown, Bill 22
Brown's Honey, Fruit & Vegetable Farm 117
Bryant, Barney 90
Bryson City 125, 153
Buffalo Bob's 43
Bullington Horticultural Learning Center 114
Bullington, Robert 114
Burgin, Wilbur 173
Burgiss, Tom 43
Burgiss Barn 43
Burke County Farmer's Market 169
Burnsville 67
Burr, Dane and Marry Etta 131
Burr Studio & Gallery 131
Butler, Marguerite 218

C

Cabin in the Laurel 76
Cabins at Seven Foxes, The 146
Campbell, Arthur and Zee 188
Campbell, Olive Dame 218
Cannon Memorial Gardens 40
Canton 136
Canton Farmer's Market 137
Carillon, Jim and Aline 191
Carl Sandburg Home 109
Carlton Gallery 27
Caro Mi Restaurant 179
Carolina Gourmet 136
Carrier Houses Bed & Breakfast 172
Carson, Bill and Judy 80, 81
Carter, Anna 41
Carter, Daniel and Robin 44
Carter Pots 44
Casey, Susan 182
Cashiers 125, 147
Cashiers' Farmer's Market 147
Cassedy, Marsha 174
Cataloochee Ranch 134
Catawba River Greenway 171
Catesby, Mark 51
Cecile's Bed and Breakfast 100
Cedar Crest - A Victorian Inn 111
Cedar Mountain 144
Celo 70
Celo Inn 70
Centennial Park 166
Chalet Inn, The 152
Chapman, Don 168
Charles Street Garden Suite 181
Chattooga Gardens 147
Cherokee 155
Chimney Rock 163
Chimney Rock Park 185, 186, 188
Chimney Rock Village 184
Chittenden, General Hiram M. 121
Chunky Gal Stables 206
Classic Garden, The 108
Claxton Farm 102
Clay County Historical & Arts Council Museum 206

Index

Cliffside Lake & Van Hook Glade Recreation 202
Cloud Nine House and Gardens 83, 115
Clyde 136
Coffey, Ralph 95
Colby House 111
Colfax 173
College Street Inn, The 169
Collis, Karen 132
Colonial Pines B&B 202
Columbus 162, 176
Common Ground 90, 107
Community Development Association of Chimney Rock 186
Conklin's Cabin 61
Coon Dog Day 183
Corn, Linda 213
Corneille Bryan Nature Center 135
Cornett, Diane 33
Cornett-Deal Christmas Tree Farm 29, 33
Coston Farm & Apple House 117
Cottage Gate, The 65, 69
Cottages at Spring House Farm, The 188
Council House Mound 155
Cove Creek 34
Coweeta Hydrologic Lab 204
Cradle of Forestry 139, 140
Craven Handbuilt Porcelain 70
Creation Herbal Products 41
Crim, Chef Mark 211
Crippens Country Inn and Restaurant 40
Crossnore 22
Crowe, Larry 174
Crowell III, Bill 181
Crumpler 46
Cryin' Shame Resort 144
Cullowhee 149
Cumberland Falls Bed & Breakfast Inn 111
Curtis, Erica 98

D

Dalmas, Joel 166, 196
Daniel Boone Native Gardens 36
Darlene's Mountain Fresh Produce 210
Darnell Farms/Corn Maze 154
Davis, Eve 93, 101
Davis, James 101
Daylily Farms & Nursery 74
DD Bullwinkel's 141
Dellinger Grist Mill 75
Dillsboro 125, 151
Doan, Randy 64
Dogwood Crafters 152
Dogwood Hills Farm 99
Don Balke Wildlife Gallery 193
Dry Falls 202
Dry Ridge Inn 98
Duckett House 61
Duncan, David 72
Dunromin Cabin 102

E

Eagle Feather Organic Farm 62
Edgewood Gardens 67
Edie's Good Things 186
Elisha Mitchell Audubon Society 96
Elk Park 18, 26
Energy Exchange 72
Ennice 44
Environmental and Conservation Organization 111
Ernst, Marian 204
Ervin, Jr., Senator Sam 169
Esmeralda Inn & Restaurant 184
Extended Garden, The 144

F

Faber, Fred and Helen 97
Fabulous Fourth 176
Fairview 106, 116
Fairview Farmer's Market 107
Famous Louise's Rock House Restaurant 194
Farm City Day 125
Farm Heritage Days 34
Fines Creek 133
Fire Mountain Inn, Cabins & Treehouses 203

Fireweed Alpaca Ranch 18, 32
Fisher, Richard 182
Fitzpatrick, Teresa 169
Flat Rock 83, 109
Fleetwood 41
Fletcher 105
Folk Art Center 88
Folkestone Inn 154
Fontana Dam 212
Fontana Village 213
Foothills Equestrian Nature Center (FENCE) 178
Forbes, Brenda 209
Forest City 173
Fourth Creek Folk Art Studio 171
Franklin 198, 202, 204, 215
Franklin Terrace 217
Fraser, John 51
Freedom Escape Lodge 101
French Broad Food Co-op and Tailgate Market 93, 107
French Broad River Garden Club and Foundation 91
French Broad River Park 92
Friendswood Brooms 58
Frost, John 94

G

Gamekeeper, The 38
Garden Club of NC 36
Garden Deli, The 68
Garden Jubilee 108
Gardener's Cottage, A 181
Gardener's Cottage, The 91
Gardens of the Blue Ridge 24
Gardens of the French Broad River Garden Club 91
Gates, Marlow and Ralph 58
Gazebo, The 217
George, Theresa 213
Gibson, Ned 90
Glen Burney Trail 40
Glendale Springs 41
Glendale Springs Inn and Restaurant 42
Glenville 148
Godfrey, Teri 86
Good Thyme Café 181
Gould, Chef Alan 150
Gourmet Gardens Herb Farm and Day Dreams Inn 97
Grace Cathey Sculpture Garden 131
Grand Dad's Apples N' Such 114, 117
Grandfather Mountain 18, 25, 50
Grandfather Mountain Nursery & Garden Center 26
Grandfather Trout Farm and Gem Mine 26
Grapestompers 43
Grassy Creek 46
Graves, Claude and Elaine 175
Gray, Asa 51
Great Smoky Mountain National Park 154, 158
Green River Bar-B-Que 184
Green River Plantation 174
Green Toe Ground Organics 70
Greenhouse Crafts 42
Griffin, Lee 175
Grove Park Inn Resort and Spa, The 96

H

Halsted Dahlia Gardens 147
Ham Shoppe, The 27
Hand in Hand Gallery 109
Hapke, Dr. Edith 99
Hardwood Gallery 131
Hawk & Ivy Country Retreat and Bed & Breakfast, The 101
Hawksdene House 209
Hayesville 199, 206
Hayesville Water Gardens 207
Haywood Community College 136
Haywood County Apple Festival 132
Heartwood Gallery 182
Hebron Falls Trail 41
Hemlock Inn 155
Henderson County Farmer's Curb Market 108
Henderson's Greenhouses 145
Hendersonville 8322, 107, 108, 112
Hendersonville County Apple Festival 108

Index

Hendersonville Home and Garden Tour 111
Henry Barnwell Orchards 117
Henson, Charles 170
Herb of Grace Farm 59
Heritage Cove Cabins 138
Heritage Festival 154
Herren House 129
Hiawassee River Garden 208
Hickory Nut Falls 186
Hickory Ridge Homestead Museum 37
High Country Greenhouses 47
High Hampton Inn 147
Highland Lake Inn 110
Highland Safari Tours 203
Highlands 202
Highlands Inn 203
Highlands Nature Center and Botanical Garden 203
Hillbilly Farm Days 67
Hillside Nursery 209
Historic Calhoun Country Inn 153
Historic Carson House 191
Historic Johnson Farm, The 107
Historic Morganton Festival 169
Holiday Toe River Studio Tours 74
Hollifield, Marshall and Eddie 86
Holy Trinity Episcopal Church 19, 42
Horseshoe 106
Hot Springs 52, 61
Howachyn, Dan 86
Howald, Dee and Tom 102
Huber, Frances 44
Huffman Native Plants 204
Huffman, John 204
Hulbert, Mike 41
Hummingbird Lodge 205
Humpback Mountain 194
Hyams, M.E. 190

I

Inn at Brevard, The 143
Inn at Old Fort, The 190
Inn at the Taylor House 31
Inn at Yonahlossee 38
Inn of the Red Thread 43
Inn on Main Street 99
Inn on Mill Creek, The 191
International Biosphere Reserve 25, 51
Ivivi Lake and Mountain Lodge 188

J

Jacumin, Jimmy 167
Jarvis Landscaping and Japanese Garden 52, 64
Jarvis, Jack 64
Jefferson 47
Jehovah-Rah Farm 134
Jesse Israel & Sons Nursery & Garden Center 104
Jewel Lake 148
Jimmy Nix and Sons 117
John C. Campbell Folk School 207, 218
John, A. 213
Johnson, Mildred 209
Jolley, Harley 123
Jonathan Creek 133
Jones, Matthew 57
Jones Pottery, The 57
Josephine's Café at Lone Beech 192
Judge's Riverside Restaurant 171

K

Karcher Stonecarving Studio & Rose Garden 151
Karcher, Collene 151
Kassab, Donna 112
Kathleen Carson Hand Painted Tiles 177
Keeran, Chef Jack and Patty 98
Kelsey Place 203
Kennedy, Aurelia 215
King Bio Pharmaceuticals 57
King, Jr., Dr. Frank 57
Kirkland Farm Produce 205
Kirkland, Ted and Vivian 205
Kituhwa Corn Maze 155
Kuralt, Charles 107

L

Lake James State Park 194
Lake Junaluska 135
Lake Louise 98
Lake Lure 163, 187
Lake Lure Tours 187
Lake Thorpe 125
Lake Tomahawk 87
Lake Toxaway 145
Lamar, Stony 182
Land of Sky Music and Arts Festival 141
Lansing 48
Lasley, Diane 43
Laurel Oaks Farm 73
Laurel Springs 19, 42
Lawarre, Joani 193
Layman, Mike 192
Leicester 57
Lewellyn Cove Walk 212
LeZurre, Janet 213
Lily Pad Aquatic Nursery 148
Lily Patch, The 133
Linville 18, 24
Linville Caverns 194
Linville Cottage Bed and Breakfast 24
Linville Falls, Town of 18, 22, 163, 194
Linville Falls 195
Linville Gorge 194, 195
Linville Lodge and Cottages 195
Lion and the Rose, The 94, 111
Little Creek Outfitters 60
Little Farm, The 44
Little Mountain Pottery 175
Little Tennessee River Greenway, The 206
Lively Orchard Outlet 117
Lodge at Lake Lure 187
Lomo's Grill, Bakery and Café 130
Long, Ben 42
Lovill House 35
Lowe, Bruce and Lori 105
Lyda Farms 117

M

MacJackson Orchard 117
Mackey, Taylor 141
Made in the Mountains 112
Maggie Valley 134
Mangum Pottery 45
MANNA Food Bank Demonstration Garden 89
Marcy, Ron and Shelley 144
Marion 163, 191
Market Place, The 93, 101
Mars Hill 52, 64
Mars Hill College 64
Martins Creek 134
Mast Farm Inn and Restaurant 27, 30
Mast General Store 32, 93, 107, 130
Mast General Store Annex/Candy Barrel 31
Max & Rosie's Café 94
Max Patch 52, 60, 61
Max Patch Cabins 60
Maxine's 146
Mayhew, Ron 137
Mayland Community College 77
McGalliard Falls 167
McKinney, Charlie 80
McMasters, Mickey and Susan 181
Mentzer, E. Hollis 112
Meytre's Grist Mill 167
Micaville 69
Michaux, Andre 50, 190
Miller Century Farm 48
Millspaugh, Daniel 143
Millstone Meadows 170
Mingo Falls 159
Mingus Mill 159
Mitchell County Chamber of Commerce 74
Mooney, James 160
Moose Café, The 104
Moretz Apple Orchard 49
Moretz, Bill 49
Morgan Mills 146
Morgan, Daniel 169
Morganton 162, 168
Morse, Dr. Lucius 186
Morton, Hugh 51
Moses Cone National Park 38
Mostly Herbs 204
Mountain Farm 71
Mountain Flower 27

Mountain Forest Studio 143
Mountain Gardens 71
Mountain Gateway Museum 189
Mountain Harvest Florist & Garden Center 116
Mountain Heritage Center 150
Mountain Hollow B&B 212
Mountain Horticultural Crops Resource & Extension Center 105
Mountain Laurel Garden Club 183
Mountain Magnolia Inn & Retreat 62
Mountain Memories 212
Mountain Pride Produce 191
Mountain Valley View Cabins 59
Mountain View Daylily Garden 69
Mountain View Nursery 136
Mt. Jefferson 19, 48
Mt. Jefferson State Natural Area 47
Mt. Mitchell Nursery & Decorative Evergreens 71
Mt. Rogers 48
Mud Dabbers Pottery 143
Mud Dabbers Studio 128
Mudcreek Basin Wetlands Trail 113
Muir, John 39, 50
Murphy 199, 207
Museum of the Cherokee Indians 156
Musilli, Susan 27

N

NC State Museum of History 189
Nantahala Gorge 214
Nantahala National Forest 204, 209, 210
Nantahala Village 214
Natural Selections 94
Nature Connection, The 151
Nature Conservancy 51
NC Clean Water Management Trust Fund 96
NC Ginseng and Goldenseal Company 62
NC Mountains to Sea Trail 128
Nelson, Nova and Mike 36
Nelson's Nantahala Hideaway 210
New Morning Gallery 91
New River General Store 46
Newland 18, 23
Niemeyer, Dennis 193
No Name Deli and Ice Cream Parlor 208
North Asheville Tailgate Market 107
North Carolina Arboretum, The 105, 118
Nowhere Branch Angora Goats 63
Nu-Wray Inn, The 68

O

Oak Moon Farm 73
Oaks Bed & Breakfast, The 184
Oaks Gallery 152
Oconaluftee Indian Village, Herb Garden & Nature Trail 156, 160
Oconaluftee Island Park 155
Oconaluftee Visitor Center and Mountain Farm Museum 158
October's End Restaurant 146
Ogden, Dan 152
Okpych, Chef Michael 184
Old Fort 163,189
Old Pressley Sapphire Mine 137
Old Reynolds Mansion 97
Old Rock Café, The 185
Old Stone Inn 132
Orchard at Altapass 77, 80
Orchard Inn 180
Organic Grower's School 111
Ottanola Farms 117
Otto 298, 204
Ox-Ford Farm Bed and Breakfast 103

P

P& R Garden Center and Produce 192
Painter, Steve and Susie 189
Painter's Greenhouse 189
Paleno, Chef Donny 138
Panes Residential Spa Retreat, The 65
Payne Christmas Tree & Horse Farm 29, 34
Pearson's Falls 163, 177, 179
Pena, Juana 182
Penland School of Crafts 76
Penny Patch Produce and Garden Center, The 168
Perdue, Pete and Joey 34
Perri Ltd. 93, 94
Perry's Water Gardens 217
Petals and Pots 169
Phipps, Teri 32
Pigeon River Scenic Walking Trail 136
Piggy's Ice Cream/Harry's 113
Pine Crest Inn 178
Pine Shadows Farm 29, 44
Pinebrae Manor 172
Piney Creek 45
Piney Mountain Orchards 117
Pink Beds Trail 140
Pisgah Center for Wildlife Education 140
Pisgah Inn 139
Pisgah National Forest 79, 134, 138, 139
Plants Direct 106
Point of View Restaurant 188
Polk County Courthouse 162, 176
Polk County Historical Museum 178
Posey Hollow Farms 177
Powell's Store 143
Price, Gertrude 206
Purple Onion, The 182
Purple Penguin 169

Q

Quaker Meadows House 170
Quality Forward Father's Day Home and Garden Tour 111
Queen's Farm Riding Stables 134
Quincy's Produce Market 22

R

Rainbow Garden Center 128
Ramp Festival 129
Randolph House 153
Raymond's Lawn, Home and Garden Center 109
Red Barn, The 132, 133
Red House Inn, The 141, 142
Red Rocker Inn, The 87
Red Roof Farms 45
Reems Creek Valley Nursery 102
Relia's Garden 215
Reynolds Farms 57
Rhododendron Festival 74
Richmond Hill Inn 103, 118, 119
Richmond Inn 78
River Farm Inn 41
River Gardens 73
River House Inn & Restaurant 19, 46
Riverside Park 187
Riverview Orchard 116
Riverwalk 24
Roan Mountain 53, 56, 75
Robbinsville 199, 210
Rock Mountain 147
RockhouseVineyards and Winery 175
Rocky Broad River Walk 186
Roeda, Carol 182
Rosenstein, Mark 93, 101
RRR Tree Farm 49
Ruane, Dennis 131
Rupach's Garden Gallery 108
Rural Life Museum 64
Rusty Bucket, The 115
Rutherford County Farm Museum 173
Rutherford County Farmer's Market 173
Rutherfordton 172
Ryan, Tim 218

S

Salmon, Alan 100
Salmonid's Trout Farm 145
Saluda 163, 180
Saluda Forge 177, 181
Saluda Grade Café 181
Salvo, Frank 95
Sam Miller Trees and Meadow Ridge Campground 28, 42
Sandburg, Carl 83, 109
Sandy Bottom Trail Rides 63
Sandy Cut Cabins 180
Sandy Mush Herb Nursery 58
Sandy Plains 162, 175
Sargent, Daphne 209
Sarpy, John and Linda 144
Saturday Farmer's Market in Burnsville 67
Saturday Farmer's Market in Mars Hill 64
Saylor Orchard 75
Saylor, Jim 75
Scaly Mountain 203
Schieferstein, David 32
Screen Door 90, 107
Sculpture Gardens at ASU Visual Arts Center 35
Secret Garden Bed & Breakfast, The 98
Senator's House 44
Seven Springs Nursery 210
Shady Grove Gardens 34
Shady Lane Farm 67
Sharp, Molly 110
Shatley Springs 19, 46
Shatley Springs Inn Restaurant 46
Shelton Farms 153
Shining Rock 139
Wilderness Area 139
Shoe Booties Café 208
Shortia 190
Sibold, Josey 182
Silvermont Park 143
Singing Waters Camping Resort 149
Sisters Three and Me 68
Sky Top Orchard 110
Smith, Amanda 41
Smoky Mountain Barbecue 47
Smoky Mountain Diner 61
Snow Hill Inn 215
Snowbird Mountain Lodge 211
Snowbird Mountains 210
Songbird Cabin 33
Sourwood Cottage 100
Sourwood Festival 86
Sourwood Grille 138
South Mountain Craft Village 168
Southern Highland Craft Guild 88
Sparta 44
Spear's Restaurant 195
Speckled Trout & Oyster Bar Café 40
Spindale 173
Spitzer, Virginia 212
Spring Park 183
Spring Ridge Creamery 204
Spring Street Café 150
Spring Valley Nursery 202
Spruce Pine 53, 77
Squire Watkins Inn 152
Standing Indian Recreation Park 206
Stearn's Park 176
Stecoah Valley Center 213
Stephenson, Clair and Eric 144
Stepp's Hillcrest Orchard 117
Stevens, Joe 207
Stevenson, Don 47, 61, 113, 157, 171
Stippich, Cheryl 112
Stone Hedge Inn 176
Stone's Throw Farm 59
Stoner, Kaaren 130
Stoney Knob Café & Patio 97
Stony Hollow Farm 211
Sugar Mountain Nursery 23
Sugar Plum Farms 22, 29
Summer House, The 183
Summit Support Services 47
Sunnyside Café 98
Sunnyside Orchard 174
Sunset Inn, The 135
Suyeta Park Inn 131
Swag, The 133
Swannanoa 88
Switzerland Inn, The 78
Sylva 150

T

Tall Pine Apple Orchard 117
Taylor, Victor 104
Taylor's Greenhouse 210
Tempest, Jeff 176
Terrell House 68
Thomas Berry Farm 149
Thomas, Journal 131
Three Oaks, Ltd. 23
TJ's Mountain Market 64
Tobin Farm Inns, The 48
Todd 19, 49
Todd General Store 19, 49
Tom Sawyer Tree Farm 148
Topton 199, 210
Trail of Faith 167
Trail of Tears National Historic Trail 156
Transylvania County Tailgate Market 142
Trout Lake 39
Trubey, Kit 80, 81
Tryon 176
Tryon Garden Club 179
Tuckasegee 149
Tuckasegee Valley 125
Tufts University 149
Tumbling Waters Campground & Trout Farm 214
Turchin Center for Visual Art 35
Tuscan Hill B&B 101
Tuscola Garden Club 135
Twigs and Leaves Gallery 130
Twin Streams Bed & Breakfast 145
Two Harts Bakery 168

U

U-Pick/We-Pick Apples Sky Top 117
Utah Mountain 132
Utter, Sandy 181

V

Valdese 162, 166, 196
Valle Crucis 18, 27
Valle Crucis Conference Center 31
Valle Crucis Fair 32
Valley Garden Market 86, 107
Valley Produce 155
Vance Birthplace 100
Vance, Zebulon B. 100
Vanderbilt, George 92, 118
Vilas 34
Village Café, The 40
Villar Vintners of Valdese 166
Vineyard Family Restaurant, The 172
Voorhees, David 109

W

Waldensian Festival 166
Waldensian Heritage Museum 166
Waldensian Heritage Wines 196
Waldensian Presbyterian Church 166
Waldrup's General Store 58
Walker Inn 210
Ware, George and Hanneke 152
Warp in Time, A 191
Warren Wilson College 82, 88
Watauga County Farmer's Market 37
Waterfalls Park 24
Waterrock Knob 159
Waverly Inn, The 107
Waynesville 124,128, 131
Waynesville Chamber of Commerce 129
Waynesville Tailgate Market 132
Weaverville 82, 104
Weaverville Milling Company 97
Webb, Betty 192
Webb's Daylily Gardens 192
Weber, Chef Monte 180
Webster, Daniel 120
We-Du Nurseries 193
Weeping Creek Cottages 112
Welch, James 40
Wellspring Farm 65
West Burnsville 65
West Jefferson 47
Western Carolina Center 168
Western Piedmont Community College 171
What Fir! 36

Whistle Stop Produce 144
WhiteGate Inn & Cottage 95, 111
White Oak Farm 65
Whitewater Gardens 144
Whitman's Bakery 130
Wildflour Bakery 163, 181
Wildwood Herbal Flower Farm 100
Williams, Ted 207
Wilson, Dr. John 87
Wilson, Julie 134
Wilson, Shelly 43
WindDancers Lodging and Llama Treks 134
WNC Agricultural Center 105
WNC Farmer's Market 104, 107
WNC Herb Festival 104
WNC Nature Center 89
Wood Farm and Corn Maze 208
Wood'n Craft Shop, The 137
Woodfield Inn & Restaurant 110
Woods, Robert 212, 213
Wray House B&B 69
Wright, Susan 34
Wrinkled Egg, The 110

Y

Yellow Branch Pottery and Cheese 211
Yellow House, The 129

Z

Zinser, Robert and Cindy 132
Zionsville 34

Credit & Thanks

Authors
Jan J. Love
Elizabeth Hunter
Mary Lynn White
LM Sawyer

Design and Photography
Scott Smith
1250 Design
Asheville, NC

Additional Photography
Jan J. Love

Other Photography
Credited by appearance

Project Coordinator (Trail Guru)
Jan J. Love

Editing and Design Associate
LM Sawyer
1250 Design

Map Design
Scott Smith
Glen Locasio
Orrin Lundgren

Map Research
Glen Locasio
NC Division of Community Assistance

Project Assistance
HandMade in America
Emily Adams
Robert Akers
Al Kopf
Alexandra Love
Brandon Love
Leeanne Murray

Printing
Hickory Printing Group

Very Special Thanks
Becky Anderson, Lynn Bender, Sue Bennett, Rod Birdsong, Norma Bradley, Pat Cabe, Sue Counts, Clara Curtis, Amy Edwards, Bob Edwards, Connie Green, Lanny Haas, Cheryl Hargrove, Robert Hawk, Johnny Hensley, Laurie Huttunen, Mary Jaeger-Gale, Betty Hurst, Carol Kline, Jimmy Landry, Patty Lockamy, John Ludovico, Wayne Martin, Kim McGill, Michael Patterson, John Redman, Ken Reeves, Laura Rotegard, Polly Smith, Carole Summers, Karen Tessier, John Vining, Lynn Williams, Kim Yates, Ross Young, Jacquie Ziller

Stay On Top of the Trails
To get on our mailing list or to order additional copies of the guidebook (for gifts or once you've worn this one out), call 1-800-331-4154.

Clockwise from left: Jan J. Love, Mary Lynn White, LM Sawyer, Elizabeth Hunter, Scott Smith

About HandMade in America

The seeds of HandMade in America were sown in 1993 when a handful of Western North Carolinians, struggling to find fresh approaches to economic development and renewal in their mountains, realized that the answer didn't necessarily lie in newly recruited industry, but could potentially be found in the invisible industry of craftspeople already working steadily and exceptionally in shops, classrooms, studios, and galleries tucked away on small town main streets and back roads throughout the Blue Ridge Mountains.

In December of 1993, HandMade in America received a three-year organizational development grant from the Pew Partnership for Civic Change. Over 360 citizens participated in a regional planning process to help determine how HandMade could establish Western North Carolina as the center of handmade objects in the nation.

We welcome the support and involvement of those in the public, private, and nonprofit sectors who share our commitment to that inspired joining of art and function we call "handcraft." Building on this support, HandMade has initiated programs in education, community and economic development for thousands of citizens in our region. Demonstrable results include a 10-15% increase in income for many of our craftspeople, and over $11 million in investment in several of the region's smallest towns.

Our Mission is to celebrate the hand and the handmade, to nurture the creation of traditional and contemporary craft, to revere and protect our resources, and to preserve and enrich the spiritual, cultural, and community life of our region.

Why HandMade, Why Here?

Every region and every community has its unique gifts and challenges. In Western North Carolina, one of the gifts is our extraordinary, rich heritage of handcraft.

As we explored how to bolster our economy and preserve that heritage, we considered our geography and how our land is used. In 1995 HandMade in America, in association with researchers at the John A. Walker College of Business at Appalachian State University, conducted a survey to measure the economic contribution of crafts in 22 counties in Western North Carolina. This survey, The Economic Impact of Crafts revealed that crafts contributed $122 million annually to the region's economy. That figure is four times the revenue generated from burley tobacco, one of the region's largest cash crop. The survey also revealed some of the challenges and needs of the craft community, including access to capital and marketing and business education services.

The Western North Carolina region is home to over 4,000 artisans whose work contributes over $122 million to the local economy.

Guiding Principles

• All work of HandMade in America is inclusive. Everyone is welcome to participate from the first-time hobbyist to the full-time, one-of-a-kind design professional craftsmen, and/or any interested citizen of the region.

• All projects are done in partnership with other organizations and institutions - all funding is written jointly or in the partner's name.

• HandMade is regional. All communities come equally to the table in resources. Meetings are held throughout the region. Board members represent the region.

• HandMade is sustainable community development. No outside consultants or businesses are used. The people of the region serve as their own best resource. HandMade is focused on long-term solutions, hence a twenty year strategic plan.

- All HandMade projects are community-based. Each community defines its needs, resources and how it fits into the strategic plan.

- HandMade is self-sustaining. All projects must fit into the operation of an ongoing institution, or be financially self-sustaining.

Our Twenty Year Goals

- To develop community strategies that will collectively enhance Western North Carolina's role nationally and internationally within the handmade field.

- To establish an academic base to promote crafts throughout all levels of education as object, subject and process.

- To develop a communication plan that establishes Western North Carolina's role as the center for HandMade in America.

- To implement environmentally sustainable economic strategies for Western North Carolina that emphasize the handmade industry.

- To implement strategies that will enhance opportunities for handmade object makers within Western North Carolina.

- To actively encourage the public, private and nonprofit sectors to develop independent and interdependent vehicles that build the handmade industry.

The Craft Heritage Trails of Western North Carolina guidebook

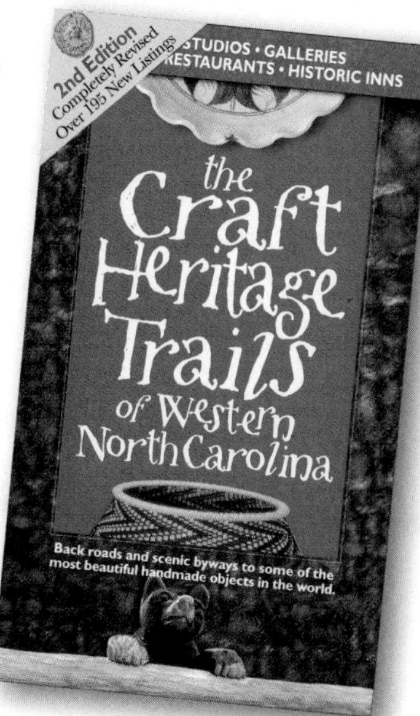

HandMade in America's guide to the best arts and craft galleries and studios throughout Western North Carolina.

Tuck this book under your arm and head for the mountains.

With over 140 pages, the full-color book offers over 500 listings of studios, galleries, historic inns and restaurants of note throughout the 22-county area of Western North Carolina. Embroidered with colorful tales, fun sidetrips, route maps and exquisite photographs, the guidebook beckons you to the mountain roads and the pleasures of discovery that await you at every turn.

Travel along one or just part of the seven driving tours that stretch out from the Blue Ridge Parkway. You'll discover handmade treasures deep in the narrows of mountain coves, across rippling streams, and in storefronts on postcard streets.

Adventures in Crafts at your fingertips

In The Craft Heritage Trails of Western North Carolina guidebook, everything you need is included: maps with each site indicated and numbered, places to stay, galleries to shop in, restaurants and cafes where you can stop and sit a spell, and how to find the craftspeople with studios in town or out in the country. Each listing has a full description and includes phone numbers if you need special directions.

There are seven regional tours from which to choose and many trails to follo within each of them: Mountain Cities, Circle the Mountain Cities, Circle the Mountain, Shadow of the Smokies, Cascades, Lake Country, Farm to Market, High Country and High Country Ramble. Each trail takes its own path and has its own special heritage.

To order your guidebook today call 1-800-331-4154. Or, fill out the order form on the next page and mail the form and payment directly to HandMade in America, P.O. Box 2089, Asheville, NC 28802. Checks, money orders, and major credit cards accepted.

The Craft Heritage Trails of Western North Carolina

Cost is $13.95 per book. NC residents, please add 6.5% sales tax per book. Shipping and handling fees are $4.50 for one book per address and $2 per additional book to the same address. Look for the third edition to be printed in summer 2002!

You can also order additional copies of this guidebook.

Farms, Gardens & Countryside Trails of Western North Carolina

Cost is $19.95 per book. NC residents, please add 6.5% sales tax per book. Shipping and handling fees are $4.50 for one book per address and $2 per additional book to the same address.

Please Send Me More...

Print name

Address

City State Zip

Shipping address if different from above:

Print name

Address

City State Zip

		Qty	Total
Farms, Gardens & Countryside Trails of Western North Carolina	$19.95	_____	_________
The Craft Heritage Trails of Western North Carolina	$13.95	_____	_________
Shipping and handling			_________
NC residents add 6.5% sales tax			_________
		Total	_________

Please charge my credit card

_____ MC _____ VISA _____ AMEX

Card number

Expiration date Signature

Notes